WELCOME TO BIOTECH NATION

WITHDRAWN
UTSA LIBRARIES

Welcome to BioTech Nation

My Unexpected Odyssey into
the Land of Small Molecules,
Lean Genes, and Big Ideas

BY MOIRA A. GUNN, PH.D.

AMACOM AMERICAN MANAGEMENT ASSOCIATION

NEW YORK ○ ATLANTA ○ BRUSSELS ○ CHICAGO ○ MEXICO CITY ○ SAN FRANCISCO
SHANGHAI ○ TOKYO ○ TORONTO ○ WASHINGTON, D. C.

Special discounts on bulk quantities of AMACOM books are available to corpora-
tions, professional associations, and other organizations. For details, contact Special
Sales Department, AMACOM, a division of American Management Association,
1601 Broadway, New York, NY 10019. Tel: 212-903-8316. Fax: 212-903-8083.
E-mail: specialsls@amanet.org
Website: www.amacombooks.org/go/specialsales
To view all AMACOM titles go to: www.amacombooks.org

This publication is designed to provide accurate and authoritative information in
regard to the subject matter covered. It is sold with the understanding that the pub-
lisher is not engaged in rendering legal, accounting, or other professional service. If
legal advice or other expert assistance is required, the services of a competent professional person should be sought.

Library of Congress Cataloging-in-Publication Data

Gunn, Moira Anne, 1949–
   Welcome to biotech nation : my unexpected odyssey into the land of small mole-
cules, lean genes, and big ideas / Moira A. Gunn.
       p. cm.
Includes index.
ISBN-13: 978-0-8144-0923-7
ISBN-10: 0-8144-0923-7
   1. Biotechnology—Popular works. I. Title.

TP248.215.G86 2007
660.6—dc22   2007008292

NPR® is a registered trademark of National Public Radio, Inc. TECH NATION® and
BIOTECH NATION® are registered trademarks of Tech Nation Media.

Printing number
10 9 8 7 6 5 4 3 2 1

CONTENTS

WELCOME TO BIOTECH NATION

CHAPTER ONE

Down the Biotech Rabbit Hole

BIOTECH? Who needs biotech? I didn't.

Although in my own secret heart of hearts, I did suspect that biotech might some day rush in and save me when I was old and blond (another tech miracle that women of a certain age rush to embrace.) But that would be later, a long time later, some time in the distant future. And by then, biotech would be pre-packaged and insurance-approved, clean-as-a-whistle medical technology, not unlike that dispensed by Bones on *Star Trek*. Everything fixed with nary a drop of blood or a thought to pain. And between now and then? The biotech folks could just work things out. Pretty much without me.

I figured by the time I got there, my personal biotech would be a lot like my car. Do I really need to know what's going on under the hood? Do I care? That would be a great big "Nooooooo." And why shouldn't I feel that way? It would be years—if not, decades—before I needed it.

Which continues to be true . . . so how was it that I came to fall down the biotech rabbit hole?

The short story is this: Biotech marched up to my door, lifted the pins from the hinges, chucked the door aside, stepped across the threshold, and took up residence in a room of its own.

The long story isn't all that much longer.

○   ○   ○

FOR OVER a decade, I had hosted *Tech Nation,* which anyone in the United States can hear on *NPR Now* and *NPR Talk* over Sirius Satellite Radio, or anyone anywhere can hear over the Internet. I thought we had talked about everything under the technical sun, and I did that by giving technology what I considered a very generous definition: "If God didn't make it, it's Technology." I also gave a big *Tech Nation* welcome to science, as science and technology are almost inextricably linked. (A new technology informs the scientists, and then science surges ahead. At other times, a new scientific insight informs the technologists, and a new technology is born. They dance together like Fred and Ginger, which means they can be a whole lot more popular together than they could ever be alone.)

With this mindset, I interviewed people high and low. There were CEOs and novelists, futurists and ethicists, journalists and politicians, astronauts and technogrinches, environmentalists and entrepreneurs. Everyone had a tech story. Or a counter-tech story.

Yet while I was talking to just about everybody, the truth was I had stayed within my own comfort zone. I had such a large comfort zone, no one really noticed—including me—but there was a big wide hole in it. You see, I was both an entrepreneur and an academic. I had advanced degrees in both science and engineering. Thanks to a Jesuit education, I had studied ethics, philosophy and theology, and a whole array of liberal arts. I worked in one capacity or another for everyone, from NASA to Intel to Lockheed to IBM to just about every name writ large on the tech scene. I even shared a software patent with two USDA nutrition scientists. From information systems to networking to robotics to scientific research to manufacturing to banking and securities, there seemed to be no limit to where my expertise might lead me. This Jill-of-all-trades background was a perfect setting for interviewing the world on the impact of technology.

So what was it I was missing? The life sciences. One course in high school chemistry is hardly enough to inform you about much of anything. Sure I had plenty of math and physics, but there was no life science in my program once I got into college and certainly not in graduate school. I had taken no biology, biochemistry, genetics, health sciences, and the list goes on.

To be sure, I didn't completely *avoid* life sciences on our weekly *Tech Nation* program, but I was pretty cagey about it. For one thing, guests had to have boatloads of credentials. A Nobel Prize would work, which let Crick and Watson through the door, as well as Linus Pauling and Kary Mullis to name a few. Others qualified by dint of their books and/or their institutions, such as evolutionary biologist Stephen Jay Gould, neuroscientist Steven Pinker or Harvard medical researcher Jerome Groopman. And who would argue that Carl Sagan didn't know what he was talking about? In a nutshell, I ignored anyone and anything that didn't already come fully vetted.

And my interview questions? I would have to say they were comparatively lame. I would rest on what a normal everyday person with no scientific knowledge would want to know, as opposed to my usual MO: studying the material, writing questions that were illuminating in their own right, creating a way to dig deep without having to spend a lot of time educating the listener, serving up the unusual insight.

And so it was in the spring of 2004 . . .

○   ○   ○

WE PRODUCE *Tech Nation* at KQED in San Francisco, that bastion of public radio (and television), and there the seeds of the odyssey began to sprout. That they didn't sprout earlier is somewhat surprising. You see, the San Francisco Bay Area is pretty much the center of the biotech universe. It was the birthplace of biotechnology, where Herb Boyer and Stanley Cohen first genetically engineered some genes onto a simple cell. Today the region is the world's largest biotech cluster. It took a great deal of studious "ignoring the obvious" to keep biotech out of the mix.

But then business and technology started merging with cutting edge science, and that spilled over into biotech. Well before I had any conscious focus on biotech, I interviewed Carol Lou. At the time she was the president and COO of Quantum Dot Corporation, which produced miniscule fluorescent dots—nanocrystals, they called them—that would cleave to and then light up individual cells. Build the attachment part of the nanocrystal to latch onto a particular kind of cancer cell, flood the area and the tumor would light up. Since this was declared one of the top scientific breakthroughs of 2003 by Science magazine, I figured it was a safe bet. Sounded like great technology to me. Of course, it wasn't just technology—it was *bio*technology. In fact, it was a specific sector of biotechnology: *nano*biotechnology, although the importance of the distinction was completely lost on me.

Many times we like to link the two interviews we air on a single show, and so the obvious second interview was one I'd been saving for a while. "Saving" may not the most accurate term here. The fact was I didn't exactly know what to do with it. I had interviewed scientist Dr. Michael West, the president and CEO of Advanced Cell Technology. His firm was attempting to do what is called "nuclear cell transfer," a technical name for "you remove the inside of a stem cell and replace it with the nucleus of an adult cell." What you would end up with is a very young cell with the genetic characteristics of the adult. Sounds fairly straight forward when we say it that way, but I had to have the fellow come back twice to finally get an interview that made any sense to me at all. (The first interview went beyond hope when he said something about "arms and legs bubbling away in a Petri dish.") After some serious discussion—and some major strategies about what would and would not work—he came back and we did the interview all over again.

Without knowing it, we had put together our first full-length biotech hour.

By pure coincidence, a few weeks later, James Shreeve came on to talk about *The Genome Wars*. We talked about the public Human Genome Project and how Craig Venter had jumped into the act while it was already underway. He changed the rules of the game—or perhaps more descriptively, moved the finish line closer by downsizing what it meant to decode the human genome. Venter went on to assemble as much gene-decoding technology as existed collectively in the rest of the world, and semi-graciously walked across the finish line, hand-in-hand with the pre-existing collective of scientists worldwide who had been at it for a while. In the glare of significant media attention, the human genome had finally been decoded—an historic event if ever there was one. It actually took several more years to complete the original goals and plan for the Human Genome Project. The entire competitive story makes patently obvious that modern day science has its own share of personalities, politics, media and money as enthusiastic sidekicks.

It turned out these interviews were the seeds. They got the immediate attention of all the publicists at all the biotech companies, and before you could spit, they began to circle.

In short order, I was invited to a "biotech media" dinner, a typical press event, where a public relations firm arranges a fancy and well-lubricated dinner and invites both its clients and the media itself.

I found myself at Le Colonial, a chic San Francisco restaurant in the French Vietnamese tradition. We might as well have been transported back to the Saigon of the 1940s—dimmed lights and Indochine decor, white-coated Asian waiters offering cosmopolitans and martinis, a crowd of swank people. Except for the journalists. For the most part, they looked cluelessly underdressed, if not somewhat disheveled.

Ogilvy & Mather's healthcare PR arm had matters well in hand. First they let the journalists imbibe enthusiastically and catch up with each other. (Journalists who have never set eyes on each other become fast friends within ninety seconds of introducing themselves.) The few hors d'oeuvres that were passed absorbed no alcohol, and the party took off like a shot. At a select moment, the PR team sent their clients into the fray, a veritable conga line of CEOs in expensively tailored suits. We journalists were separated like a good break on a pool table. The CEO before me related the story of his company. I loved it. I said, "You must come on *Tech Nation*." He quickly turned and introduced me to the CEO beside him. Another fascinating story. "Oh," I declared, "*you* must come on *Tech Nation*." And then I became alarmed. We only had two interviews in each weekly show. I couldn't make *all* the interviews biotech. But I was getting my sea legs.

The next fellow introduced himself, and I repeated "That's fascinating!" about six times before he gave up and turned me over to the next guy. While settling in for the spiel, I caught arm-waving out of the corner of my eye. I turned, and there he was—the last CEO. He was gesturing madly to the first two CEOs, and he wasn't happy. You didn't need to be a rocket scientist to guess he had just figured out that he hadn't been asked on *Tech Nation*. I looked back at the CEO before me, who hadn't broken cadence, even though I wasn't even listening. I abruptly announced, "We're going to do a weekly segment on biotech."

It was as simple as that.

By my own hand—and undoubtedly with some help from my vodka martini, or was that a cosmo?—I confidently climbed up the ladder of the high dive that happened to be positioned directly over the Biotech Rabbit Hole. The only thing left to do was jump.

The act of jumping was a problem for tomorrow, for like many decisions made under pressure, you are just so relieved to have a workable decision, you forget that you will have to act on it. That I actually knew nothing about biotech would not occur to me until morning.

Still, I was able to manage pretty well through the rest of the night, since I could honestly say that I still had to find a producer. I spoke with people from the Salk Institute, people from database management companies, people from healthcare policy organizations, people who were cancer researchers, people in marketing and people from sales. I understood about half of what I heard—the non-biotech half, so you might say I understood almost none of what I heard.

I didn't know it yet, but that *Alice in Wonderland* sense of listening to people who weren't making any sense was beginning to happen. They looked like normal people. They spoke English, when they weren't randomly inserting some strange biotech language in every other sentence. And they looked me straight in the eye and expected that I understood everything they were talking about.

They spoke rapid-fire with emphasis on certain unintelligible phrases and alternate nodding and shaking of their heads. The nodding and shaking was matched by others within earshot, and from time to time apparently also contained some amusing content.

Besides what I took to be brand names and obvious scientific terminology, there were abbreviations and catchwords, as well as everyday-words-strung-together—individually comprehensible, but together they no doubt meant something very complex. There were references to companies not in this room, scientific theories not yet proven, biotech products not yet available, and venture capital funding not yet confirmed. Or about to be confirmed, but could not yet be spoken of until the final papers were signed. Or recently confirmed, the news for which was delivered in a manner which telegraphs they believe they are giving us a real "scoop."

As the targeted journalist you are expected to immediately grab your fedora with the press card stuck in the brim and prop it on the back of your head a la Jimmy Olsen. Your reporter's spiral notepad and a stubby pencil should then materialize out of nowhere. Your eyes must bulge and then slide into mere slits. You lean in and intone "Tell me more" to get an original quote all your own. You are then supposed to rush into the hallway shouting "Where are the pay phones?" and call it into the night editor. Even today, when cell phones are as available as paper napkins, there's something about being with the press that brings out the 1930s movies in all of us.

Of course, I'm sure I looked like a complete dunce. I was smiling like someone being described the highlights of the local scenery by a townsperson who only speaks French. Because you don't speak French, you understand nothing, and so you smile appreciatively and nod and say "Aaah!" and "Oooh!" until eventually someone or something rescues you.

And yet . . . there was something very familiar about the whole scene.

It was reminiscent of the heady days of the dot-com boom. Only these weren't kids with PowerPoint presentations stenciled on their T-shirts. Or geeks, fresh from their garage, hoping to strike it rich. These people weren't the hip-techno-chic, the disdaining-venture-capital-cool, or the predatory-value-added-board-member-parasite who inhabited the South-of-Market MultiMedia Gulch parties that were going every night during the run-up to the bust. These appeared to be real people. Professional people of one sort or another. If you had one advanced degree, you likely had another. And markedly, few were young. You know, like early-twenties young. "Young" in this crowd meant in your thirties, and most were in their forties and fifties and even beyond. Perhaps the PR team would have a few young ones, and a few journalists could be described in those terms, but for the most part, this was a refreshingly older crowd. Refreshing for me, at any rate. So what if I didn't understand a word they were saying.

I found myself standing alone—as one can do in an excited, packed crowd—and I wondered how this parallel universe could have existed and I knew nothing about it. These people were gripped by an entire industry, an industry based on science that I knew nothing about. What had I stumbled upon? These people spoke *as if they were at the center of the universe.* How could I have missed it?

I was reminded of a vibrant marketplace in India. Inside the bubble of an air-conditioned SUV, we had just come in from the countryside and were abruptly stopped in traffic at its crossroads. Swarming around us were people on foot and horses and oxen and carts and motorbikes. I looked up to see a wide street teaming with people and dotted with makeshift stalls. The crystal-clear sun lit the iridescent clouds of kicked-up dust. There was the din of raised voices, bodies moving everywhere, colors flashing, hands going up and down, the crowd hemmed in solely by three-story buildings lining the street on either side, each fast against the other as far the eye could see. Ground-floor shops could barely be seen through the stalls and vendors and hanging wares; laundry hung from above and handmade signs with strange symbols were everywhere, but what drew the eye was the moving crowd. Not an inch was vacant for long, for as each space emptied in one direction, it was immediately filled from another. There were no apparent lanes or paths or order or organization. It was like a "Where's Waldo?" book come to life and set on "high speed" in India. I let out a breath. The driver said, "You have places like this in the United States, no?" I said, "We have nothing like this in the United States."

Our driver looked quizzical. To his eyes, he understood what he was looking at. Because he had seen it so many times.

I thought it must be like learning to do Sudoku puzzles. The first ones can be very hard, but as you do more and more puzzles, they reveal themselves. They reveal their patterns. There is an order, a logic, a solvability, even when you cannot see the whole. No doubt this was true of that marketplace in India. Our driver might know there were tailor shops and dry goods and pharmacies and more. He could guess from the time of day and the day of the week why particular people might be in the street and what business they might be about. He might know whether the buildings held businesses or apartments, and what those apartments might be like. How many people might live there. In the heat. Would it be better to be out on the street or stuck in the still hot air? The problem was, I could discern nothing about what I was looking at. It was all so new I couldn't take a single item and assign it a comprehensible place.

This was how it felt being thrust into biotech.

I sometimes wonder where that CEO is today, the one who was the sole member of the audience at the first announcement of our new series *BioTech Nation*. Did he see the light bulb over my head? Did he even hear me? Was he so wound up, having to push his company in the PR equivalent of speed dating, that he had too much drama of his own to deal with?

As it turned out, I never did interview anyone from that first dinner. I put them all off with the fact that a new weekly segment was "in planning." And planning began in earnest the very next day.

And so it was with biotech and me. I didn't know it then, for I had just come in from the countryside and thought I was momentarily stuck at a jammed intersection . . . but I was fast sliding down the biotech rabbit hole.

CHAPTER TWO

Shy Beyond Words

I MET Clive at the genetically modified food lunch.

I didn't want to. Not meet Clive, that is. Clive's great. What I mean is
that I didn't want to meet *anybody*. Here we were—Mark Andrews, my
trusty new *BioTech Nation* producer, and me, the ostensible host. Well,
maybe not "trusty." That word didn't really begin to apply to either one of
us. Not only had I never intentionally done a biotech interview, he had
never produced anything. Ever. But that didn't appear to faze him whatsoever. Which may have been my fault.

I had repeatedly assured Mark that he was more than capable of doing
this . . . and I was convinced that he was. San Francisco is a town awash
in capable radio producers, but who knew biotech? I couldn't risk it. I had
to find someone who could nod along with the gang from Le Colonial, so
Mark was my mark. He was the only person I knew who knew anything
about biotech. And I had done a whole lot of hand-waving to get him to
agree. The initial flurry of this hand-waving took place in New Orleans,
a mere month earlier.

I laid out my proposition about this new segment while we were having lunch in the French Quarter. (Mark's kind of bi-coastal—the Gulf

Coast and the West Coast, and he is—among many things—a biotech patent attorney.) I told him about my idea for this new segment and how I had planned to go to the big international BIO conference, fortuitously being held in San Francisco. Surely, out of the 16,000 people predicted to be in attendance by the Biotechnology Industry Organization, we could line up the initial roster of interviews. So, I slipped the proposition in as transparently as that. "I" became "we" in the matter of half a "dressed" oyster & shrimp po' boy. At least, *I* was saying "we." The "we" could have been me and any number of people. It could have been a Queen Victoria "we" for all Mark knew, but I knew exactly where I was going with this slippage of the pronouns.

I needed a person to go through all the exhibits at the conference and dig up potential guests, and then convince them to get in a cab and come over to KQED where I could interview them. The producer had to troll the receptions and the hallways and the sessions and anywhere else he could find. He needed to tell people that we were already an established show and we would start airing biotech segments in just a matter of weeks. The job was to find as many people and as many topic areas as possible. So, after my meandering all over the place, and not getting called outright on the "we" business, I finally told him that the perfect producer would be . . . oh . . . ah . . . ummm . . . him!

In full Southernspeak, he exclaimed, "You want me to be a carnival barker?!?!"

And that pretty much summed it up. But I needed him to do *so* much more. I needed him to explain biotech to me, as I was completely clueless. His bachelor's degree in biochemistry would have to serve us both. And having tested it, I already knew there was no one who explained science like he did. No one. Imagine this son of the South raising one hand and shaking it in the air, like an updated Andy Griffith. "You see, you got yuh enzymes here." His other hand would rise up from behind his head, fingers wiggling. ". . . And you got yuh molecules here." Then the enzymes hand would start to move on the molecules hand, which started showing signs of actual distress. Well, you had to be there to fully appreciate it. "New Orleans science" is what it was. And a good part of the time I actually understood what he was talking about. Most of the time it was all I could do not to fall off my chair into fits of giggles, but the bottom line was that he could explain it to me.

Without that, I was sunk.

There was another thing. Besides lining up the guests and laying out the science, he needed to tell me what the point of the interview was. A minor professional detail . . . knowing where you're going when you ask the questions. Remember, I had already had my first conscious brush with biotech seared into my memory from that fateful biotech press event at Le Colonial. *Oh, you're a small molecule company? . . . Well, I hope you become a big molecule company some day! . . . Oh, they're intentionally "small" molecules? . . . because that . . . saves on shelf space?*

Nevertheless, somewhere in the middle of this single, calorie-laden New Orleans lunch, Mark and I managed to strike up a deal. Never mind that what little we actually discussed, we hadn't really agreed upon, but once he got the bit in his teeth, he was off. He announced that he wanted to teach the world basic science. Which was the last thing *I* wanted to do. I just wanted to find out what the point was. The point of all this science. The motivation behind all this biotech. The future that they were all working so hard to create. The good that could ultimately be done. The downsides, for there always are downsides. And most definitely, exactly who all these people were who worked in biotech, and how they managed to make a business out of it.

Like so many deals, in the end, the price was right. From my corner, the price was "free." Cash-wise, that is. I was "paying" his expenses and giving him unprecedented access to everyone in biotech. From his corner, he could actually go to BIO without having to pony up the several thousand dollars it would normally cost the average attendee. But the media goes "free."

○   ○   ○

WHICH BRINGS us back round to the genetically modified food lunch. I had wasted no time signing us both up for media registrations for BIO 2004, and I arranged for Mark to fly out. What happened next was Mark's instant immersion in professional media. Which means that nothing happened. For a while. Until about a week before the conference. Then his e-mail exploded.

We were invited everywhere and anywhere. Suggested press topics came in from every direction, and for starters, there were all the states that wanted to get into biotech. MichBio (Michigan), Bio in Ohio, BioIowa, MDBio (Maryland), Genetown (Massachusetts) and BioGarden

(New Jersey). The purse is so big in the biotech race, states even got together on the deal.

Pharm Country—say it out loud and it will become clear—is the brotherhood of Connecticut, New Jersey, New York and Pennsylvania. BioMidWest is the collective venture of Iowa, Indiana, Illinois, Michigan, Missouri, Nebraska, Ohio and Wisconsin. (There's no truth to the rumor that this group meets at Big Ten football games. I should know. I started it.) It seemed that every state in the union was interested, and every territory to boot. Remember that Puerto Rico manufactures most of our blockbuster drugs, and they are all labeled "Made in U.S.A." Technically speaking, it is the U.S. It's just not one of the S's. And the big news from them is that they've decided to call it "Bio Island." You would think that being called Puerto Rico would be snazzy enough, but if you're in biotech, the fragment "bio" almost certainly has to be tucked in there somewhere, and there doesn't seem to be a really workable runner-up.

But names are just names. Mark had been around the biotech industry, and he knew the lay of the land. He knew that no matter how many press releases were sent out heralding the glories of one purported biotech region or another, there were really only a handful of thriving biotech centers in the United States, with the granddaddy of them all being right here in San Francisco. The numbers—as they frequently do— tell the tale. Of the 5,000-plus biotech companies worldwide, over 1,500 are in the United States, and over 800 of these are within spittin' distance of San Francisco. That means over half of the American biotech companies are within fifty miles of each other. The remainder of Yankee biotech enterprise spreads itself throughout the rest of the country except for a big chunk that hangs out in San Diego, while several third-tier regions should be counted, as well. Which means there ain't a lot of biotech left to go around.

But biotech is all about the future. About potential. About the promise of both miracle cures and miracle-caliber financial rewards. So while it's true that most states have little biotech to speak of, without a doubt every state wants in.

A frequent ploy is for states to claim *they're already huge.* They have state colleges whose scientific research is being published "at this very moment" in refereed journals. Their towns have been home to pharmaceutical plants for decades. The expertise—they argue—is *already in place.*

From there, they promote the broad vision of the state. Perhaps there are favorable laws, or they've built biobusiness incubators, all meant to show their readiness to prime the great pump of commerce. Pennsylvania, for example, spent its settlement from Big Tobacco building biotech "greenhouses," where they tell you they actually "grow" biotech start-ups. Besides some very good start-up efforts, their formidable economic development team is fronted by public relations pro's and jet-fueled by spin. They serve up visions of an economically booming future, no doubt atop their own hefty slice of the biotech pie. And while Pennsylvania is a reasonable example, Mark figured out pretty quickly that no matter what the actual status of a state was, everyone had the same message: "We're open for business!"

Scanning the incoming waves of e-mail on his laptop, he'd shout it out to no one in particular. The press releases, phone calls, and spiffy mailings didn't fool him one bit. Most, he explained, were only *getting ready* to do business. They'd committed to building buildings—or had actually built them under the "if we build it, they will come" doctrine. Many had hired staffs, eager and willing to engage and filled with talk about what was *going* to happen. There were offers to talk with a bevy of ingénue start-ups, but they were so new, they were still opening checking accounts and unpacking boxes. The prize for worst offense came some months later when one city (which won't be named) put a bunch of us journalists in a van, drove us to an empty lot, and told us that this was where they were *going to build* the building. (It got ugly. The journalists turned on them.) But at BIO 2004, in response to pitch after pitch, Mark countered with his big booming voice: "'We're open for business' is not a story!"

After a while, he even made it work for him. His Southern accent would go into overdrive. "We've heard 'We're open for business' till our ears bleed! You got any scientists?"

He was deluged with inquiries, and he loved swimming in them. We could be anywhere and he'd grab the cell phone from his belt and negotiate a story, a guest, a time, a day. Phone pressed between shoulder and ear, his schedule of openings on papers in one hand, his fountain pen in the other. (Yes! A fountain pen! He tells me "It's a Southern thing." Or he may have said, "It's a Mark thing." Either way, it was hard to ignore it waving around in the air.) He attacked this job with relish, and *every* time was a *good* time to talk. It was obvious from the start he was the man for the job.

But the hungry states were only part of the picture. Also over the transom came pushes from individual companies, pleas from policy consortiums, notices about press conferences and thinly-disguised social invitations. Which is how we got to the genetically modified food lunch in the first place. The topic and the luncheon sponsors were identified, but it's always the draw that gets the journalists into the room.

○   ○   ○

THE LUNCHEON had been strategically set for the first open day of registration—the day *before* the conference officially started. Members of the press would already be in town—especially since it was San Francisco, and there would be little competition from other official distractions. It was clear our hosts had paid dearly to get the venue—it was all of ten steps from the press room. And the draw? It was a speaker everyone wanted to see in the flesh—David Kessler, the former and controversial commissioner of the Food and Drug Administration and the current head of the prestigious UCSF Medical School. This was the very same place where Herb Boyer first figured out how to splice-n-dice gene fragments back in the 1970's, leading to the founding of Genentech and giving birth to the entire biotech industry. Today, the University of California at San Francisco med school has even risen higher as a font of innovative research, and so there was a possibility we could get two stories for the price of one.

But why was Kessler controversial? Well, the "Google trail" tells it all. In fact, it's an object lesson in science and American politics.

The first President Bush had appointed him to head the FDA in 1990, and President Clinton kept the party going when he came into office. Certainly, there was no question about Kessler's credentials. The man had enough for two stellar careers: Phi Beta Kappa, Amherst. JD, University of Chicago Law School. MD, Harvard Medical School. Internship and residency, Johns Hopkins. Medical director, the hospital at Albert Einstein College of Medicine. Various teaching gigs included expounding on food and drug law at Columbia University. Add to that the awards, board memberships, and the capacity to eventually produce a best-selling book after his FDA stint was over.

But it was during his FDA years that he earned his reputation. On the controversial side, there didn't seem to be anything he didn't want to regulate. He established his capacity for zeal by seizing somewhere between 24,000 and 40,000 gallons of orange juice because it was labeled "fresh," when in fact it was made from concentrate. Even today the FDA is still proud. Visions of Elliot Ness and his boys raiding bootleggers are proudly alluded to in Kessler's official FDA biography, which stretches painfully in an attempt to make "Elliot Knessler" both a sound-alike and read-alike play on words.

On a more serious side, Kessler decided that the silicone breast implant folks had had more than enough time to complete further scientific studies, and he pulled silicone breast implants off the market, declaring them bad for women's health. He lobbied pharmaceutical companies to stop providing MD junkets to fancy resorts so that doctors could be "educated" on the latest treatments. And he became positively infamous for trying to bring tobacco under the control of the FDA, arguing that nicotine was a powerful addictive drug. Although he was unsuccessful, by the time it all played out there was no doubt America understood that tobacco was addictive.

The launching and tending of *FDA v. Brown & Williamson Tobacco Corp.* took both passion and fortitude. Newt Gingrich, then Speaker of the House, called Kessler "a bully and a thug," a sample of the public abuse Big Tobacco also threw at him. The case ultimately wound its way to the Supreme Court, where O'Connor, Rehnquist, Scalia, Kennedy, and Thomas essentially sided with the tobacco companies, and Breyer, Stevens, Souter, and Ginsburg didn't. One justice in a different direction, and the FDA would now be regulating tobacco. And regulating it to the hilt, if David Kessler had his way.

Still, Kessler did have one visible *positive* role early on in his FDA career. He was the enthusiastic "explainer" of food labeling, now as common as Kleenex and the law of the land. Proudly stated on the FDA's website, "Kessler himself . . . appeared on major news and entertainment shows to unveil the agency's new 'Nutrition Facts' food labels. Designed with bold new graphics, they were intended to make food labels more useful to the consumer and soon became one of the most recognizable graphic formats in the world."

I think the reason he did so well with it and didn't get into trouble was really pretty simple—it wasn't his baby. He *inherited* the requirement to label food. He didn't invent it. He didn't have to fight anybody. He didn't rile anybody up, take a chunk out of anybody's food chain, or have to deal with the politics. The fight was over before he showed up. And we know this because the FDA website reveals one very important fact: "Dr. Kessler was sworn in on the same day that the Nutrition Labeling and Education Act (NLEA) was signed." So while David Kessler became the face of food labeling in this country, it was hardly his idea, his passion, his personal crusade, like the orange juice debacle or the crusade against tobacco addiction. It was already a full-fledged act of Congress and became law on the very day he got his shiny new government employee ID and was looking around for the coffee machine. Food labeling was simply his first order of business.

Best of all, he got to make the rounds of TV, radio and the press—the fun part! Which he did enthusiastically and well. Yes, he was the loud and booming voice of food labeling in the interest of public safety, but there's always a difference between simply telling *the* story . . . and telling *your* story. And it was never *his* story. I know the difference. I can hear it in the studio with the headphones on. Are you telling *the* story? Or has it become *your* story. It doesn't have to be about you. It's about whether you are gripped by it . . . or not. It's easy to guess, he wasn't.

Now, let's get back to lunch.

It had been some eight years since Kessler left the FDA. He had gone on to Yale medical school, and was now happily the dean at UCSF School of Medicine. The press hadn't seen him lately, and there was great interest on everyone's part—both from the American press and the international contingent—in seeing what David Kessler had to say *now.*

I on the other hand was simply following orders. Mark had arranged the entire thing, the first stop on a breakneck schedule he had engineered so that we would miss absolutely nothing. It was late Sunday morning and I was really kind of groggy when he took us down to Moscone Center, made sure our press credentials were properly in order, and took me for a quick glimpse of the press room, which he had already checked out. "No time to dawdle!" Mark expansively declared, before rolling me across the hall to lunch.

We entered the room and reported our presence at the entry table. Our names dutifully checked off, we were handed weighty folders of press materials, and I looked up to see that the room was jammed with elegantly set tables, at most three feet apart, and pretty much every seat had been taken. There was one last empty table of ten in the farthest corner, and without consulting Mark, I snaked my way along the back wall, trying to be unnoticed. The presentations had already started, and instead of just Kessler, there were no less than five people cheek-to-jowl on the tiny stage up-front. (I suddenly remembered that old bait-and-switch tactic. Yes, other names had appeared on the invitation. They were just in smaller type and a bit below Dr. K's.)

It was tough going as everyone and everything was packed so tightly. I began to wonder if this had all been checked out by the Fire Department, but then I realized the Fire Department probably only asked how many people would be in the room. There was no local ordinance on the number of giant screens that can be placed at every possible turn. It was an old media ploy with new technology, making sure you couldn't miss whatever it was they wanted to show you. *No, no! You can't make me look! You can't make me look!* But try as I might, PowerPoint slides of huge data charts and flashing bullet points zipped by, weirdly accompanied by a too-loud and out-of-balance speaker system. (This last you can't completely blame on them. I tripped over one cable almost immediately, and you can bet the sound system suffered any number of insults from the get-go.) Still, no matter which way I turned my head, there was this parade of startling images, strangely reminiscent of Orson Welles in the funhouse hall of mirrors scene in "The Lady from Shanghai." That same sense of vertigo, also familiar to those who favor sitting too close to the screen at drive-in movies. But the unspoken deal was that if they were feeding you lunch and serving up David Kessler for dessert, by golly, you were going to get blasted with the message.

I had finally reached the empty table when Mark tugged on my sleeve. "No!" he said in an insistent whisper. "We have to make friends!" *Please, no. Don't make me do this.* Pleading, I looked up at him. He held my gaze while he pointed with a twist of his hand to the next table, like a practiced docent leading a recalcitrant group through a high-class museum. Two people sat there, side-by-side, staring at us. They seemed above the assault. Or just possibly, they considered our presence an assault. No doubt, they preferred to keep the only other empty table of ten to themselves, and wondered why we wouldn't do the same, since we had the clear opportunity. Or possibly they had watched us trip and fall across the room, only to be followed by our animated *sotto voce* exchange and pantomime. No matter. In the blink of that moment, they both registered alarm.

Obviously, this was no time to make a scene, so I smiled and circled around to sit next to Clive. *Yes, finally Clive.* Between the changing rotation of speakers and the food arriving by practiced wait staff in practiced succession, we had all introduced ourselves. For the very first time, I had to describe to a fellow journalist what we were doing. A fellow *biotech* journalist. Two of them, in fact, who had probably spent years honing their craft, studying the science behind every detail, ensuring that what they wrote was precisely correct and provided no room for misimpressions. They drilled down into the topic making sure every fact they would report was in context. And here I was, knowing essentially nothing about the topic, and presuming to be doing biotech interviews as soon as Mark could corner a willing victim. My unconscious rose like a freight train comin' at me, and I nearly froze with fright.

Clive and Nuala (she was the other journalist) buried their alarm and introduced themselves. Clive turned out to be Clive Cookson, the science editor for London's *Financial Times,* and Nuala Moran, the current senior editor with *Science|Business,* although at this particular conference, she was serving in her role as the U.K. correspondent for *BioWorld.*

In short order, the waiters placed a salad before each of us, and each sported three gargantuan shrimp. We all looked down. We all looked up. We looked at each other. Were all the foods we were eating genetically modified? Were these huge shrimp originally destined to be teeny-tiny, but with a little clever tinkering had been switched to jumbo? What about the butter which we now noticed had been pushed into strange space alien shapes? Had it popped out of some genetically modified cow this way? By the time David Kessler got up and started talking about obesity, you were either in . . . or you were out . . . on the GM food before you. Not unlike Heidi Klum's abrupt dismissal on *Project Runway.* "You are out. *Auf wiedersehen.*" I had lost my appetite completely, while Mark was eating with great gusto. The man's constitution made him a natural member of the media. Perhaps he had finally found his true calling.

In the end, Clive and Nuala kindly let us know that nothing really new had been said. Then Mark, the perpetual scheduler, surprised me by asking them if they would be at the British reception the following night. We all agreed to keep an eye out and I momentarily posited that they were completely sincere, but meant that they would then run in the opposite direction. Still, I had made it through my first explanation of what *BioTech Nation* was going to be, and no one called the journalism police. I had made the acquaintance of actual biotech journalists, and I had actually somehow managed to see David Kessler in the flesh. Maybe this was going to work after all.

Of course, I was off my game. That was for sure. Normally, I would have cornered Kessler for an interview, but in that moment, I didn't know any more about him than the average person. And Mark was so new he didn't realize he should have leaped up and organized it. The only mistake the folks hosting the luncheon made was not bombarding Mark with misrepresentations. That would have gotten his attention. And Mark would have wanted to schedule the man and not the message. But be that as it may, Mark had plenty on his plate.

Suddenly Mark spun up like a CD inserted in a laptop. Like the White Rabbit in *Alice in Wonderland,* he looked at his watch and pronounced, "No time. No time. We're late. No time." Then he grabbed my arm and marched me out of the convention hall to find another David—this David being Lord Sainsbury of Turville, then parliamentary under-secretary of state for science and innovation in the U.K. He was about to speak to an international audience at the Marriott a few blocks away.

Of course, the David Kessler story didn't end there. Any member of the press will tell you that good stories never end. Always keep an eye on them, they'll tell you. Even after people die. Sometimes especially after people die, what with the bracing truth-telling of DNA technology. But technology or no, there's always more to be told, more to unfold, more to be revealed—as was the case with Dr. Kessler.

○   ○   ○

WHAT I'VE been casually referring to as "the genetically modified food lunch" was hosted by Fleishman-Hillard, a global public relations firm. F-H represents a whole gaggle of global biotech clients including (funnily enough) Procter & Gamble, the very folks from whom Kessler's boys had blatantly nabbed the orange juice. That was a decent angle in itself, but to tell you the truth, it was not exactly clear how Kessler had come to be on the podium. *Why* he was there could be guessed at. He was talking about science, and after all, Kessler was a scientist in a prominent position. He was dean of one of the most prestigious medical schools and research centers on the planet. Clearly, it was his job to come out and educate the public, and if that meant educating the media so *they* could educate the public, that's even better. More bang for the buck, as we say. He wasn't pushing a product. He was pushing the challenge of obesity and how science might just help with a solution.

He could easily have been speaking for himself, for his institution, and/or for his field of science. And he could also have missed the good old days when he merely had to blink and the press would arrive right on cue, hanging on his every word. Even when they asked rude and challenging questions, *they were listening to you! You were the center of attention! The center of the universe!*

Certainly, the press's interest in David Kessler had grown cold in recent years, as had his media trail. No one was really tracking Kessler, or they would have been aware of a single public announcement from one year earlier: Fleishman-Hillard International Communications had added Dr. David Kessler, then dean of Yale University School of Medicine, to their international advisory board.

Whatever Procter & Gamble felt about him at that point had clearly been happily resolved. Any questions about his inclusion in that august assembly had been asked and answered. But the announcement itself is rife with other implications. Dr. Kessler would be joining a number of other luminaries on this board, including Republican and former House Speaker Newt Gingrich of thug-and-bully fame, as well as a cadre of federal cronies that anyone would like to see (or not see) in the same room: Leon Panetta, former White House chief of staff; Louis Sullivan, former secretary of Health and Human Services; and Mickey Kantor, former secretary of commerce and U.S. trade representative. Former, former, former, big shot, big shot, big shot was the order of the day.

And wow! What a cast of characters. Fleishman-Hillard certainly knew how to cover its bets. But this was hardly news at the time of the GM food lunch. In fact, at the time Kessler was added to its international advisory board it wasn't even news. Although F-H had apparently hoped it would be. By happenstance, I found it on the Internet in an aging press release from PR Newswire, which is where you go with all your press releases. PR Newswire disseminates them far and wide, and it's so convenient for the media. Press-perfect copy, quotes from the powers that be, et al., are fully approved and ready to insert into anyone and everyone's newspaper. Even better is when the release catches the interest of a bona fide journalist, who will then call for an interview or to clarify information. It's like seeding the clouds to make it rain.

When it works, the PR Newswire reference will fade down the list of references on Google, and you won't even know it was how the ball got rolling in the first place. Once an item gets researched and expanded upon, and it lands in *The Washington Post* or is picked up by the Associated Press, the number of Internet links to those news items far exceed the PR Newswire release. If you look for it, you can find it on Google. It may be reference number 286 or 286,000.

In the David Kessler case, it doesn't look like anyone cared to pick up the hint. I found it in the first couple of references, and I only found it because I went out to Google to see if there might be a transcript of what David Kessler talked about at the lunch. Or a reference which might be helpful. How was I to know what gold I would mine when I typed in "David Kessler Fleischman-Hillard"?

The PR Newswire item was unusual in that it also noted that F-H declined to say how much Kessler was being compensated.

David Kessler was being compensated to be on the International Advisory Board?

I guess that's reasonable . . . I mean, he's spending time, obviously. I thought nothing more about it. What did it matter how David Kessler came to be speaking at the lunch? What did it matter, his relationship with Fleishman-Hillard? What did it matter if and how much David Kessler was paid? Why should they reveal how much he was paid? . . . *Yet why put the refusal to divulge his compensation in the PR Newswire release? Was it bait to get a journalist to call and ask?*

Well, it didn't work. No one called. Or if they did, they didn't write about it or anything else about David Kessler joining their advisory board. It withered on the vine. As of this writing, David Kessler and the boys are all listed in a row right out there on the Fleishman-Hillard website under the description of its powerhouse public affairs practice. And that shouts one very important message for F-H: *These fellas are on your side if you hire us! And they are just a sample of who's on our international advisory board. We'll introduce you around after you come on board!*

But here's a great example of how a good story never ends.

In October 2006—three years after the advisory board announcement and a full two years after the genetically modified food lunch—David Kessler got back in the news in a completely unrelated dust-up. This time, it was a local California story having to do with excessive pay packages for University of California executives.

It turns out that David Kessler, as dean of the UCSF School of Medicine, earns a salary of $545,000 a year. This is more than three times the salary of the top-ranking elected official in the state, California Governor Arnold Schwarzenegger, who is entitled to a yearly salary of $175,000, which he tastefully declines.

Dr. K then reported publicly that in addition to his salary, he had three outside gigs for which he was paid: the Fleishman-Hillard advisory board, for which he receives $100,000 per year; the board of the non-profit Kaiser Family Foundation, for which he is paid a modest $20,500; and the PepsiCo health and wellness blue ribbon advisory board, ringing in at $50,000. (The F-H connection is one thing, but *$50,000* from *PepsiCo?* That would be how many lifetimes worth of high-fructose-corn-syrup-laced Pepsi? Do they drink gallons of the stuff at board meetings? How does he square this with his work on obesity? What is he doing on the board of a company that produces reservoirs full of soft drinks no healthy person should be consuming? . . . *!!!*)

I don't mean to be picky about all this, but these are easy pickins.

And I'm prepared to be reasonable. If all David Kessler—that possible thug and bully—had to do to protect $100,000 in annual income was get along with Newt—that creative name caller—for a couple of meet-ups a year—well, heck, why not let bygones be bygones? And to be truthful, the accusations weren't all coming from Newt's side. Dr. K threw some mud over the fence himself. In his 2001 book, *A Question of Intent,* he tells us that Newt called him "a thug and a bully" immediately prior to boarding "a plane owned by a tobacco company."

Now, now, boys! You're both going to have to stop all this and play nice. Here's $100,000 for you. And $100,000 for you.

Yes, it's true. Journalists can be sooooo picky. And yes, it does matter that Kessler was being paid by Fleishman-Hillard. It matters very much. You see, when people accept such sums of money, both their actions and their words immediately become suspect, even if they really are straight arrows. It's hard for these fellas not to appear to be in league with the big boys, whoever the big boys are. And it's hard for most mortals to give up $100,000 a year for probably not doing all that much. But, hey! Let's give credit where credit is due. A special "hats off" to Fleishman-Hillard! What a crowd they've assembled. And expensive, too.

But wait a minute! We only know what David Kessler gets. What does Newt get? Of course, now Newt knows what David gets. So does Leon and Louis and Mickey. And what do they get? You know Newt's got to believe he deserves more than any of them. Unless you're Mickey. He's got his own argument for why he's so gosh darn valuable. And Louis? He can't possibly expect to get as much as the rest of these boys. Or should he?

Oh, to be a fly on the wall. You know this is gonna cost Fleishman-Hillard big bucks. If it hasn't already.

CHAPTER   THREE

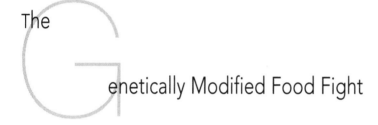

The Genetically Modified Food Fight

WE WALKED out of the convention hall and into the open arms of the riot police.

Whoa! *Riot police?* Those plastic shields in front of their faces really give you the creeps when you're up close and personal. The paramilitary stances, the rigid straight-ahead faces, the identical navy blue uniforms— they make you wonder what planet you landed on. Especially because nobody was there but us chickens on this beautiful, sunny, clear San Francisco day. It was a day like any other day . . . only there were riot police.

This was my first BIO convention, and I was about to learn that the people who object to genetically modified food don't just voice a polite objection. No, they're pissed. Angry. And they are said to follow the BIO convention around like so many Deadheads. The 2004 conference had 18,000 attendees from fifty-nine countries, and to be sure, the conference is really about the business of biotech, as opposed to the science.

From the protestors' standpoint, that was the problem. They objected to the science alright, from genetically tinkering around with seeds to using animals to test products to the very idea of stem cell research. No, they didn't all object to everything, but they were united in that their gaze landed directly on the profit motive. To them, the profit motive tainted all the attendees and the convention as a whole.

Of course, the conference attendees didn't quite see it that way, nor did BIO, the big Biotechnology Industry Organization, that was throwing the three-day shindig, and that's the side the riot police were taking.

To get a picture of what all the shoutin' was about, there's a pretty clear outline out at FoodFirst.org, where Margaret MacSems and Kathy McAfee have published "The Activist's Guide to the BIO 2004 Conference." They went through the conference program in detail and ran down the major objections. They also pointed out that the biotech industry was well aware of the activists, citing official program verbiage. One session, "Animal Extremism—A Growing Threat to Biotechnology," reads as follows: "This session will review the escalation of animal extremism, critically analyze the threat to the biotech industry and provide advice on how to prevent, prepare and respond to activist attacks."

Hey, you must be "real" if they have sessions about you! Unless I missed a click-through button, the FoodFirst website was simply an analysis of the issues. There were no directions to upcoming protest or hints on when they might be scheduled. Still, the blogs revealed there was clearly some grassroots organizing going on. But that wasn't my mission. I wanted to see what riled these people up into a frenzy, and I pretty much found the full list.

Weaving our way through the police line, which had formed in anticipation of early protesters, we were told that the first *known* protester activity was actually going to be that evening before the official opening party. Apparently, the protesters were going to stage a genetically modified food fight. They may be furious, but at least they had a sense of humor.

o   o   o

IN ITS INFINITE wisdom, BIO had staged the opening reception down at Fort Mason, a retired Army post with huge old buildings, most of which were built on piers sticking out into the Bay. Where else could you pack in 18,000 of your closest friends and be reasonably sure the protesters couldn't crash the party?

Most people had boarded buses at their various hotels downtown and were placidly driven across the city. Since we were local, Mark and I decided to drive and take our chances. Even if we had to walk into the venue, we could then leave any time we wanted.

If you're not familiar with the entrance to Fort Mason, it's fronted by a big parking lot and marina, and a road runs alongside the lot, separating it from a big Safeway store, a veritable bastion of genetically modified food. What luck! They could have as big a GM food fight as you wanted, and it would be hours before they ran out of food!

We drove in from the other direction, thinking we might make an end run around the convoy from downtown, and we almost made it before traffic started backing up. As we came around the curve we could see two small groups of protesters, one on either side of Marina Boulevard, shouting and raising their fists. And there were lots and lots of police. Just like downtown, there were more police than there were protesters. And the police were all over the place. In the middle of the road. Lining the curbside. Police cars parked at various odd positions.

Waving our press credentials out the window and talking fast, we were turned back once by a policeman who ordered us to move and "Move now," yelling in that scary way they're all trained to do in difficult situations just like this. One more circle around, and we made it past him. Then we were told to move up twenty feet and stay put in the intersection, right on top of the remains of the genetically modified food fight.

Either they'd run out of money, or they'd made their point, or the same fella who turned us back the first time had spoken sharply to them, but the crowd had stopped tossing any more stuff into the road. Only shattered watermelon rinds were still recognizable, as the entire area was smeared with fruits and vegetables, tamped down into one big organic slick. Or would that be a genetically modified slick? The protesters were only shouting half-heartedly while we were in front of them, but the pause in the action didn't last for long.

Just then a line of riot police startled us, jogging in military precision two-by-two around our car. The shouting rose into a loud chant. Coming head on, chartered buses jammed with conference attendees were suddenly fast-tracked in front of us. Then the main traffic cop spun around and pointed at the entrance to the parking lot. He circled his arm around and around, pointing and shouting, "Go! Go! Go!" We went. And were lucky not to have spun out in all the goop. It was a real relief to finally drive through the gates of the fort, park, and start making our way over to the reception hall.

Then we looked up. And stopped in our tracks. There were police lookouts positioned above us on the hill. Now that was unnerving. This was my hometown, and I'd been coming to this place for years. I've never associated it with violence, or even the thought of violence.

Inside the huge reception, everyone questioned whether the threat was real, and the votes were mixed. As the week progressed, the action appeared to escalate. Coming in and out of the conference, we were met with rows of barricades and lines of police. They were standing at attention, helmets strapped to their chins, four-foot billy clubs clamped to their belts. A few had video cameras on long poles, no doubt to record arrests and counter charges of police brutality.

Each time we left, security would ask us to take off our badges to avoid being recognized and harrassed, but even so, we stuck out like sore thumbs against the ragtag protesters. One science researcher, whose life work now involved racing against the clock to stave off his wife's cancer, was shaken by a verbal assault while entering the convention center. A woman said she didn't feel safe enough to walk alone from her hotel. And while the newspaper reported that one CEO had actually engaged in a civil conversation with several protesters, I happened to know that his company's efforts will reduce the need for animal testing—no doubt, that was the message he delivered.

E-mails and telephone calls came in from friends all over the country, concerned for our safety. Yet I could find no one who witnessed anything akin to the footage playing out on the TV news. Of course, if they arrest a bunch of people and put them in jail for three days, by the time they get out, the conference would be over. I guess you had to be there at the right time in the right place. After all, *someone* got the television footage.

What I did hear was rumors. All from the attendees. They went like this: The protesters were regulars, well-known to the police, and who always showed up to protest everything. Or they were shipped in from Seattle. They were locals from the surrounding bad neighborhood, just out to make a nuisance of themselves or wanting in on a little "street theatre."

Whoever they were, the protesters were more or less effective. At times, the entirety of downtown San Francisco would unexpectedly go into gridlock, and then, just as suddenly, traffic would begin to flow again. By the closing reception, a half-block walk from the convention center, the police had shut down all of Market Street, something I've never seen in all my years in San Francisco. Streetcars were lined up and silent. Riot police were clustered in the middle of the street, drawing a motley crowd of protesters. There was sporadic cheering, a weird tension in the air, a sort of a seedy street carnival atmosphere. One scruffy fellow had a video camera and a black leather jacket hand-painted with the words: "Legal Observer." And there was a large empty white bus with locked and barred windows parked in the middle of the street and bearing a sign advertising jobs with the sheriff's department.

I found myself asking one question again and again: How much did these protesters actually know about what they were protesting? That led to a more important question: How much did I know?

The truth was . . . not much.

○   ○   ○

OH, I'D HAD inklings that biotech was thriving, but frankly, for many years, I wasn't paying all that much attention. Still, it seemed to me that some time ago I'd actually done an interview on genetically modified foods with someone who seemed perfectly reasonable. Who was it? *When* was it?

I started looking through the *Tech Nation* archives, and since I keep all my interview notes on my computer, it was just a matter of checking all the female names I didn't recognize. And there it was . . . in 2002. It turned out to be one of those *Tech Nation* interviews that I had unwittingly done on biotech and didn't really grasp its importance at the time.

The guest was Kathleen Hart. A longtime journalist, she worked the science-tech-government-policy side of things, and over the course of her career had reported on nuclear power for McGraw-Hill's *Nucleonics Week,* as well as on health and the environment. Some of her articles had appeared in *The Boston Globe,* and she had also covered agriculture and biotech for *Food Chemical News.*

If you're not familiar with this later publication, I don't blame you. It's been around for fifty years and has its roots in the days when publications were named descriptively, if unimaginatively and with no regard for the impact on the human soul. Truthfully, it's really only of interest to people in a particular end of industry and government, and it carries an expensive annual subscription. Let's be very clear, though—this is journalism. The information reported in *Food Chemical News* must be correct and up-to-date, and the price and smallish circulation only reflects the fact that there's a limited audience. This is no beach read. Those who need this information, need it very much. Government policy and regulations are complicated and can change every day of the week. Knowing that they've changed—and what that means—is crucial.

Food Chemical News is a whole lot like its sister publications, the equally-enticing *Pesticide & Toxic Chemical News,* and *HACCP & Food Compliance News.* Most people won't know what HACCP is. It's an FDA term that stands for Hazard Analysis & Critical Control Point, and the FDA website explains how to pronounce it: "hassip." The website has everything you would ever want to know about HACCP and more. It turns out that the FDA regulates the "low-acid canned food" industry, the seafood industry, and the juice industry. HACCP policies are also in place over at the USDA for meat and poultry processing plants.

And if you haven't had enough of this already and really want to lose your appetite, please be advised of this statement, direct from the FDA: "The need for HACCP in the United States is further fueled by the growing trend in international trade for worldwide equivalence of food products and the Codex Alimentarius Commission's adoption of HACCP as the international standard for food safety." If there ever was a more deserving bunch to be protested, I don't know who they would be. These Alimentarius folks sure *sound* scary, especially when you realize that the Latin word *alimentarius* roughly translates as "the food police".

At the same time, know that you're looking straight into the nitty-gritty of federal government regulation. It's how the government goes about keeping America's food supply safe. And the FDA sure does know how to regulate—you gotta give it that.

But that's not why or how Kathleen Hart had found her way to *Tech Nation.* Nope. She had simply written a book entitled *Eating in the Dark . . . America's Experiment with Genetically Engineered Foods,* and it just happened to come across my desk. For some reason, I must have thought it looked interesting.

The wisps of fog were beginning to clear from my brain, and I was starting to remember. It was from Kathleen Hart that I heard the European joke: "What do you call an American supermarket with no genetically modified food?" . . . "Empty!" It was from Kathleen Hart that I learned that genetically modified food is the same as genetically engineered food. It's just a different term for the same thing, in all likelyhood media spin, since nobody likes to think they eating anything that's been engineered. It was also Kathleen Hart who had laid out just exactly how much GM food had made it into our food stream. From corn and soy, to high-fructose corn syrup to fillers, it was in just about every kind of packaged food you can buy.

And it was also Kathleen Hart who had answered my exasperated, off-the-cuff question: "How did we suddenly get all this genetically engineered food in our supermarkets?" She responded with a snap: "Why, we have Dan Quayle and the President's Council on Competitiveness to thank for that!"

What?!?!!

It was such an important answer, I knew I had to go back and check it for myself. Actually, not at the time of the interview. Right then, it just seemed like a surprising answer. I almost couldn't believe it.

But now, as I was on the verge of becoming a biotech journalist, and I was seeing all these food protesters, I thought, what a good question. How *did* we get here? And what *is* this whole hullabaloo surrounding genetically modified food? How did GM food come into our semi-pristine food supply? Surely, the information was a matter of public record.

Turns out, the action pretty much happened between 1990 and 1992.

○   ○   ○

AUGUST, 1990 brought us the first President Bush's "Four Principles of Regulatory Review for Biotechnology." Like all documents—even short ones—it takes time before we learn which sentences, words, and phrases will turn out to haunt us.

In hindsight, my vote is this sensible and seemingly innocuous sentence:

> Biotechnology products that pose little or no risk should not be subject to unnecessary regulatory review during testing and commercialization.

There's that *regulatory* word. And what's the word *unnecessary* doing next to it? In a federal government document? I thought these guys always moved for control, not lack of control. Ah, but growth requires being unhampered by too much regulation. It's that old "free marketplace thing," as Bush Senior himself might say. Okay, so no unnecessary regulation. I'll go for that.

And of course, that principle would be tempered by the part that reads "little or no risk". But how would we determine if a biotechnology product poses "little or no risk"? Well, that answer's simple. Science. What was there to worry about?

Separately, a Biotechnology Science Coordinating Committee was formed to include the US Department of Agriculture, the Environmental Protection Agency, and the FDA, as well as the White House Office of Science and Technology Policy. Eventually, this committee produced a report, which was sent over to the President's Council on Competitiveness, headed up by none other Vice President Dan Quayle.

Now we're onto Kathleen's trail.

Since so much of the focus in genetically modified foods is on corn, let me break right here and point out that Dan Quayle hails from the reasonably big corn state of Indiana, although Indiana does trail Iowa, Illinois, Nebraska, and Minnesota. Still, those are the Big Five when it comes to corn production, and I have to believe that Dan Quayle knows his corn. Weak on the spelling of the word *potato*, but for Dan, "corn" is not a four-letter word.

We could talk about what things were like back in 1990, but what things are like today is far more germane. Despite the reputation we have in the world, *not all the corn we grow in the United States* is genetically modified. To be sure, 85 percent of our soybean crop is genetically modified, while three-quarters of our cotton crop is, as well. But let's stick to the corn.

According to the USDA:

In 2004, 55% of the corn acreage planted in the U.S. was 'Non-Biotech'

And the footprint that US corn makes on the world?

In 2004–2005 (the October thru September Marketing Year),

- ○ The U.S. grew 43% of the world's corn.
- ○ The U.S. exported about 17% of the corn it grew, and kept the rest of it—some 83%.

A good question is: What portion of the 83% that we keep, do we actually make into other products that we then export—well, I couldn't really figure that out, but I do know this:

The U.S. grew 66% of the world's corn exports, i.e., the corn which was shipped from one country to another as corn.

In rough terms, there are two main points to be made here:

1. Exporting corn is big business.

2. For every ear of biotech corn we grow, we also grow an ear of non-biotech corn.

Which leads anyone to ask: What kind of corn are we eating when? When is it biotech, and when isn't it? When is it genetically modified or genetically engineered or GM or who cares what, and when is it the good old-fashioned kind?

Hold on. Not quite time yet to answer that question.

Let's finish this aside first.

In the interest of full disclosure, Dan Quayle is also a lawyer, and when he's not eating corn, he's been known to enjoy a good "potatoe."

Now let's get back to the early 1990s, the GM trail, Dan Quayle, and the President's Council on Competitiveness.

Dan and the boys had marching orders to come up with "steps to implement the goal of maintaining and improving U.S. competitiveness in biotechnology." In fairly short order, they came up with the slickest solution imaginable. You see, GM seeds increase crop yield by orders of magnitude. The council could boost both agribusiness and the biotech industry in a single stroke.

Let me repeat that. *The council could boost both agribusiness and the biotech industry in a single stroke.* We could feed ourselves *and* the world, and the U.S. balance of payments would get a spectacular shot in the arm. It was a terrific idea on all fronts.

The only hurdle was that GM crops weren't approved for planting or for consuming. You've got to know that the members of the council went back and studied that single sentence from the president's "Four Principles" until they were blue in the face: "Biotechnology products that pose little or no risk should not be subject to unnecessary regulatory review during testing and commercialization."

The council was looking to create an optimal economic landscape for biotech. If GM seeds and the crops they produce were to be successfully commercialized—*without regulation*—the council would have to ensure that there was "little or no risk."

What to do? Umm. What to do?

Why not just ask science?

Well, unfortunately, there wasn't all that much science to be had. We hadn't grown a lot of GM crops. We hadn't eaten a lot of GM food. There wasn't a lot of science to go on. The first level of science was to make sure the modified seed did what it was designed to do. But as for the impact on humans and the environment—that's another level of science. That couldn't have been done to any great degree.

But given that so many people in Washington, D.C. are lawyers and not scientists, it's not surprising that they came up with a way to dissect the words and to use what science there was . . . to *argue for* safety.

They had the answer!

They would declare genetically modified foods safe . . . *there being no scientific evidence to the contrary.*

That argument almost sounds rational, until you realize that such a claim works especially well when there is no scientific evidence whatsoever.

Now, don't get excited here. I'm not arguing that GM food is unsafe. I'm just saying that from a strictly scientific viewpoint, GM food was not extensively tested. That didn't mean they were unsafe. It didn't mean they were safe. It meant the foods were *untested.*

You see, in science, we don't have an "innocent until proven guilty" clause. That's a legal concept.

It also means that science can't declare something "safe, until it's proven to be unsafe." We have an "untested" state. And then we have a "tested in these particular ways and under these circumstances" state.

So who exactly should be deciding if a GM food is safe? Well, there's the FDA, the USDA, and the EPA. They—in their various areas of responsibility—would decide what level of testing would be appropriate. This is what we would call the "regulatory environment." And regulations do change as we learn more, *scientifically,* about any situation.

Still, to my way of thinking, this "safe until proven unsafe" argument—while very innovative—wasn't the final step to actually opening the door to GM foods. It was a very important way station on the road, without a doubt. But while the council came up with the idea and the rationale, it didn't have the power to act.

For that, let's move on to February 24, 1992. That's a date in history that anyone can go out and research on the Internet. Of special interest is a document issued by the White House Office of Science and Technology

Policy. It also contains and/or refers to all the documents I've been talk-ing about, which makes it immensely handy.

```
EXERCISE OF FEDERAL OVERSIGHT WITHIN SCOPE OF
STATUTORY AUTHORITY: Planned Introductions of
Biotechnology Products Into the Environment

Office of Science and Technology Policy

AGENCY: Office Of Science and Technology Policy
Executive Office Of The President

ACTION: Announcement Of Policy
```

Let's stop a moment and enjoy its very title: "Exercise of Federal Oversight Within Scope of Statutory Authority." *Hey, this ain't no position statement. We got the power, and this is how it's gonna be. Right here at the Executive Office of the President. You gotta problem with that?*

And then there's the subject to appreciate as well. "Planned Introductions of Biotechnology Products into the Environment." *Finally! Clarity from Washington.*

While you would expect some combination of Washingtonspeak, governmentspeak, and let's-obscure-our-intention-speak, this is refresh-ingly clear: Biotechnology products are coming, and this is how we're gonna do it.

And that's it. That's how we got genetically engineered foods into supermarkets across the entire nation. Remember when people used to wring their hands wondering "How are we going to feed the world? There are just so many people." You haven't heard that lately, have you? And why not? GM crops are really a marvel.

o   o   o

NOW IF YOU think the story I've just told is all very interesting, you might find the next one interesting as well. Why is it—with all the food labeling we have going on—you can turn over any food package every which way, and it doesn't say anything about genetically modi-fied anything???

Well, I'm so glad you asked!

But I think you already know the answer.

Who's in charge of food labeling?

The FDA.

Did the FDA know that GM wasn't going to be on the label?

Well, remember, the FDA was a participant in the Biotechnology Science Coordinating Committee. The same committee that sent its report over to the President's Council on Competitiveness. The same report that was cited in the executive order issued by the White House Office of Science and Technology Policy. That would make the answer, "Yes. They knew about it."

Which brings us right back to David Kessler.

Independent of whether or not he thought genetically engineered foods were a great idea, it was his responsibility to enforce the Nutrition Labeling and Education Act (NLEA), the very same one which was signed into law in 1990, on the very same day he started as head of the FDA.

To be clear, GM wasn't in the food labeling law, and the FDA commissioner was only precisely responsible to implement what was in the law. And GM wasn't in the law for a very good reason. GM crops *weren't permitted to be grown* at the time the NLEA was in the making. So they couldn't be eaten. There were no GM foods in the American food supply. With all the complicated machinations that any legislation undergoes before it becomes law, why would Congress legislate against something that arguably didn't exist? It's hard enough to get legislation through both houses of Congress, and then get the president to sign it. "Genetically modified" wasn't anywhere in the final food labeling bill, and presumably that left David Kessler off the hook.

Which left the consumers pretty much in the dark.

American food producers had to pony up the calories on the tiniest packages imaginable, but they spent no time at all tracking whether the product contained anything that was grown from GM seeds. Neither did they track if any part of the GM seed still remained in the product they are hoping consumers would wolf down without a moment's hesitation.

What's clear is that David Kessler was far more excited by the idea that concentrated orange juice might be labeled fresh, than the prospect that Americans didn't know that the food they were eating came from genetically modified seeds.

It would be easy to give almost any other FDA commissioner a free pass on this one, perhaps suggesting that Congress needed to direct him on this matter. But this was David Kessler—the man who launched enormous campaigns to expand the purview of the FDA. Like seeking to regulate tobacco. He was unafraid to stretch the FDA's reach, unafraid to stare down powerful global companies with major political ties, unafraid to drive an issue all the way up to the Supreme Court. But he just didn't see that it was all that important to say, "Hey, it's okay with me if you want to let in all this GM food, but don't you think we should put it on the labels?" And then when they said "No," you would expect David Kessler to pull a David Kessler and escalate the situation into total bedlam.

Word had it that the administration of the first President Bush was tiring of his zealotry, and it was just a matter of time before he would be replaced. But then came the unexpected Clinton win in 1992, giving Kessler's FDA career new life. "To the victor belongs the spoils" tells us to expect a fresh slate of newly-minted appointees with each new administration. But there's more to it than that. "To the victor also belongs a long list of prior appointees, and if you don't think you have a problem and have passed out all the rewards, don't fix it."

To all outward appearances, David Kessler appeared to be a go-along-to-get-along guy. When the Clinton team rolled into town, Kessler rolled with them. The new folks in the White House weren't so trusting of biotech as the Bush-Quayle administration had been, but by then it was a done deal. In truth, there was no scientific evidence *to the contrary*. Maybe that decision was in fact visionary, even if it didn't come down on the side of caution. Besides, money speaks in every administration. There'd have to be a pretty good reason to shut a thriving agribusiness proposition, and there wasn't any. There would have been plenty of blowback, and President Clinton had other challenges in his hands. (Remember that Hillary was in charge of coming up with a new, all-encompassing healthcare plan?)

But why didn't David Kessler put on his crusader's cape and pick up the food labeling sword? Seems to me that sort of thing was right down Clinton and Gore's alley. I don't know if even David Kessler knows. In the absence of any indicators to the contrary, I think we already know: It just wasn't his baby.

And the result? Today, GM foods are as American as apple pie. Or at least as American as high-fructose corn syrup, which, incidentally, former President Clinton now touts as one of the main reasons Americans are becoming obese.

We can readily count our calories, fat, sodium, carbohydrates, and proteins in the food we buy . . . but we have no clue about whether or not it came from seeds which were genetically modified.

In seeking out more on this whole genetically modified food debate, it was clear to me that I couldn't talk to anyone in the United States. They were all wildly pro or wildly con. And the same went for people in Europe, except they were all pretty con. Africa was a mixed bag: Six countries were staunchly against, South Africa was definitely pro, and the rest said they had other problems to solve, so let's delay the decision. South America was a real surprise, because after the United States, the world's largest producer of genetically modified foods is . . . Argentina! While we were licking our wounds from the dot-com bust followed quickly by the devastation of 9/11, we were way too involved to notice that Argentina's economy was headed for the ditch. Argentina's big decision? Become a major producer of genetically modified crops for export and plug the gaping hole in its economy. It worked. That left the only place where I seemed to get an arguably balanced answer: Asia. What were they doing that kept them out of the fray?

○   ○   ○

DR. GURINDER Shahi is both a physician and a scientific researcher in molecular biochemistry. He holds a masters in public health from Harvard, and at the time I spoke with him at BIO 2004, he was the chairman and CEO of BioEnterprise Asia in Singapore. He continues to hold this position today, but now he is also the director of the Global BioBusiness Initiative in Southern California and teaches at USC's Marshall School of Business.

I wanted to know about the *public sentiment* regarding genetically modified foods in Asia, in addition to the public policy. He explained.

"Asians are pragmatic when dealing with GM. Two concerns really need to be taken care of. Number one, people are concerned about safety. Number two, they're concerned about environment, and making sure you don't have environmental contamination. When people can be reassured that these two considerations have been taken into account, they tend to be very open to GM. So, now, the two largest countries in the world, China and India, have started growing GM crops, and I think the impact or significance for the farmers has been very positive. They've actually seen better yields, better income, so there's a lot of interest in moving in this kind of direction."

With basically half the world's population living in Asia, I wondered if all these countries were looking to simply grow more food, or if they were looking to put certain nutrients into the diet to achieve a healthier populace. According to Dr. Shahi:

"Again, it depends completely on the kinds of crop you're talking about. The reality is there is an opportunity there to actually improve nutrition, depending on what's incorporated into the particular crop or plant. One of the great developments over the last decade would be Golden Rice, where we've incorporated Vitamin A into crops like rice which traditionally have lacked the ability to produce carotene, for example. It impacts eyesight, it affects night blindness, and so on. It means a source of Vitamin A for people who otherwise might not have access to this."

I noted that a number of African nations objected to receiving food aid in the form of genetically modified corn. Did Asia have any social or government reactions to GM technology?

"There was some initial reaction. The important thing is that you don't force GM on people. People have got to see the values, the benefits, the advantages that it brings. And the safety concerns, the environmental concerns really need to be taken into account."

You don't force GM on people? Hmm. What a fascinating idea. Then he continued.

"The position in Asia is actually intermediate, I would say, between the very liberal US position and the very conservative European position. Many countries in Asia require labeling. Countries like Japan and Korea, for example. They have labeling laws, but they have no qualms about having GM food in the market. The idea here is to say, 'Well, maybe we don't know everything about GM, but it should be an individual choice whether you want to have

GM food or not.' So we should separate that. Whereas the United States is very strongly against labeling of any sort, and so that's a point of difference with the way things are done in this country. So, in Asia, people say, 'Well, yeah, okay. If you want to take something which is genetically modified, go ahead take it. Twenty years down the road, if something happens, at least you know. I've been taking these products—GM or non-GM.' Then you can actually do real studies along the way, whereas if you mix everything up, it's difficult to tease out what causation might be."

Now that's interesting. Since we don't know what we've been eating, if there turns out to be a problem—and if there's a long lead-time before it rears its head—then we might have a hard time figuring out which GM source caused it—if one did. Or whether it was something else all together.

Then I asked my serious question. Dr. Shahi is an MD in addition to being a scientist. He's very familiar with testing for safety in the interests of public health. I asked him how long it would take to do proper clinical trials on the effects of genetically modified food. To his way of thinking, what would it take to really test genetically modified foods? He slowed down his pace and replied carefully.

"The reality is that human experience has been one of experimentation. We've got something like 30,000 chemicals out there that we use. Less than 600 of them have been properly evaluated, but lots of stuff that's out there in the environment that could have significance in terms of possibly being carcinogenic or having all other kinds of other impacts on us.

If we look at GM foods, because you're actually having very controlled mutations, it's actually probably going to be safer than much of the stuff that we grow naturally. For example, we create cross-breeds of different types of fruits. The kiwi fruit is a human creation, produced by taking very gross types of genetic combinations and hoping something interesting comes out of it. This is traditional, and people say 'Yes, this is natural.' But the reality with GM is that you actually are making very, very specific, pinpoint-type changes in the plant or the animal that you're dealing with, You're coming up with, therefore, an end product that can actually be measured subsequently in terms of how it's performing, how it grows, and what impact it has—whether you've put a nutrient into the whole thing, whether you've essentially allowed the organism to produce a new protein, for example, that was not there in the first place."

And how long would that take to test?

"Back to your question about how long it would take to do the testing, it depends on what you are looking for. If your endpoint does this—now produce Vitamin A—where it didn't in the past, that's a relatively fast test. And if you're going to clinical studies to see whether you take a product with one set of nutrients [as opposed to] the other one, it's a relatively short thing to do. In six months, a year, you can get good results.

If you're looking at carcinogenicity, you're probably looking at three to five years. If you're looking at mutagenic change, for example, teratogenicity [the effect on the fetus], then you need to look at intergenerational-type work.

My hunch is that the kinds of changes that people make in creating genetically modified organisms are so minimal that you're not going to see a massive impact in any of these types of conditions. But to reassure the public, I guess there's a real need to say that 'yes, we've done the testing and we can show that it doesn't have this impact or that impact.'"

Hunch? This is just your hunch?
Of course, it's a hunch. There is little science. Unless you count the great science experiment that is the American food supply. Even then, there is no long-term, multi-generational science. There can't be. There hasn't even been a full generation since we started planting the stuff and eating it.

Still, Dr. Shahi wanted to address some common concerns posed by GM food critics:

"Some of the examples that people have been using about negative consequences include, for example, the Brazil nut protein. If you incorporate that into an organism, and someone is allergic to the Brazil nut, you then have an allergic reaction to the protein. These are very special circumstances that we need to take care of, and be aware of, and deal with in a responsible systematic way."

Wouldn't the solution be labeling?

"Absolutely," he said. "Labeling might really help in this situation, so sometimes I get a little confused at the anti-labeling perception with the U.S. government."

You get confused? What about the rest of us?

○   ○   ○

DR. SHAHI shed light on a number of issues in the debate. For starters, there are a number of issues—not just one. 1) Has GM been thrust upon Americans without their knowledge or consent? 2) Was it brought to the market with sufficient scientific testing? 3) Is it being appropriately tested now? 4) Why isn't the presence of genetically modified seeds or residue written on the infamous food labels *now?* 5) How much genetically modified food has the average American consumed already? 6) Have we already hurt ourselves from a safety standpoint?

There are more questions, to be sure, but these alone are enough to get a perfectly reasonable person riled up and out of his seat, ready to join the protesters. As you can see, this is a snake ball of issues, with each one seeming to lead to another, and none look to be resolved in the near term.

At times like these, engineers try to dissemble the problem. Is it just too obvious to simply put GM on the food label, and see what happens from there? Let the consumer choose. Let the producers charge what they may. Let the marketplace speak. Let the protesters re-arrange themselves. It sure beats an act of congress, although that's exactly what we needed the first time around just to get food labeling into place. If this situation is like everything else, once everything is labeled, different people will make different decisions, and we won't all do the same thing.

One person might not want to eat genetically modified food, but may be perfectly willing to have GM plants grown in a field in Iowa and converted into ethanol to burn in his car. In fact, he might welcome it. Genetic modification could make the feedstock used for ethanol require fewer natural resources and be cheaper to boot. Another may want GM all the way, and for another, GM-nothing.

As for the science of it all, that bears some serious looking at, but it's now a lot trickier. We can examine the population of the United States and see how we're doing, but we've had so much of GM mixed up in our food supply over time in untraceable ways, who knows what we've done. It's as if we've had one big clinical study going on, and unwittingly everyone seems to be a part of it. Except it's not a clinical study. We don't have one group with and a control group without. We don't have the careful addition of one element, and precise combination of others. We don't have the scientific tracing of various markers. Who of us can say what part of what we are eating is GM? And even if we wanted to know, isn't that information lost forever?

Perhaps the most important question of all is this: Is it possible to at least get food labeling of GM into place without a full-scale, nationwide, genetically modified food fight?

If we can't, then we might remember the words of Paul Brodeur, the well-known environmental reporter for *The New Yorker*. He was on *Tech Nation* years ago, and he had some simple advice. "Follow the money trail. It seldom leads you wrong."

CHAPTER FOUR

n a Roll

SIR RICHARD was scanning his guests with an eagle eye, and only he knows why he was on high alert.

The reception in the Garden Court of the Sheraton Palace Hotel in San Francisco was well under way. Drinks, food, and lively interchange were in full abundance. Mark had gotten us there in a timely manner, for this was the Brit reception that he had talked about with Clive and Nuala. We had already located Clive, and he had introduced us around. Periodically, Mark would turn to me and give me the old "Don't turn around now, but that's so-and-so." I would eventually turn, and there he or she would be.

Of the several dozen or so other snazzy and not-so-snazzy events that evening, this was definitely the classiest. The Garden Court was originally the carriage entrance to the Palace Hotel in early San Francisco. It was an open-air courtyard, and the hotel wrapped completely around it. When horses were eventually jettisoned from San Francisco proper, the Palace got the bright idea to cover it over with glass and deck it out. During the day, it's a jewel, capturing sunlight at every hour. At night, it's a dazzling room with mirrored walls, ornate columns, and twinkling sconces. That night was such a night, and the room was packed.

We had earlier received an inquiry from David Lord Sainsbury's homies, and we were to meet with his local delegation liaison, Emma Stevenson, at the end of this very reception to go over general lines of inquiry for the science and innovation minister. We had set a tentative schedule for the formal interview at KQED, but she needed to take a good look at us, if only to make sure we bathed regularly and could watch our manners.

In the mean time, Mark was meeting old friends ("old" in the one-hour-to-two-day sense of "old") and making new ones, at breakneck speed. His Southern accent would wax and wane at inexplicable intervals, as he ebulliently worked the room. From time to time, he would whip out his pad and uncap his fountain pen. This was the signal that he was reviewing available times and offering to pen in someone. He had a bead on the British delegation and their guests as well.

I was exhausted, having survived my very first ever day of *BioTech Nation* interviews. As we had agreed, Mark would be over at the conference while I would be over at KQED. Most of the time, I hadn't a clue who would be coming to the station, but I was assured they would arrive in the KQED lobby with a *BioTech Nation* work-up sheet. I had generated it on my computer in about ten minutes the night before, and it looked like it would work beautifully. Name of guest. Official title. Contact information. E-mail and website. Publicist contact, if any. Pre-interview/Definitions. Interview Topics/Questions.

First on the scene was Dr. Jorgen Thorball, Vice President of Novozymes. He had arrived with the company's American publicist, Roger Friedensen, and it was Roger who had the paper in hand. Mark had passed it to him after quizzing him closely and said—as he would say so many times that week—"Give this to Dr. Gunn. You'll see her before I will."

I thanked Roger and gave the work-up sheet a quick glance. What a perfect example of wishful thinking. Mark had filled in the form, alright, except for Pre-interview/Definitions and Interview Topics/Questions. Being about to interview this person, and being patently clueless, all I could think was, "Great! Here's the thrill of jumping without a parachute! Swinging on the high trapeze without a net!" Maybe thrilled wasn't the word, but it will do.

I walked them to the elevator and, as casually as I could, asked, "Tell me about Novozymes." Roger did the PR heavy lifting, and before you knew it we were ready to go. Between Jorgen's Danish accent and my on-the-spot *Cliff's Notes* quizzing of what an enzyme was, we managed to get in an actual interview that seemed to make sense. Of course, I had to keep poor Dr. Thorball there for a half-hour just to get a seven-minute interview. We would have to start and stop. I would have to ask a question for myself. When I saw where he was going with an answer, I might re-ask the question for insertion in post-production. Roger would wave at us from the engineer's booth, and then he would tell us to be sure to get in this point or that concept. Dr. Thorball would throw in words like peptides and polysaccharides. Hyaluronic acid and eyeballs. Rooster combs and streptococcus. Bacillus and bioethanol. I was hanging on for dear life.

In the end, every great guest always pulls it out. So it was with Dr. Thorball. He ended by saying, "Your body's full of enzymes, and it's the way nature has designed how to move processes forward. People then [began to use] chemicals and other mechanical solutions to try to change things, but nature's way of changing things was using enzymes."

Roger was delighted. Dr. Thorball was a gentleman. I say that because he had to have thought I was as dumb as a post, and he didn't let on. He did say I should meet the president of Novozymes. Now, *he* was a really interesting guy, and that suggestion turned out to be prophetic.

As for me, I was relieved. We had made it through our first interview! I had to re-listen to determine if it would work, but I pretty much knew that it would. Escorting them back down to the lobby, I asked Roger how he had met Mark. "I was standing as close as I could get to the press room. Mark was looking over the shelves where they let publicists leave press materials. I figured someone from the press would come out and look at them. When he showed up, I pounced." We laughed about it and, with that, the elevator door opened. There stood a nice man with a now familiar piece of white paper in his hand. I might as well have called out "Next!" It went just exactly that way for the next five hours. Who I talked to, what they said, what they were doing here—it was all one big biotech blur. And then came the British reception.

o   o   o

YOU CAN imagine that my mind was mush, as I looked around the Garden Court. I could see Clive talking to a tall blond surfer dude. When I pointed him out to Mark, he rolled his eyes and uttered in complete frustration, "That's no surfer dude. That's Professor Sir Chris!"

Huh? Clive was deep in intense conversation with him, while people pressed in all around them, occasionally sneaking side glances. Professor Sir Chris was definitely the fellow they were interested in. "I'm trying to get him to come in for an interview," Mark explained. "He didn't seem too impressed. I hope Clive is telling him we're real people. *We owe Clive if we get the interview.*" We owed Clive for not calling security the moment we walked in the door. Whatever he was saying—well, who knows? I refuse to ask Clive. I simply insist on taking the position that we owe him indefinitely.

Mark was in full swing, while I was really exhausted. I decided to go to the very back of the room, where I could get a full view of the crowd, in case Mark needed me. With any luck, no one would try to tell me their biotech story. Pray God, they not tell me their biotech story. I'd heard quite enough for one day.

It was then I noticed Sir Richard. I don't even know how I knew who he was—Mark, no doubt, or maybe Clive had told me. He was Sir Richard Sykes, former chairman of GlaxoSmithKline, and now rector of Imperial College, London. Imperial integrates science, technology and medicine—the precise elements that combine to create breakthroughs in biotech. (And for you Americans, "rector" would be the same as a university president.) He was a scientist, I'd been told, and I now realized that I spied someone who was actually interesting to me. He was a scientist *and* he had worked his way up to top management and onto the board, as well as becoming its chair. He had then become an academic, breeding the next round of scientists. And with that, he spied me. He took three steps toward me and introduced himself. Well, introduced himself in that way people do when they're hosting a very large social event and they are only trying to welcome you and ensure that you have something to eat and drink and everything you need to have a wonderful time. I assured him I did, and off he went.

He was on the move. Quick, quick, scanning the room. He must be wild to have as a boss. You'd have to be on your toes and quick, quick, quick. I made a mental note and mentioned it to Mark when I saw him next. "Do you think we could get an interview with Sir Richard?" His response was classic. "Don't worry, baby! Mark's on it!"

Eventually, the room cleared, and we had a sit-down with Emma. We guaranteed the availability of a KQED studio at such-and-such a time, and she guaranteed absolutely nothing. Although she was lovely about it, I must say. And at that point, it really didn't matter. We had interviews in the can already! We could start our *BioTech Nation* segments at any time.

We had no idea we were in for an embarrassment of riches.

○   ○   ○

WHEN THE appointed time for Lord David Sainsbury's interview arrived, we were assured he was coming, but indeed, he would be arriving a bit late. Would we mind taking Sir Richard first? *Would we mind? We'd love it!* They explained that Sir Christopher Evans was also on his way and would be even further delayed, and would that be alright? *No! Leave, the lot of you!* Only kidding. We had scored—or were about to score—and we had scored big time. Mark had brought home the bacon. (Or would that be rashers?)

Sir Richard was a dream. He understood what it took to develop people who could push the scientific borders. And his excitement was palpable. (When you read this excerpt from our interview, think Sean Connery!)

"This is the Golden Age of Biology. There's absolutely no question about that. And that was going back to the fifties with the discovery of DNA, from then, the understanding of what that means in terms of genetics, and today almost any problem is solvable in the human sense. Understanding the human being. Understanding how it works, how it operates, how it thinks, how it behaves, how it's susceptible to disease—all these things are possible now. All the technology, all the information, is there for us to do that. It's gonna take a long time, and I think this is a problem that people don't realize. We're capable of doing anything—it's just time that we need. We will understand the brain. We'll understand how the brain works. But it'll take time. It won't happen next week. It's gonna take a long time, but everything's possible now. We have all the templates. We have the information. We have access to the information. All we need to do now is understand it—understand how it interacts with every other bit of information. And so, this is an amazing period. I think to be studying science today is the most exciting thing that anyone could do."

And he spoke English! After two solid days of learning science-by-surprise, my brain had reached critical mass—nothing more could go in, even if I wanted it to. I had just thanked Sir Richard when I looked up to see Lord Sainsbury and his entourage coming into the adjacent engineering booth. Lickety-split, we made the switcheroo, and Lord Sainsbury sat in the seat Sir Richard had just vacated. Sir Richard, for his part, was having a sufficiently good time, so he decided he'd stay for the festivities. There was a full boat of people on one side of the glass, all crowding around our engineer, Danny Bringer, while Lord Sainsbury and I were on the other side of the glass, like fish in the aquarium.

His lordship was a public official, and he did a stellar job with every question I threw his way. But he had a precise job to do. I never got a single original thing out of the gentleman, and if I could have, he would not have been the man for the job.

Still, I kept looking at him and remembering my interview with Sir Edmund Hillary. We had a running joke about him finding me a member of the aristocracy to marry. You see, I had always wanted to be Lady Moira—I think it came from all those old British black-and-white movies from the 1940s that I used to watch with my mother. And stack upon stack of her Agatha Christie novels. Yes. Lady Pamela. Lady Claire. Lady Moira. Has a nice ring to it, no? But that's a purely American take. (Hey! We think Lady Queen Latifah rolls off the tongue!) But Ed—as he likes to be called—had another idea. He wanted to encourage me to personal achievement. "Why not Dame Moira?" he said. "Do it all on your own." But I had to disappoint Sir Edmund. It was Lady Moira, or burn. Looking at Lord Sainsbury, I was tempted to joke with him as well. "Are you single? We could get married, and I'd be Lady Moira, and I really wouldn't be a bother whatsoever!"

But Lord Sainsbury kept any sense of humor he possessed under deep cover, so I didn't dare risk it. I had the impression that Sir Richard, watching from the other room, would have howled, but then there was the stalwart Emma—she would have had a stroke. No, I just couldn't risk it.

I thanked his lordship, and with that, everyone, including the entourage, jumped up. Sir Richard swept into the room with his camera and said, "Let's get a shot." He snapped away as Lord Sainsbury and I stood posed. Then Sir Richard cracked, "I'll send it over to *The Daily Mail*," which was clearly a cheesy London tabloid. We all had a good laugh and took pictures of each other in various assemblages. Right then, Professor Sir Chris showed up, and we all said goodbye. Sir Richard shook my hand and gave me a kiss on one cheek, and then he quite naturally went to give me a kiss on the other, but in midst of all this excitement, I had pulled my head back. *Like a dolt! An American dolt!* He had nothing to kiss, so he tried to make it look as if he hadn't really just kissed the air. He smiled nicely, shook my hand again, and said good-bye. *Shoot me! What an idiot!*

○   ○   ○

THEN I SETTLED in with apparent surfer dude Sir Christopher Evans, who this time was actually wearing a surfer shirt. It turns out he had spent the early portion of his scientific career in the U.S., as well as some time in California. The look, if not the lifestyle, had stuck. Today, he's the Founder and Chairman of Merlin Biosciences, the largest biotech venture capital fund in Europe. He's Welsh, so when you read what he has to say, think . . . Timothy Dalton, who played in several of those James Bond movies. Or think a youngish and blondish Sean Connery, perhaps in his first James Bond role. Even though he's Scot, you can't have too much Sean Connery.

The obvious question to ask him was why he named his company "Merlin." "I was called Merlin about ten years ago now, because I'm Welsh. I'm Celtic," he said. "Merlin was an alchemist, one of the original pharmacologists, working for King Arthur, of course, and I became known as the Welsh Wizard, for good or bad reasons in the national press in the U.K. And so, it stuck. So, Welsh Wizard, Merlin, alchemy—it's all about that. Turning lead into gold."

His early time in the States definitely had an impact on him. "If you talk well enough and long enough in America, and impress a few people," he said, "they usually offer you a job. And that occurred."

I thought he was a good person to ask to compare entrepreneurs in Europe with entrepreneurs in the U.S.

"There is a big people thing. I mean, the science is comparable. There's some superb science in the U.K. and in Europe, particularly the U.K., very strong. We've got a good venture capital base. We've got lots of money. We don't have such a dynamic stock market, I'm afraid. London is nowhere near as dynamic as say, NASDAQ. So then you come down to the people thing, which is the management of the science, of the scientists themselves, and the commercialization of the science on the international markets. I've got to be honest with you. The Americans do that better than anybody else in the world, and I think the British are—to be honest—learning from that.

But there's a more conservative, cautious, less risky nature about British managers, as opposed to their American equivalents. That's something I often beat the drummer (sic) about, and I just think you're very naturally enterprising in America. It's not so natural in Europe. But it's getting better, it's getting better."

It's always hard to dare, isn't it?

"Yeah."

Unless you're Merlin ...

"Ay! I'm up for it! Big time! I spent three years in America. I learned a lot, and I love the culture over here, and I think it's an injection of fresh air in the U.K. to have an 'Americanized' organization, as we call it, but Merlin is very American in its attitude. We're very flexible, creative. We work incredibly long hours. We work weekends, and we love what we do. We're highly committed, and everyone's pretty energized. I lead from the front, and just go over the top, and off we go."

Now, that sounds American . . . Sir Chris was on a roll.

"We love doing it, and I think there are other firms now that have appeared on the scene in venture capital who are similar to Merlin, and you can argue we were similar to some American firms many years ago. We're trying to throw out the old establishment way of doing things, and do things in a very entrepreneurial way, which is typical of America.

I've built about thirty-odd companies now. Thirty-three companies—twenty-three of them are from [universities] in the U.K., so I have a lot of knowledge about what makes them tick. The biggest mistake is rarely to do with the science. It's the ambition of the management team and the boldness of developing the company quickly. To do that, you need a lot of money, of course. . . . [S]tock markets are less ambitious, venture capitalists take less risks than the Americans, and as I said earlier, British managers tend to be a little bit less ambitious and go-getting. When you combine the three things, you tend to create a sort of slowness within these organizations, compared to the American equivalents, which seem to go extremely fast from the word 'go.'"

Since I was new to biotech, I thought I'd ask him to draw me a map of "The Biotech World, According to Chris Evans":

"America is dominant. America is the dominant nation in biotech. It's way ahead of the second nation in the world, which is the U.K. Britain is a clear second. I think the U.K.'s well ahead of Germany and France and Scandinavia, etc., and Europe. You've got Austral-Asia, of course. The Australians, of course, have built a good-quality start-up science base there, but they've got a long way to go yet to develop really big international companies. Of course, China's a threat that everyone talks about—when are the Chinese gonna do what they're gonna do? Well, let's see what happens. There's lots of activities in Korea and Taiwan, and some in Singapore, as well. But I think it's Europe versus the U.S., and I think you should be comparing the two because a similar number of companies [are being] created in biosciences in Europe as there are in the States, but they're a lot bigger in the States. They're a lot more profitable ones.

Whether we'll ever catch up with America? . . . Hey! We can dream!"

Chris Evans may be Welsh, but he sounded American to me.

There was no doubt that with this trifecta—in addition to all the other interviews that we had already done at BIO 2004—we could produce a full-fledged weekly segment on biotech. We were off the ground and running!

We didn't know it then, but in the years to follow, the Brits would provide *BioTech Nation* with any number of fascinating people and interviews. There's Dame Judith Polak, a Professor of Endocrine Pathology at Imperial College and one of Britain's longest-surviving heart/lung transplant recipients. There's the Yank transplant, Dr. Roger Pedersen, who left his prestigious post at UCSF to go to the University of Cambridge so that he could freely and fully pursue embryonic stem cell research. And there's the completely original Baroness Susan Greenfield, a professor at Oxford and the director of the Royal Institution of Great Britain.

Much later, while moderating a debate in front of an audience of 250 people at the BioAgenda Summit 2006, I was able to formally ask her, "Hey, Susan! How'd you get this Baroness gig?" Which is always an interesting question. Certainly, it was in Susan's case, as her father is reported to have been an electrician, and her mother is said to have been a dancer. The award of any title is ready fodder for the press, and the press eventually became interested in two of our three guests in that single fateful hour in 2004, when we snared two knights and a lord, and staged our own *BioTech Nation* version of an episode of *Masterpiece Theatre.*

○   ○   ○

TWO YEARS later, in the spring of 2006, it came to light that a number of people, who had been put forth for peerages by Tony Blair, had recently made large loans to Blair's Labour party. They had clearly been coached, as it was pointed out to them by relevant officials that they need not report these transactions. Under British law, direct donations to political parties must be reported, but loans do not.

Speculation was rampant—one doesn't donate millions of dollars in public and act surprised a few weeks later when your name suddenly appears on the short list for an accolade. If a loan was in the works—out of the public eye—well, you can imagine that the press had a field day.

The initial investigation spread to scores of people, and it turned out that upwards of $25 million was lent to the Labour party by a dozen well-heeled blokes . . . and none of these loans had been disclosed. On the list? Well, anyone could figure Sir Chris Evans to be there—he's just the sort of fella to be in the middle of anything wildly creative. But that leaves one more person, and that would have been a surprise either way. Still, it was shocking to find that the other gent was David Lord Sainsbury.

This all came to light under what became known as the "cash for honors" or "cash for peerage" scandal, which spread as the weeks went by. The investigation is scheduled for completion in January 2007, and all the while, Tony Blair's government continues to be under fire. At this writing, the ultimate fall-out is not known, but fall-out there already is.

It's hard to schuss together, because both David Lord Sainsbury and Sir Christopher Evans had already received their peerage and knighthood, respectively. But that didn't stop the implication of impropriety. Accusations and imaginings flew in all directions.

In September 2006, Sir Chris Evans was actually arrested, after it became known that he had loaned Labour nearly $2 million. At around the same time, he had been appointed head of the UK Stem Cell Task Force, and Tony Blair became affiliated with his charity, the Stem Cell Foundation.

Professor Sir Chris was outraged at the arrest, although he has not yet been charged, and he may never be in the end. Was there a quid-pro-quo? The loan in exchange for the leadership position on the task force? But wait. This scandal aside, if you were building a UK Stem Cell Task Force, Chris Evans would have to be on your short list. If you wanted the task force to actually do something, he would be at the head of your list. At this writing, he insists his loan was perfectly legal (to which all agree), and he's now demanding that his loan be repaid with commercial interest forthwith, as called for in the original loan agreement. Since the Labour party is reportedly broke, that shoe will be falling some time soon.

His lordship, on the other hand, was in the loan pool for something under $4 million, but Lord Sainsbury got into hot water for an entirely different reason. Truthfully, he has donated far more than that amount publicly and directly to the Labour party on numerous prior occasions. When asked about this particular loan, he denied it, standing by his belief that he had fully disclosed all his contributions. Then he apparently realized that he had confused the loan with an earlier donation of a similar amount. Yes, the loan had been made. His confusion was completely reasonable and his explanation entirely possible, although some would like to think not. Whatever it was, it was embarrassing.

After serving impeccably as the science and innovation minister for a very long and successful eight years, he has now resigned citing "personal reasons." He claims that the scandal had nothing to do with it. I must say that the first time I met him some five years into his service there were rumors of his imminent retirement, so a retirement at any time would not in and of itself be surprising. Of course, no one but David Lord Sainsbury in his own private moments knows the truth. Or ever will.

So, what's to be made of all this?

Certainly, it proves how difficult it is to be in the public eye, no matter who you are. From this side of the Atlantic, it appears that these two gents simply came to the aid of their party, and given their already-exalted stature had nothing to gain from their loans. It also shows that connect-the-dots can be more than an innocent parlor game—sometimes it leads to the truth, but at other times, it amounts to savage undermining and political opportunism.

In truth, there is more to know about this story than we will ever know, and less to know than some people would like to imagine. There is also the problem suffered by every democratic government when trying to foster action. When seeking out people to join cabinets, commissions, and task forces, leadership looks for those who can actually make things happen. That they might also eventually benefit is highly likely. They're in the game, are they not? They want the field to succeed . . . as does the government. And yet, if leadership instead turns to others with no connections, who will never benefit and who have never been to the center of the tornado, these people cannot understand the issues on a first-hand basis. Nothing substantive is likely to get done. Or a very wrong turn can easily be made.

In the end, all we may see here is our old pal—the good story. And this is a very good story, indeed. If unfortunately, a particularly unhappy and potentially destructive one.

CHAPTER FIVE

And Baby Makes Three...Four... and Then Some...

"YOU WANNA interview Brooke Shields?"

"What! Who?" I sped out the door of the studio and around the corner, rushing to the closest window in hopes of getting some decent reception. I had a few minutes between interviews at KQED, and the shielding on the soundproof recording studios pretty much squelched any chance of a reasonable conversation. Besides that, Mark was likely standing in the middle of the exhibit floor, trying to talk to me over the din of 10,000 of his closest friends. I was trying to listen and speak on the run, all the while heading for the cell phone sweet spot.

"Who? What!" I repeated.

"Brooke Shields."

"Brooke Shields?"

"Brooke Shields."

"*Brooke Shields* Brooke Shields?"

"How long is this gonna go on?"

Finally, I said, "Why would I want to interview Brooke Shields, and why are you whispering?" He was in a public place, alright, but it was quieter than I expected. And Mark's voice was deep and hushed, that muted *sotto voce* reminiscent of sports announcers commentating on Tiger Woods' next-to-impossible next putt. And why is that? Tiger can't hear us. Is it just some extension of the etiquette of golf courses, where we're all supposed to be hush-hush while someone else swings? These guys are in a booth back at the clubhouse. Or riffin' from their comfy studios in New York or Atlanta. At the same time, I'm watching and listening from the comfort of my home, flipping to the next channel if Tiger doesn't get a move on. Still, they're hush-hush-hush. And so was Mark . . .

"Brooke Shields is here at BIO, thanking biotech for making it possible that she could have her baby."

Still incredulous, I asked again, "Why would I want to interview Brooke Shields?"

"I don't know. She's got a tattoo."

"She's got a tattoo? Huh? She's got a tattoo? Is that biotech?"

"I don't know. I just know she's got a tattoo. On her ankle. I just took a picture of it with my digital camera."

Then I remembered. Some time after the David Kessler lunch, I had said something like, "Oh, we should have cornered him for an interview! We can't miss these opportunities." Mark's a quick learner, that's for sure. He wasn't going to let another one get by. At least, he wasn't going to be blamed for it. Clearly, I had brought this on myself.

My position was simple: Brooke Shields knew things that I could only begin to imagine, but I couldn't trust her to know enough about science to be on the air.

Then Mark played his hole card.

"Actually, there's a doctor standing next to her, and she answered the one question that was technical and scientific."

Ah! Finally, I got the picture. He was at a press conference. Brooke had spoken at some big BIO event, and then afterward they had rolled her up to somewhere near the press room. I'm sure they had a podium and mics and audio and video feeds and the whole nine yards. Mark has since learned to open with, "I'm at a press conference," but these were early days still.

"Yes," he said. "In fact, I like her. The doctor, I mean. She can talk about *in vitro* and pre-implant testing, all the stuff that it took to make a baby pop out of Brooke. Shall I get her to come on?"

Now we were talking.

Ever since test-tube baby #1—Louise Brown—was born in 1978, the technology of *in vitro* fertilization (IVF) has taken off like a shot. In fact, without the overwhelming desire of humans to procreate, it's arguable that stem cell research itself would be foundering.

Let me explain.

○   ○   ○

THE STEM cells primarily being used for stem cell research are derived from those teeny-tiny cells produced soon after a sperm invades an egg. *Yes, it invades! Look at those pictures! It's quite rude, actually! Does the sperm look like it asked permission and waited around for a positive reply? Well, anyway* . . . Once the egg and sperm get together, it becomes a new single cell, and that cell divides into two, and then each of those cells divides again, clinging altogether in an ever-evolving clump, and they keep this activity up until they don't any more.

If inside a healthy female and all goes well, in nine months time, you've got yourself a baby. Well, that's what happens if the whole process happens inside a woman in the normal course of events.

For people who are having a hard time pulling that off—or may have some disease or condition that they are worried about, this can be problematic. And so, technology steps right in.

That's what I wanted to talk to Dr. Carolyn Givens about. She is the associate medical director of the Pacific Fertility Center and a former assistant professor of reproductive endocrinology and infertility at UCSF School of Medicine. She was the lady standing next to Brooke at the press conference, and she doesn't have a matching tattoo. (She was wearing a skirt the day she showed up. All I had to do was look down. Sometimes being a journalist is soooo easy.)

Harvesting eggs from a human female is very do-able, although definitely hard on Mom. It's basically a hormone-induced ovarian frenzy, followed by surgery to try and scoop up as many eggs as possible. Harvesting sperm from a human male is covered elsewhere in this book and is not to be missed.

Since both essential ingredients are in separate containers, I asked Dr. Carolyn how Mama's eggs got mixed with Daddy's sperm. She didn't even blink.

"We can just incubate eggs and sperm in a laboratory together, and let the best sperm win, so to speak," she explained. "Or if there's a significant male factor, we can pick out a single sperm and inject it right into the egg."

Now I think we're back to that permission thing, only now it's the poor sperm. Does every sperm have to be a hero? There are so many of them. Millions and millions and millions, like stars in Carl Sagan's galaxies. I envision one of those Aussie blokes with a sizable carriage stepping up to the bar of his favorite pub. He's raising his arm with the first pint of the day clutched in his hand; his only mission is to bring it to his lips. If this guy was actually a sperm, he would be perfectly happy to let his mates get there first. You never see one of these guys abandoning his brew for the cute gal who just sashayed through the door. No, that's for those other sperm. You see, not every sperm needs to be humanity bound, just as every bloke doesn't need a girlfriend. But just then Dr. Carolyn's sperm police sweeps in and nabs him, interrupting forever his hallowed ritual. It could happen to any sperm. It could happen to any Aussie bloke. Your fortunes can change dramatically if Dr. C takes a liking to you.

"Once the egg is normally fertilized, then we just leave them alone," she tells me. *Finally, some privacy!* "We leave them in the incubator for at least two days, and if it's a normally fertilized egg and does not have any serious chromosomal problems, it should start to divide and within two days—ideally—it has about eight cells."

No kidding. It takes two days for a single fertilized cell to divide into two cells, to each again divide for a total of four cells, and then each again, to eight cells. In forty-eight hours. 1-2-4-8. In 48 hours. Somehow, I thought it was a lot faster than that. Of course, later on, it really gets going.

"But we can see anywhere from two to twelve cells," she added, "two days after the fertilization process has happened."

Twelve cells? I can do the arithmetic. What happened to the 1-2-4-8? Turns out the cells don't all make it. And that's just life. Nature. Some make it; some don't. Nature's messy, even though we like to describe it as if it were clean, neat, orderly and predictable. Mechanistic is the word that springs to mind. And what Dr. C and her staff does to these tiny cells is nothing short of remarkable.

"The individual cells are called *blastomeres,* and we perform what's called a 'blastomere biopsy' under a dissecting microscope, where we actually go in and gently hold on to the embryo with a little suction pipette. And we use a glass tube—or now we're moving to actual lasers—to create an opening in the outer protein coat around the embryo. We can go in and actually just gently extract a single cell, leaving the remaining seven cells behind for that embryo to go on and keep dividing. And perhaps eventually become a fetus, if it's found to be normal and transferred back."

Okay. So you got your eight cells, or thereabouts. And you hold the clump of cells (which she's calling an embryo) with a teeny-tiny suction thing on one side, and on the other, you stick in what's effectively an even tinier glass needle—and you make a tiny puncture. Then you go in and pull out one of the cells. Or you can do it with lasers or whatever kind of technology you want. But that's basically what they do.

So, let's make the point. We've got the technology to *insert* one sperm into one egg. To *see* these embryos at one, two, four-plus cells. To *slip in* and take one cell out.

Now what are they going to do with that one little cell?

Dr. Givens talked about two kinds of testing: PGD and PGS. PGD is "pre-implantation genetic diagnosis," while PGS is "pre-implantation genetic screening."

"PGD is pre-implantation genetic diagnosis where we're actually looking for a specific mutation that the parents are known to carry. Therefore these parents are at risk to have a child with this specific disease. So they want to test their embryos prior to putting them in, rather than just rolling the dice, waiting until after they became pregnant and had to make a difficult decision about whether to terminate the pregnancy, because they're going to have a very ill child."

There are more than 200 different diseases that can now be diagnosed—and this number increases constantly, as the genetic bases for particular diseases are discovered. Included today are Cystic Fibrosis, several types of muscular dystrophy, hemophilia, Huntington's disease, certain types of leukemia and sickle cell anemia, to name a few.

And PGS? Dr. Givens explains:

"PGS [preimplantation genetic screening] is a little bit different. PGS analyzes that cell for the chromosomal complement. As you know, we're all either 46 XXs or 46 XYs. [That would be girls and boys.] But if an embryo has '47 XX or XY plus 21' that is Down syndrome—an extra Chromosome 21. And there are many other chromosomal abnormalities that can result in either disease or miscarriage or simply infertility. So we can actually screen a population of embryos to look for which embryos have the right number of chromosomes.

So we're looking for two signals from Chromosome 21. We're looking for an X and a Y, or two X chromosome signals. Basically right now, we can test for about nine chromosomes . . . Those are the most common chromosomal abnormalities which are seen in miscarriages or that could be present at the time of an amniocentesis. . . . Those are the ones we're looking at to have to terminate a chromosomally abnormal pregnancy."

Bells started going off with every other sentence. . . . "we're all either 46 XXs or 46 XYs" . . . "amniocentesis."

Let's take the last one, first, because I will never, ever forget the time I got an amniocentesis.

○   ○   ○

I WAS PREGNANT with my second child, when it was recommended that I get an amnio, so up we traipsed to UCSF. (If you've learned nothing from this book, you should be getting the picture that's there's a lot of hot stuff going on at UCSF. It's not the only place, but ignore it at your own peril. You might need it some day.)

They put us in a little room—or should I say "closet?" Inside was a really short version of an examining table. They don't need a big one, because they have you—fully clothed—half sitting up with your big belly out in front of you and your knees up around your shoulders. This is so the doc can get to your belly. You'd think they'd give you a little more room then that, but they didn't. Any way, my then husband stood over 6'6" tall. He was on my right, squeezed into the "V" created by the table being slightly angled out from the wall, and on my immediate left was an ultrasound machine. Next to the ultrasound was the wall, so you begin to appreciate the closet-like qualities of the place. Before you could say "boo" a nurse had gelled up my tummy and was searching around for kiddo. And there he was! She had to tell us we were looking straight down at the top of his head—as if we were standing directly above him. But what were those two antennae coming on out of his forehead and wiggling all around? Oh! They were his hands! They were two little fists, and they were punching the air (or would that be amniotic fluid) like a prizefighter getting ready to come into the ring. It was instant love. And in the next instant, I knew that the news had better be good.

I wasn't at all sure I could backtrack on this pregnancy now. But heck, we were here. Knowledge is power. Let's get a-goin'. Before you knew it, the doctor opened the door, the people standing re-arranged themselves so that he could get into the room, and then he shut the door behind him. At this point there was no room left whatsoever, so if you wanted to bring your lawyer with you, someone would have to leave. Fortunately, my husband was a lawyer, so this particular challenge never came up, but let's say, you brought your mother *and* your sister along. It would have been a problem. So now the doc takes over from the nurse, who has set up all the machines, and he's giving the once over to what the nurse already found with the ultrasound. Then he says, "Okay, let's go."

At which point the nurse brings out the biggest, honkin'est hypodermic needle you've ever seen, unless you're a vet and you work on horses. It had to be six inches long. And thick. I didn't care that the point at the end of the needle was sharply angled. I don't like needles to start with, but I really don't like needles that are so big you could see the sharp angle from three feet away. Especially when they're fixin' to stick it in my tummy! Yaahh!!! Or anywhere near my baby.

This must be a common reaction, as now both the doctor and the nurse began rolling out stories in that monotone that's supposed to temporarily anesthetize you. About how the needle isn't going to puncture the baby. It's just like an orange bobbing in a tank of water. The orange might come up to the needle, but it just bounces away, unscathed and scar free. Only afterward do you realize that an apple would have been a far more obvious choice—the old bobbing for apples thing. But obviously this didn't calm anyone. Everyone has torn an apple skin with their thumb and finger if it was overly ripe, and then you have the second problem, that a baby's skin isn't anything like an orange, and this needle would have handily punctured Godzilla. While in a bit of a panic, I'd set my mind on this course of action, so I steeled myself.

I'm sure I was an easier sell than some. I'm not exactly someone who can be led placidly to the gallows with a little hot cocoa and some soothing words, but I do tend to stay committed to things sometimes longer than is wise. Still, I distinctly remember saying, "Let's get this over with."

The doc began to feel my belly for where the baby was and pushed it around a bit, telling me that he wanted to come in at an angle and find a nice pocket of amniotic fluid. Sounded like a good idea, if it avoided nicking little "Bucky," as we had jokingly nicknamed him. (Actually, we also called him "Trixie," in case he was a she, but my husband was relentlessly rooting for boys all the way, so Bucky was pretty much the favored reference.)

The doctor grabbed my stomach and stuck in the needle. I'm pretty sure he said, "Don't move." I hope he said, "Don't move." It would have been irresponsible otherwise. I certainly said it to myself. But this was one of those times when you know for sure you're between a rock and a hard place. You want to run, but you can't possibly. For a relatively simple reason. *Hey, girlfriend! There's a horse hypodermic needle sticking out of your abdomen!*

He had slid it in carefully with his left hand, and then with his right hand crossed over to pull back on the plunger and extract the precious amniotic fluid. But nothing came out. He tugged gently again. He pulled the whole needle back a bit and tried to reposition it, turning it at a slightly different angle. He tried extracting fluid again. The only sound to be heard was heavy breathing and the whirring of the machine. Then he slipped the needle out several inches and decided to turn it and try for a radically different direction. I see his right hand move over but instead of trying to pull out the plunger again, he grabs *the entire hypodermic needle apparatus!* I see his left hand leave and move slowly over to my six-foot-six husband, who is towering head and shoulders over everyone in the room and fixated on the horse needle. He is pale and starting to wobble. All the time holding onto the hypodermic needle stuck deep into my belly with his right hand, the doctor takes his left hand and pushes my husband straight back into the wall behind him and then slides him down to the ground. Then he points at him and says, "Stay there." The next try proved successful. I quickly got a little bitty bandage for my puncture wound, and the doctor proclaimed, "You can get up now." Presumably, he was speaking to both of us.

Hopefully, the amniocentesis experience has improved since then—things usually do with technology. Smaller, faster, cheaper. It's the humans who remain pretty much the same.

○   ○   ○

THERE WAS another bell that went off inside my head when talking with Dr. Givens. It was about the nature of being human. This XX-XY business, and the idea that "we're all either 46 XXs or 46 XYs," either full-fledged girls or full-fledged boys. Except that I distinctly remembered my interview with Johns-Hopkins science writer Deborah Rudacille, the author of *The Riddle of Gender.*

"I think it's very important to begin by defining a few terms. We use the word *sex* and *gender* synonymously these days, and that's sort of a misnomer. They're not exactly the same. When we talk about sex in the context of science, we're not talking about sexual orientation, and we're not talking about desire. We're talking about the biological markers of sex.

First, we have chromosomal markers. Most people think you're either XX or XY, but there are people in this world who are XXO, XXY, XYY, so there's variation, chromosomally. Another biological marker of sex is gonadal sex. Again, most people think, 'Well, you have two testicles, or you have ovaries.' Well, that's true, but some people have a mix of testicular and ovarian tissue, so again, a little bit of variation there.

"Endocrine. Males and females produce both androgens and estrogens, but in different balance. What's the balance? Morphological sex. Your body shape? How is your fat distributed? Do you have facial hair? Again, variation.

"Genital sex. You know, people think you have a penis or a vagina. Well, some people have incompletely-differentiated sexual organs. And then finally we get to the really confusing one. Gender. Gender identity. Your sense of yourself as a male or a female. Increasingly, this is becoming apparent as 'brain sex.' How you are sexed in your brain.

"Variation can be introduced at any level. Although in most people, these biological markers of sex are congruent, in some cases, they're not. And we're learning that in maybe 2.2 percent of live births, people are 'intersexed' in some way."

2.2 percent? Intersexed? Some intersection of the two sexes? Deborah Rudacille was now hitting her stride.

"In any one of those ways that we've just discussed. For example, XXY people—Kleinfelter syndrome—feel male because they have the Y chromosome. Some identify as women. Some identify as men. Morphologically, they are male."

There are 6 billion people on the planet. . . 2.2 percent of live births would be. . . 132 million people? Who aren't precisely boys and aren't precisely girls? 1 out of 50 live births?

"Not a minor number," Rudacille concurred.

The child of someone I know was actually declared a boy for two days before the medical community took a more studied look. Admirably equipped in a number of ways, the medical professionals soon advised the parents that she should really be a girl. Today, she's a grown woman in her forties. She has three biological daughters of her own and a great husband, but at her birth, her parents were truly confounded. The options presented to her parents ran from bewildering to grotesque. I wondered what happens today when a couple gives birth to a child who is "intersexed."

Deborah Rudacille was once again direct.

"There's been a sea change in the last couple of years. Since the late 1950s, early 1960s, it was thought that it was important when children [were born] with anomalous genitalia, that a decision be made as early as possible as to which sex the child would be assigned. It was considered a medical emergency.

Very often indeed, most always, those children were subject to so-called *normalizing surgeries* to normalize their genitalia, and then in puberty were dispensed hormones based upon that original sex assignment. But when those children grew up, many became intersex activists and argued that this should never have been done to them without their consent. And increasingly that view is being adopted within the medical community. There's a wonderful pediatric neurologist named William Reiner, who was originally at Johns Hopkins, and now is at the University of Oklahoma. [He's] done studies of intersex children, which show that with time they can tell you who they are, and there is no reason to perform surgery prior to the child actually telling whether they are a boy or a girl.

That view is increasingly being adopted in the medical community. There are still a few holdouts, of course, but things are changing."

Now, it's one thing when you can physically observe that there may be something going on with your baby that is, "incongruent with expectations," shall we say. It's quite another if it's at the endocrine or chromosomal level, for example. You wouldn't test for it, unless you had a reason to.

"Exactly," said Rudacille. "And very often, those situations aren't discovered until much later in life." She explained further.

"I think it's important to stress that these are *naturally occurring conditions*. Biological variation is part of life on earth. In cases like that, very often when it is discovered, there is, again, pressure for the child or the young adult to be pushed in one or another direction, but of course, by then they can tell you who they are.

I interviewed some people for the book [including] a neuroscientist at Stanford. In late adolescence, he—at that point, she—had a condition called Mullerian agenesis, absence of vagina and uterus. As he tells it, the doctors were, like, 'Well, you're XX, you're a girl. We're going to construct an artificial vagina and uterus for you.' And he said, 'I didn't really want one, but it was never really asked. It was just assumed that because I was chromosomally XX that I would have a vagina.' And of course, much later in life, this person, who always felt very uncomfortable with a female gender identity, decided to transition to male."

And today is a neuroscientist at Stanford? "Yes. Yes. Brilliant, brilliant guy." Deborah continued.

"One of the really interesting things that's happened in the last couple of years [is that] previously it was thought that female was the default sex. That without a sharp burst of androgens in the second month of pregnancy most embryos would develop in the female direction. But now because of all the new technology, we're discovering that an interaction of a number of genes *probably begins to sex the brain* even before that sharp burst of androgens. So again, we're learning more about this all the time."

I have another friend. She's adorable, as pretty and feminine a female as you can imagine. Has been all her life. She's never been able to conceive, and in the course of trying to figure out why, she found out that she was XXY. In some ways, she says, it was a relief. Knowing why she couldn't conceive. But she has wondered out loud: If she were going through IVF today, would she pick herself? Or rather, an embryo like her? Would her parents have picked her? Or discarded her? In her words, "it's seems so trivial a fault, if it's a fault at all."

o   o   o

SO BACK TO Brooke's Dr. Carolyn Givens, who looks for more serious conditions in the work that she does. At this point in my conversation with her, she's telling me how she just nicked a cell and sent it out for testing . . .

"They can actually do the analysis which can tell whether that particular cell carries the mutation for the disease of interest—or not. They can simply fax us back a report, and by Day Five, we can have a report on which embryos are normal, which ones are perhaps carriers of the disease like their parents, and which are affected and we don't want to transfer.

Then we can look at how the embryos have done in the laboratory in the last couple of days. Have they continued to progress from an eight-cell stage? Are they viable? Those viable embryos [which] are unaffected will then be transferred back to the mother."

Okay, five days have gone by. How many cells are there now? "Usually about 100 to 200 cells," Dr. Givens explained.

"At an eight-cell stage, the embryos have not yet differentiated into which cell is going to become the placenta, or which cell is going

AND BABY MAKES THREE...FOUR...AND THEN SOME...   **69**

to become the embryo itself, which is going to become the kidneys or the head or the brain. So we can take a single cell, and it is representative of all the remaining cells.

But over the next two days—between Day Three after fertilization and Day Five after fertilization—the embryo does start to differentiate. You can actually see cells that are starting to line what's called the *blastocyst,* and those outer cells are going to be placental cells and the inner cells—or what we call the 'inner cell mass'—are actually going to become the embryo itself. And so, at about 100 to 200 cells, this embryo is now starting its destiny of differentiation and development.

And it's at that stage that we transfer these embryos back to the uterus."

I asked Dr. Givens, how many good embryos might be produced in a single IVF procedure.

"Well, it totally depends on the age of the woman, because the younger she is, the more likely she is to make more eggs. We might have anywhere from two to twelve embryos. It would be rare that we would have more than twelve Day Five embryos, because not every egg that we remove from a woman gets fertilized, and not every fertilized egg develops out to Day Five. There [are] so many points in the process where embryos stop developing."

I wondered if you have as many as twelve embryos, how many would you put in the woman at any one time?

"We try to limit it to two, particularly if we're doing a Day Five transfer, because these embryos are already pre-selected for which ones might be the most viable, the most likely to cause a pregnancy. And because we don't want to create triplet pregnancies.

If there are excess good quality embryos, we'll freeze them, so that if a patient wants to come back in a year or two and have another baby, we may have some embryos that are viable and we can just simply thaw them and put them in, without going through the [whole] process."

And the rest of the embryos? What happens to them?

"If we have more embryos than a couple may want to use to create their own family, they're given a choice about what they [want to] do with the embryos. In fact, every year we contact everybody we have embryos on, and we say, 'What would you like to do? Would you like for us to keep them stored for another year? Would you like to thaw them and discard them? Would you like us to donate them for research? Or would you like to let somebody else receive them to try to get pregnant? Sort of like an adoption of embryos? They are all given these four options, and most of our patients choose to either discard them or give them up for medical research, if they don't want to take them back themselves.

I have this conversation with my patients once or twice a week, because it comes up a lot. We have a lot of patients who have children and they have embryos frozen. It's hard for them to really think about taking the embryos out and thawing them and discarding them. [These embryos are] similar to their other children that they already have, but they don't necessarily want to donate them to somebody else. That again is a very difficult emotional choice. Many of them find [donating the embryos to scientific] research sort of an in-between choice. They're allowed to let the embryos live out their life doing something useful, but not necessarily being used to create another baby."

If you thought that donating these embryos to science was something that happens to be just the particular policy of the Pacific Fertility Center, you'd be wrong. It's a California law. Fertility clinics must notify their patients that this is one of the options. Still, the PFC doesn't donate the eggs blindly. "We have a collaboration with researchers at UCSF who have a non-federally-funded laboratory that is receiving our embryos, and using them for very useful research," Dr. Givens explained. "I would estimate that between 400 and 800 embryos a year are actually donated from our center."

While there are no absolute ways to do the counting, pretty much everyone is in agreement, that at this writing, some 400,000 embryos are currently on ice in the United States. Obviously, we've gotten really good at making embryos.

At the same time, there are couples looking for donor eggs. They would use someone else's egg but Dad's sperm to make a baby. Today, the Pacific Fertility Center pays $6,500 as a first time egg donor, and then $7,000 for subsequent donations. (Before any of you gals get too excited about how you're going to spend this windfall, remember that you have to inject yourself daily with hormones, be available for repeated testing, and subject yourself to a surgical procedure, all the while attempting to generate plenty of good eggs and trying to get on the same cycle as the aspiring mother.)

And for those couples who can generate great embryos, but have problems carrying them to full term, they can always contract with a "gestational carrier." Your egg. Your sperm. Someone else's body. Your baby.

It seems like technology is zipping along, handling just about every aspect you can think of, except for the ethics of it. And the emotions of it all.

But let's not forget that these babies and these embryos are the exception. Most people in the world have their babies the good old-fashioned way. Unexpectedly. *"Uh, honey? Remember the night that Joe and Alice came over, and we went bowling? And to O'Reilly's Pub afterward?"*

You should know that Brooke Shields went through seven IVF procedures and a miscarriage, a roller coaster of emotional upheaval, physical effort and serious expense, well in excess of $100,000, before she brought her first baby to term. Much to her reported surprise, her second baby arrived without having to return to the technology well, and thank goodness, she made that clear publicly. Brooke's children are in the eye of the paparazzi storm. The good she was able to do speaking up on behalf of pregnancy #1, opened the door for questions about pregnancy #2. The least she could do for her second child was circumvent complete strangers idiotically intoning, "You used to be frozen."

So Brooke, you go, girl! And just wondering—how old will your girls need to be before it's okay for them to get a tattoo?

C H A P T E R   S I X

Washington, D.C.! Here We Come!

HE "DECLINES to take the meeting."

I read the e-mail again. Mr. X "declines to take the meeting." *What does this mean? He declines to take the meeting? He declines?*

Let me back up here.

When we started recording *BioTech Nation* segments during the big BIO convention in June 2004, a certain Mr. X was the head honcho for communications for BIO, the Biotechnology Industry Organization, which runs the conference. We'd never met him, but we had made friends with a number of his staff.

After the conference was over, and we had started airing the *BioTech Nation* segments, the obvious next step was to go visit BIO headquarters and meet with Mr. X, as a professional courtesy. After all, we had come out of nowhere and we instantly had national and global reach. It was appropriate to tell their communications staff what we did and didn't cover, how we preferred to get information, and what wasn't appropriate. For example, there was no reason to rush us late-breaking news. We don't do late-breaking news. But we would do topical interviews. That meant they should be thinking about qualified guests, along with their stories.

Also, these guests should be able to come to our San Francisco studios, as we hesitate to do "phoners"—they just don't have the audio quality we generally look for.

In addition, we wanted to hear from BIO, the organization. From their end, what did it think were interesting or brewing issues. BIO had both national and global members, and their staff was a font of information. We needed to know the industry stance, and as journalists, we could fill in the rest of the picture—where the self-interest lies, no matter who the "self" in question is, in business, in public policy matters and all the rest. It's always better to do this in a collegial manner, rather than in an adversarial one.

So, in that fall of 2004, we told one of our BIO-insider friends on the communications staff that we were coming to Washington, D.C., to meet with Kingsley Smith over at National Public Radio. Which was true. It was time to sign another contract for the *NPR Talk* and *NPR Now* channels on Sirius Satellite Radio. And whenever we go to Washington, we try to kill six or seven birds with one stone. One bird targeted for this trip was to come by and meet with Mr. X.

"Oh . . . Er . . . Ah . . . I don't think he's going to want to meet with you," our friend had stammered.

And my enthusiastic response? "Of course, he will," I said. "Why wouldn't he? He's in charge of communications. He's supposed to get BIO and biotechnology out there in the public eye. We've got a new weekly radio segment on biotech with national and worldwide reach. It's his job to know us. In fact, it's *his job* to be on good terms with us."

She said she would try, but then her e-mail arrived.

Mr. X "declines to take the meeting."

I called Mark, the *BioTech Nation* producer, who immediately said, "Well, that's that."

That's that? I responded. "That" is never "that" in the journalism business.

Mark was a little taken back at my response. "Why would you continue to pursue this?"

"Well, it's appropriate," I said. "Whoever has his job is *supposed* to do this." Besides, you never know who we will meet along the way, what we will learn, or what might happen. We can't be the only ones he's treating this way. My journalist nose told me that we shouldn't let this lie. If there's something big happening that the Biotechnology Industry Organization knows about, then the whole communications branch should be on us like white on rice. They know things that we could only hope to find out later. They can aid us in directly contacting people who might not take our call otherwise. We couldn't be on the outside on this stuff.

"Okay," Mark said, not completely convinced, but knowing there was no point in arguing with me. "What's our next move?"

I said, "Absolutely nothing."

Faced with a situation like this, there's only one thing to do. You don't go back. You go up. That's right. Go up. Who was above Mr. X in the organization? That was easy to tell from the website. He reported to one and only one person: Carl Feldbaum, the longtime president and CEO of BIO. Well, that wouldn't be so easy. He was so pressed by the demands of the BIO conference, he didn't do many interviews. Mostly, it was all he could do to answer quick questions about the anti-GM food protesters and the riot police. Still, it would be do-able. We just had to be patient. Until Carl Feldbaum wanted to talk to us.

As if on cue, several weeks later one of X-man's underlings (a person other than our friend) called to tell us that Carl Feldbaum was coming to San Francisco to speak at the Biotech Investors Conference. Could we manage to interview him while he was in town? You bet! Certainly we could make room for Mr. Feldbaum. And we did.

He came to KQED, arriving with no less than two people in tow. He came into the big atrium, and right away said, "I don't understand who you are and what you want to talk about. I have to tell you they schedule these things for me, and I just go along with them. I hope you don't mind me asking." He was completely direct and very polite, although I wondered: How odd? *They* called *us*, and they hadn't briefed him. Sill, any journalist can work with that. So I sat him down and told him what we had in mind. Then the two of us squeezed ourselves into a single-person recording booth (the normal ones were being refitted at the time) and we did our interview.

Everyone else sat outside in the engineering booth and listened carefully, in case Carl let some bad ju-ju out by mistake. I don't know what they would have done had any ju-ju hit the fan, but they clearly felt it was their jobs to listen to every word intently with concerned looks on their faces, ready to leap up and correct the record. *Fine with me! Just don't scare the horses.*

As the interview progressed, he loosened up, telling me how the annual conference drew 18,000 people now, but when he started it was just hundreds. How he initially mistook the angry objections to "human cloning" as objections to "human clothing." He was especially supportive of cancer research in the biotech field because of his personal experience with the disease. It all went swell, and I was ready to pounce, because I figured that I knew what was going to happen next. It doesn't always happen. If someone is grilling a guest unfairly or accusing them of something they didn't do, post-interview fury might be what you get next. But most interviews, even tough interviews—when they are over—create a short-lived phenomenon I call "post-interview euphoria." And why?

First of all, any anxiety about being on the air is instantly gone. It's over. Over! Add in the fact that the guest has just spent some amount of time with the interviewer hanging on his every word. Everyone likes to be paid attention to. Ask the unexpected question where the guest gets to shine, and the guest finds himself both acknowledged and at the center of the universe. Actually, he *is* the center of the universe. Mix in the evacuation effect of finally getting to say what he's really wanted to say for the longest time, and bank on the natural excitement of being at a spiffy high-class radio and television station . . . post-interview euphoria.

Believe me. It's the time to ask for just about anything you want.

I asked President Feldbaum if we could come and see him in Washington in a couple of weeks, at the same time we were coming to talk to NPR. It would be a quick drop-in visit, just so we could tell him a little more about our show and hear any suggestions he might have, since he had headed BIO all these years. He said he would be delighted, and his assistant would arrange it. I got on the horn to his office and also sent an e-mail right away. Before the hour was out, we had our appointment in Washington, D.C.

I wonder exactly when it was that the hairs on the back of Mr. X's neck stood straight out. If he felt anything, I'm sure he cast the notion aside—his control was so utterly complete.

Mr. X was something of a legend around the press room. A bad legend. As a member of the press, you are used to people pushing stories on you, and you are also used to people being exceedingly nice in the hopes that you would at least consider what they are not so subtly pushing on you at some later date. But Mr. X hated the press. He was barely polite, and it wasn't just me. One top journalist volunteered after a subsequent BIO conference, "That was a wonderful BIO! I managed to get through it without laying eyes on Mr. X."

Fortunately, Carl Feldbaum didn't feel the same way as Mr. X. My producer and I flew into Washington from our respective coasts—the West Coast for me and the Gulf Coast for Mark. At the appointed time, we made our way to the modern high-rise that houses the inner sanctum of BIO, zoomed up the elevators, and entered the expensive and tasteful glass lobby. Right on time, Feldbaum's assistant came out and ushered us into the great man's office. Or would that be the man's great office? Why not. It was a great office. With a great view looking out on a pleasant Washington street. He look relaxed as he sat there in his collarless shirt—neat and pressed and casual.

I started in with the small talk, and he immediately stopped me. He said, "I'm sorry. *Who* are you? And *why* are you here?" Oooh. Is this how he started every meeting, recalling our first encounter at KQED? Or had he totally forgotten us? I played it both ways.

"Well," I said, "you may remember our interview recently in San Francisco?" He nodded. "We wanted to come by and tell you about ourselves . . . and since you're at the center of the biotech universe, we wanted to ask you—or at least a representative of BIO—to be on our advisory board."

"Oh!" he said. "Actually, you have to understand. I've announced my retirement, and it will be several months before Jim Greenwood takes over. I must say I'm enjoying this 'lame duck' period. The guy you really want to talk to is Mr. X. And he's the guy who should be on your advisory board, too. I'll have my secretary set it up."

"Great!" I said. Then we spent the rest of the time talking about how he was going to enjoy his retirement.

Mr. X was out of town that week, but it didn't matter. He wouldn't dream of crossing Feldbaum. After all, this was Washington. You served at the pleasure of your boss. Even an outgoing one. To the victor belongs the spoils, and no position gets replaced faster than the head of communications. I was going to have my meeting with X, even if X didn't know it yet. Wouldn't it have been great to be there when he found out. . . .

○   ○   ○

THE MEETING was on, and the next time only I could travel to Washington. A month had gone by, and it was December, sharply cold and snowy. It's a wonderful time of year to be in the District, especially with all the holiday decorations and the excitement of Washington bright in the air. Washington is a very "do-able" town, unlike New York City. It's small and beautiful. It has its sophisticated spots, its old homey spots, and its elitist hangouts. People mostly only stay for a fixed time in Washington, because they've come for a reason. The time may be two years or one. Two decades or four. But most come only for a set period. And, unmistakably, where money is the aphrodisiac of choice in New York, power is the player in the Washington. And power comes in many forms.

Not so long ago, it was always fun to look up and realize you were driving right by the White House. Yes! The White House. Today, roadblocks cordon it off, but despite these minor visible changes, from whatever vantage point you see it, you get a thrill—this is *Washington, D.C.!* You can feel that you're here as surely as you feel alive.

Even the hotel rooms speak volumes. Washington is home to some pretty nifty places and highest on my list is the suite I once had at the Hay-Adams. What a place. My driver (I was lucky that day—it was before I became a journalist) drove me under the portico of what appeared to be a large and stately mansion. Inside, the dark carved wood of the reception area was gleaming, while the actual space for check-in was relatively tiny. I supposed it dated from a time when there wasn't a need for computer terminals and printers, for electronic key card writers and credit card readers, for large banks of phones, and all the wires and cables that go with them.

It didn't matter. From the moment the doorman has opened the door of the car, I was never alone. My personal Ghurka (you should have seen his smart uniform and wonderfully bronzed skin!) asked me for my name and credit card as I stood comfortably in the foyer. He ran back and forth to the tiny reception desk and handled everything there was to be handled. They managed the whole thing by having the reception people *out in front* of the desk. And I must say, it worked beautifully.

Would Madame wish to have dinner in the Lafayette Room tonight? I can make a reservation. Would Madame like us to take her bags up to her rooms? Perhaps Madame would first like an aperitif in our "Off the Record Bar?" Please know that Madame's suite has a full bar available, and we have 24-hour room service. Does Madame yet know if she would like a wake-up call? And would Madame like to be awakened fifteen minutes earlier or fifteen minutes later to be sure that she's on time?

Oh! Let me tell you what Madame wants! Madame wants to live here for the rest of her life! Madame wants to be called Madame until Madame tells you to stop!

Especially since Madame's young kids were at home at that very moment letting the hamster run through the maze on the living room floor, which they had constructed out of those oh-so-educational wooden building blocks. "Madame! Oh, Madame!" Such music to my ears after "Mommy! Oh, Mommy!" Both M-words—an infinity apart.

In truth, I would have been happy if they showed me to a closet. (I'm soooo easy once I've bought your act.) But no. My Ghurka held the key up, and said, "We have a special room for you!" What could that possibly mean?

We got out of the ancient elevator and wound down and around the narrow twisting and turning corridor. The inside was a polyglot, while the outside spoke "elegant digs." Perhaps this is how they built hotels in days gone by. He led the way, still clearly excited by the proposition, just as I began to lose faith that there was much to look forward to. All this twisting and turning. Suddenly, he stopped, opened a door and charged in ahead of me.

He waved over his shoulder to the left. "There's the bathroom," he said, and kept on moving. The hallway was dark and narrow as well. So far, I wasn't impressed. I could see the king-size bed in front of me when he made a snappy right and disappeared. I emerged to find him across the room and opening the drapes on the windows. I looked to my right and realized that there was an entire living room with a Victorian fireplace and ornately-carved white ceilings. It was beautiful. He cast aside the drapes of the very last window and spun around. Silently, he extended his hand, palm up, towards the windows, as if to say "Look." I looked. Through the window, there was all of Lafayette Park, still and perfect as the sky was turning sunset pink. And beyond? A complete and unobstructed view of the White House.

The lights had just begun to come on; the facade glowed in the twilight. I walked to a window and looked out. Then I turned and looked back at the room. The Madame chorus came back in full voice. "Madame, the drinks cabinet is here. Madame, the ice has already been laid in. If Madame would like anything, she need only press the button on this phone here, or that phone there, or any of the phones anywhere." I gave him the biggest tip I had ever given anyone who showed me to my hotel room, and was thankful that I hadn't had time earlier in the day to go to a bank machine. He might have been able to buy a condo.

He left with a smart turn, and I rolled my luggage into the closet, not wanting to spoil the effect. And I wondered, Who could have previously inhabited this room? Presidential wannabe's, gazing across at the White House, so palpably close? Even the hotel's literature informs you that you're as close as anyone can get to staying at the White House, short of being invited by the President. *In fact, I think I see him there in his shorts, right now!* Well, it wasn't that close. But pretty darn close.

And the tasteful, period furnishings shouted Washington. Everything bespoke power and money. Its gain. Its loss. Its appeal. Through the years, this room had stood and continued on, impervious to who won, who lost, or how. This was Washington. When you were here, you were somewhere indeed. And still it was immensely peaceful and comfortable. And better yet, it was all mine.

I stared out the window for what seemed like ages. At the White House. At the beautiful park below. I couldn't tear myself away. The night sky went to dark. The White House glowed with light, becoming even larger in the darkness.

Finally, I turned and went over to the drinks cabinet. I poured myself a drink, sat down on the couch, and called every friend I could think of.

○   ○   ○

WHEN I'M ON my own dime, things are different.

The Tabard Inn is my usual haunt when I'm in D.C. Three old houses strung together chockablock near Dupont Circle. Every room is different, and a handful of rooms actually share baths. I've stayed in rooms that were converted from ladies' dressing rooms and other rooms that spanned the entire width of a single building. I've stayed in the wonderful rooms that look out on the handsome trees on the street, and I've laid in a chaise lounge by the window next to funky Victorian couches and an obviously defunct fireplace. You can count on encountering an eclectic mix of rundown furniture in the hallways and rooms, as well as pictures of inexplicable provenance on the walls. Half the plumbing looks like it was put in by my Uncle Hen, who would really have preferred to be out putting a fiver on the fifth race. I love the place. Each morning you go down to breakfast—which is included—and you see people from the embassies near by. It means you see people from all over the world. You hear a cacophony of languages in the early morning breakfast murmur. At night, this same dining room becomes a great restaurant and the darkened cocktail lounge/parlor out in front presents a veritable fleet of horsehair couches—*where do they get these things?*—and more of the same kind of decor featured in the rooms. In warm weather, the action spills out into the courtyard, and at night there are tiny twinkling lights, the waft of great food, the tinkle of glass and knife to plate, the sound of people excited just to be there.

◯   ◯   ◯

IT WAS AFTER one such lovely morning breakfast, about a month after Carl Feldbaum's assistant "set it all up," that I walked to my rent-a-car and drove back to the high-rise that housed BIO. I re-traced my elevator journey up to the lobby, where Mr. X's assistant came out and got me.

She knows better than to be friendly to the press, although it's clear that she's not an unfriendly person. She seems to be a wonderful person. It's just her job. Or, at least, it's her job if Mr. X is writing the job description. Everyone is in agreement that her demeanor is more a result of having to please-her-boss, please-her-boss, please-her-boss—the number one rule for getting ahead on the job. Or at least, most jobs. "Never follow the idiot off a cliff" is a corollary to this theorem. I had interacted with her ever since I first tried to register as media for BIO 2004.

I know, I made it sound as if I signed Mark and me up as press for BIO 2004 in a flash, but the truth is she had seriously questioned every press credential I offered. It was astonishing how much was required. At no other time or place have I ever had to provide such materials. I finally got her on the phone and said, "Look, how can we get this done? I can't have my boss write a letter on official letterhead. I am the boss."

"Oh," she said. I told her to bring up the Tech Nation website on her computer. I told her to go out to the NPR website. "Okay," she said. And so we finally got our press credentials. What was self-defeating was that during BIO 2004, the press room was deader than dead. Where were all the journalists? Driven into ditches trying to establish their credentials?

But now she came rolling into the reception area to pick me up, and she was relatively pleasant since she wasn't officially on guard shack duty. She escorted me to just outside Himself's office, where I cooled my heels for ten minutes, standing at the end of her cubicle. *Why no seat? Does no one visit her? Does no one visit him? Aaah . . . no duh.* About ten minutes went by and then suddenly the door to his office flew open. She leaped to her feet as Mr. X rat-a-tat-tatted several orders in quick succession. All the while he eyed me up and down and twice again, as if he was sizing up the hostess at an expensive men's club where they encourage guests to drink copious quantities of bourbon and branch water and smoke big ol' smelly cigars. It was a little unnerving from five feet away. Thank goodness he ran out of orders to give her.

He turned around and briskly walked back into office, saying "Follow me" as he walked away. I presumed he was talking to me, and so I did.

He sat down at his desk, looked across at me, and said, "Okay, you got your meeting. Speak." I laughed and said, "Oh, good! I'm so happy!" I put a big smile on my face and started in. I had a briefing packet for him that matched my own. He took it out of my hands and dropped it on his desk, without giving it so much as a glance. *Might as well keep talking. What did I have to lose?* About ten minutes into my spiel, I stopped and asked him a question. Silence. He stared at me. I stared at him. Any salesman can tell you, the next person to speak loses. He lost.

He started telling me about how they had built this huge, first-class television studio downstairs, and no one ever used it. *Golly, I wonder why?* He would love for it to start being used and kill to have biotech stories all over the media. At precisely, half past the hour, X's assistant knocked quickly and opened the door. It was obviously pre-arranged. She started saying, "Your next appointment . . ." He interrupted her and barked, "No. Go away."

We sat for another half hour, and he asked me what I could do to help him. He called downstairs to locate the guy he wanted me to talk to. He wouldn't be there until the next morning—could I come back then? I was busy the next morning. Could I come in the afternoon? And he had other ideas. Could I do this? Sure. Could I do that? You bet. Let's have a conference call about it. The minute hand snapped straight up on the clock behind his head. A full hour had passed.

This time a furtive knock came. Then a second one. His assistant timidly opened the door a crack, speaking as she did, so as not to be cut off. "Mike *really* is here." X interrupted her any way. "Tell him to cool his heels." She shut the door, and we continued talking. He said, "Look. Get together with this guy. I wanna hear what he has to say. Give me some options. OK. I gotta move on." And he walked to the door and opened it. His assistant was still standing there. He gave her the scoop, and exchanged me for the next guy.

You'll never guess what happened next. Or maybe you have. So it won't be a surprise . . . what happened next was . . . nothing. That's right. Nothing. X's assistant straight-armed me on the next three trips I made to D.C. She straight-armed me on every phone call, every voicemail, every e-mail, every way to Sunday. It was as if the television studio (which I know is still there and quite lonely) had disappeared. It's as if the person in charge of it forgot to come back to work. My own call is that Mr. X had a relapse. He must have realized his mistake shortly after I left. Perhaps it simply came to him. Perhaps his staff looked at him, and said, "What's wrong, X? You've never acted this way before?" At the very least, he said to himself, "What could I have been thinking?!?!!"

Maybe we made our mark. Maybe it was an exercise in futility. We'll never know. Time passed. Mr. X did his best to ignore us at the next BIO, and yet patience proved to be our friend. By the time the BIO conference of 2006 in Chicago rolled around, Jim Greenwood had taken the reigns as the organization's new president, and Mr. X had moved on. The folks at BIO came to us directly, and asked if we would consider recording in a radio studio they were building inside their BIO-TV studio. It overlooked the exhibit floor at Chicago's enormous convention center, McCormick Place. "What would we need?" they asked. We were delighted. And we were grateful. And continue to be so. We've learned that with any luck, we can record more than half of our annual interviews at this single conference, and they are not just any interviews. Most of the year we are situated in San Francisco, the largest biotech cluster on the planet, and we are also able to take advantage of visiting journalist trips from time to time. But it's our relationship with BIO that ensures a first-quality *international* production. And that was the point from the beginning.

Even with all the trouble we went to, for some reason, I was not discouraged. I still subscribe to that old saw—you never know what opportunities will come your way, just by showing up.

CHAPTER SEVEN

The mazing Chakrabarty

HE WAS A small man, but dynamic down to his DNA.

Dr. Ananda Chakrabarty came into my KQED studio bursting with energy. Circling sixty and maybe beyond, he sat down to tell me the story of how he came to be the first person to be awarded a life science patent, which could mean just about anything as far as I was concerned. My first thought was simply to ask, "What exactly did you patent?" and hope for some sort of comprehensible answer. Unfortunately, I already knew the odds were against me.

I'd done enough of these interviews to know that if I asked a wide-open question like that, the scientist might actually answer me, and the answer could be completely incomprehensible in terms of radio. Then I would need to ask further clarifying questions and sometimes that only made it worse. Another approach I tried was the pre-interview—doing a mini-interview off-mic, until I finally understood. This also backfired on a regular basis. If the guest was not experienced with the media, it was hard to put the same authenticity into the second take. It was even dicey to ask a guest to simply say something over again, substituting an everyday term for a scientific one. In the worst cases, they'd repeat what I asked them to like a bad robot.

The most horrific experience, bar none, happened at BIO 2005 in Philadelphia. My guest was an eminent senior scientist, and he was one of those people who won't look at you when talking to you. I'd ask him a question, and he'd look away and start answering it. One sentence after another spewed forth. One *incomprehensible* sentence after another. I had to lean over and wave at him whenever I wanted to get his attention. I'd talk to him off-mic, and then I'd say "Okay. Let's do it again." But he always left something out, or unexpectedly threw in a new term, and we'd have to start over. Finally, he erupted with displeasure.

"I have explained this to many different groups and many different people! You are the only one who doesn't understand! If you will just listen . . . [dramatic pause] . . . you will understand it!"

"Alright," I said, "Go." Once again, it was complete gibberish.

Sometime later Mark came up to the booth and caught me in between interviews. He asked me how it went with Dr. Biobabble. As I was about to answer, he quickly interjected, "And let me introduce you to Dr. Biobabble's public relations person, right here." *Yikes! Okay, how do I do this? Telling the truth always helps. As does sugar-coating.* "He was great, and very patient with me. The problem was it's . . . ah . . . well . . . very complicated stuff. And . . . ah . . . very hard for people to understand on the radio. Er . . . but he did well. He did very well."

Turns out Biobabble was furious. I had apparently insulted him. Mark suggested to the PR person that he could listen to the recording of the raw interview, to see what he thought himself. We set the flack up with earphones, and he sat there listening intently. Quietly, he put down the earphones and looked up at me. He said, "Actually, I've been with him at all kinds of meetings, when he's been explaining this approach. I never understand what he's talking about."

Exactly! And from the lips of his publicist!

I was afraid of a similar experience with Dr. Chakrabarty. The idea that he had genetically modified some bacteria didn't exactly sound like great radio. If he hadn't gotten the first gene patent, I probably wouldn't have done the interview.

The first stumbling block was realizing that the word *bacteria* was plural.

When you say, "Hey, Doc! Is this caused by a bacteria"?—hoping to get your flu over quickly with a course of antibiotics—you're actually asking about a crowd of critters and not just one. For sticklers, it's grammatically incorrect. One "bacteria"—so to speak—is a "bacterium." (Let the Latin endings spring forth from the dusty high school sector of your brain.) So "bacterium" was the proper word to use in the interview. Dr. C had genetically modified a *bacterium*. But everyday people don't say bacterium. They say "bacteria." We had a lot of ground to cover and before we even started, I was getting stuck on "You say to-may-to, and I say to-mah-to." Only "to-mah-to" was dead wrong. I told my brain to go with bacterium. It forgot to tell my mouth.

After the voice check, I spoke right up. "So you invented a new bacteria?"

So, shoot me.

o   o   o

Ananda Chakrabarty was a young scientist, fresh out of the University of Illinois at Urbana-Champaign, when he went to work for General Electric. He had moved from that ivory tower of research to the bastions of R&D at a for-profit company, and the year was 1971. As he tells it:

> "I was researching how certain bacteria could degrade certain components of oil—hydrocarbons. This was all very basic research without any thought of application, as people do in the universities. But then, when I went to GE and the price of oil was going up, there were certain parts of the world—like in the Middle East—where oil was cheap, but protein was very expensive. So British Petroleum and Imperial Chemical Industries in England, they were actually trying to make protein from petroleum. They were using yeasts, the same kind of yeasts [you use in bread], and of course, yeasts are consumed by people. They're harmless.
>
> Because I used to work on bacteria which could actually degrade many different components of oil, it occurred to me that I could actually shuffle genes from different bacteria that could [degrade] different components of oil, put them altogether in a single bacterium, so a lot more [of the] oil would be utilized and give rise to more bacteria. And like yeasts, bacteria are also 75 percent to 80 percent protein. So basically what you are doing is converting crude oil into protein!"

Appetizing, no? Could a Chakrabarty Crude Oil Energy Bar be far behind? Undaunted, I went on, asking, "You actually took different genes from different bacteria and put them together, sort of like a jigsaw puzzle?"

It was the wrong metaphor. It was more like a cut-and-paste job, cutting genes from several bacteria and then pasting them onto another one. He took different groups of genes from various bacteria and inserted them into what would become a super-duper bacterium.

Now it was Dr. C's turn to be undaunted. "Something like that." *What a nice man!* Then he continued:

"I could transfer the genes that would allow hydrocarbon degradation from, let's say, four different bacteria, and these different bacteria would all utilize different kinds of hydrocarbons. So when I put all the four types of gene clusters—as we call them—into a single bacterium, that bacterium could now degrade multiple components of oil, which any single bacterium couldn't.

I constructed a new type of bacterium. But do remember, though, that I started with a natural bacterium. That bacterium was there in nature. It could degrade only one or two components of oil. What I did was I endowed on this bacterium the capability to degrade many more different components of oil, so that it had a more voracious appetite for oil than it had when I started with it.

In nature, you do not see such bacterium, and therefore [it] became what's called a patentable invention."

But patenting the bacterium wasn't his idea. In his words, "I actually didn't know anything about patenting." Which is a sign of the truly lucky.

What happened was that he was invited to give a talk in Israel, and it was GE's policy that such talks needed to be written up for approval. And then luck came out of left field. He explained:

"GE is a very large corporation. Many people go and talk about their work, and I was assured that there would be no problem. So I submitted [the request.] Apparently, it ended up in the hands of the vice president, who I happened to know once in a while. Because I was really, really interested in this work, I would come to my lab in GE during the weekends, I would work after-hours, and the vice president, he was a workaholic. It so happened we would meet each other on the weekends or after-hours in the men's room. So after a few months, he [asked] me, 'Who are you?' and we would just have a pleasant chat. When he received the abstract that I submitted, he apparently read it and he got intrigued, because I said that this kind of microorganism could be used either for making protein from petroleum . . . or for cleaning up oil spills, and oil spills were becoming a problem. That's what I think attracted [the vice president's] attention.

The next Sunday, I met [him] in the men's room, and he said, 'Oh, by the way, I read your abstract. How confident are you that this will actually work?' I said, 'I don't know, but it's really different from what other people are doing with yeasts.' He said, 'So if you think it's really going to work, have you submitted a disclosure letter?' And I said, 'What is a disclosure letter?' Then he said, 'Well, you write a disclosure letter for filing a patent.' And I said, 'What is a patent?'"

Sometimes the universe just insists that you are going to be the guy.

By the time the patent was issued, Dr. C. knew bunches about obtaining a patent, as well as about filing disclosure letters, even if it was a little puzzling to start out with. His management had told him he could go to Tel Aviv, but he couldn't make a presentation. The patent filing would not be done in time. You can imagine the reaction of his esteemed colleagues for whom science was science—that would be "open source" in modern speak. He approached the dais and announced he had come all this way and couldn't talk about his work . . . because they hadn't finished filing the patent. A patent? It was unheard of. Plenty of chuckles all around. And I'm sure he made quite an entertaining show of saying nothing. Then he went back to the United States and back to work, but the wheels of patenting his bacterium had begun to turn.

To be absolutely clear, there were two parts to this patent, and it was the second part that caused all the commotion. The first part simply asked for a patent on his *process* for using genetic engineering techniques to construct such microorganisms, and it was granted in short order. However, the U.S. Patent and Trademark Office objected to patenting the bacterium itself. They said it was "a product of nature," and therefore, couldn't be patented. To which, GE objected. These bacteria don't exist in nature! They only exist because of human intervention! Up General Electric went to the appeals board, and the appeals board agreed. These were *not* products of nature. *Yea!* However . . . they were living, and living microorganisms cannot be patented. *Darn!*

And so the long and winding road continued to unfold for Dr. C and GE. From the Patent and Trademark Office to the Court of Customs and Patent Appeals to the Solicitor General and twice to the Supreme Court—well, you'd have to be patient and wildly interested to pay attention to it all. But eight years later—in 1980—Dr. Chakrabarty was awarded his patent.

Of course, this was simply the U.S. patent, and there are international patents as well, which Dr. C. was very interested in. He points out that "science is universal, but different countries have different patent laws." And no place has been more rife with intellectual property conflict of late than India.

○   ○   ○

IN SOME WAYS, India is a highly developed country—huge economy, educated populace, advanced technology. And in some ways, it's a developing country—grinding poverty, overpopulation, famine, public health problems, and every trouble in between.

But these are just words. And nothing—nothing—is like going there and witnessing it for yourself. I made reference to an Indian marketplace in the opening chapter, and this was just one of many, many startling experiences I had there. I can only say that anyone who has not been there cannot begin to understand what it is like. Strangely enough, after a person goes there, they often say that they understand far less than they did before. For the average American—and possibly for almost anyone anywhere—India is incomprehensible.

Its cities are teeming free-for-alls of honking, beeping traffic with bazaars offering up a cacophony of sounds, smells and visual impressions. People tramp everywhere, beggars tap insistently on car windows, and hawkers accost you at every turn. This impression fades fast as you pass into placid country villages, where life seems primitive, a throwback to an earlier century, when people lived in huts and simply off the land.

But India is India, and that means you should expect the unexpected. An elephant lumbers in the slow lane on the crowded road from Delhi airport. Cows recline lazily on the median strip. Monkeys and even dancing

bears are on leashes, ready for the tourist photo op. In main thorough-
fares, oxen pull carts, while the occasional camel manages a heavy load,
cheek to mechanical jowl with buses jammed with people. There are
three-wheel taxis with entire families packed aboard and hanging off the
sides, next to scooters driven by Dad, with Mom on the back and tiny off-
spring standing on the floorboard staring straight ahead into traffic.
Seeing is believing. Or is it? Just as I was wondering why someone had
put mothballs in the sink, my beer arrived in a teapot.

Everything—just everything—is perplexing.

Perhaps the most challenging of all are the slums. They roll out for
unbroken acres, corrugated sheets of metal assembled like so many playing cards, tilted this way and that in haphazard array, with dirt pathways
winding through. I'm told they have electricity and their own city coun-
cils. I can see for myself tidy schoolchildren emerging in clusters, their
uniforms impeccable, the girls' braids perfect, the boys' hair precision-
cut. And why not? Open-air barbershops are everywhere, yet humans create waste, and that fact is undeniable as well.

No matter where I turn, there is always so much I don't understand.
In airports, going through security, I find myself guided to a separate
women's line. It's the same as the males, except I must enter a booth with
curtains to be wanded down by a female in male guard's clothing. It's like
any other airport in the world, but why must this ritual for women be
kept from public view? What don't I understand?

In my final hours, being driven to the airport in the dark of night,
passing body after body deep in slumber on the sidewalks, my friend tells
me a story that offers a glimmer of understanding.

Many years before she volunteered at a home for the blind, where
young Indian boys lived through grade school and beyond. Each boy had
a clean room and clean clothes, a full education, medical attention, and
three meals a day, more than they could ever expect their families to provide. Some of them might go home only once or twice a year, while others went home more often. One boy in particular loved going home and
toward the end of each week would grow excited with anticipation. He
couldn't wait to go. And one day he invited my friend to come have tea
with his family.

He told her the street and to look for the fourth lamppost on the left.
She said, "There must be a house number or a name on the building."
"Oh, no," he said. "The fourth lamppost on the left." Sure enough, that's

where his family lived. On the sidewalk at the curb. It was there that she came to understand the boy's excitement—his parents loved him so dearly, he loved to go home.

Eventually, the blind boy grew up and went on to university. And my friend continued to watch the lamppost. One day, she saw that the family had moved which is a good sign. In India, when a son succeeds, the fortunes of the entire family rise.

It's hard to imagine growing up blind on a Mumbai sidewalk: cars and motorcycles just inches from your head, the incessant honking and screeching of brakes, people all around you cooking their meals on tiny open fires and doing everything that humans do, and yet loving it so completely, because you were there with those you loved and who loved you.

While India is vast, it is a nation of individuals. And it's hard to think that India's agreement to join the World Trade Organization could reach down and touch the lives of all these people. But it has. It's been in the works for over a decade now. In truth, it started even earlier than that.

○   ○   ○

AFTER THE BRITISH left India in 1947, India was in difficult straights. Among other things and for various good, bad, and complicated reasons, the flow of medicines from Europe and the West had effectively ceased. With famine and disease rampant, India's problems seemed overwhelming. As a result, a tradition of producing generic drugs came into being to address the social need. Foreign drugs under foreign patent were reverse engineered and produced by private concerns cheaply . . . for the good of the people. Eventually, the greatest problems became arguably manageable, and the leaders of Indian commerce saw that perhaps intellectual property protection of a sort might be a good thing.

In 1970, a legal structure of patent protections was put into place, but not the kind of patent protection people in the West generally think of. The patents didn't protect the drug. They protected the processes by which the drug was made.

In broad terms, let's say a foreign company invented a new drug, demonstrated that it worked through clinical studies, got its patent protections in line, and then started selling it. If an Indian company could figure out a way to manufacture it, India could issue a unique "process patent," and the Indian concern would be open for business. *And* the

Indian company would have protection from its Indian competitors, as long as none of its competitors figured out a different way to manufacture the drug. If they did, a competitor could also obtain a process patent. Then both drugs could be on the market, each manufactured in a different way.

And what about the foreign company that developed the drug in the first place and did all the safety work bringing it market? Bubkes.

Time passed—decades, in fact, and the world went global. In this regard, India was no different from any other country. It became a member nation of the newly-created Word Trade Organization in the very first round and at the first possible instant: January 1, 1995.

If India, like so many countries, wanted to emerge from being an economic backwater to assume its rightful place on the vastly lucrative global stage, it had to play by the rules. And one of the WTO's absolutely non-negotiable rules is its specific take on intellectual property.

In the case of pharmaceuticals, that meant "product patents"—not "process patents."

Every member country was required to sign what is called the TRIPS agreement. That would be the agreement on Trade-Related Aspects of Intellectual Property Rights. You can find out all about it at www.WTO.org, but suffice it to say you probably need a lawyer to steer you through it. For starters, there are the references to the Paris Convention, the Berne Convention, and the Rome Convention, with an added nod to the Treaty on Intellectual Property in Respect of Integrated Circuits. Actually, only specific articles from each of these documents are relevant, so you've got to separate the wheat from the chaff. It's not an exercise for the faint of heart.

In broad strokes, the basic idea—as far as drug patents are concerned—is that having been awarded a patent, the patent holder has twenty years exclusivity to manufacture and sell the drug in the marketplace. In exchange, the inventor must fully disclose the invention (i.e., the drug itself). And if the inventor also sought patent protection on the process of making it, that would have to be disclosed as well. No matter how you cut it, the patent holder has two decades clear run before anyone else can manufacture and sell the drug.

Now let's get back to the TRIPS agreement. What's important to remember is that WTO member countries were initially given five years to come into line on intellectual property. And yet some member countries with special circumstances were given longer. In India's case, five years longer. That made the official date for India to conform to the TRIPS agreement January 1, 2005, a pretty darn interesting date if you're the $5 billion Indian generic pharmaceuticals industry.

The WTO does suggest a path in its TRIPS provisions, yet each nation still must take action within its own sovereign domain. There was no doubt India had some serious work to do. It needed to transition from where it was . . . to where it was going, and that was tricky.

What about all the drugs that were already under patent before everyone joined the WTO and signed the TRIPS agreement? To level the playing field, a simple decision was made: Any drug patented by WTO member organizations prior to 1995 just plain didn't count. If a company had a blockbuster drug patented in 1994, too bad. It wasn't part of TRIPS.

But what about that ten year period between January 1, 1995 and January 1, 2005, and the roll-up to a full product patent system? Well, two main actions came into play. First, India developed a "mailbox system" wherein pharmaceutical companies from WTO member countries could mail patent applications for new drugs that were invented from 1995 on. Then, around the time of the millennium, pharmaceutical companies could also obtain "exclusive marketing rights" for their drug applications, and these marketing rights would extend for five years. The presumption was that those five years would be enough time for a new Indian patent law to be voted in and a re-worked Indian patent office to get its act together.

Sure enough, India's parliament passed its shiny new TRIPS-observant patent law, and when the mailbox was opened in March 2005, there were 8,926 new patent applications. The big winner was Pfizer with 373 patent applications, followed not far behind by Johnson & Johnson with 262. Needless to say, approving a drug patent is not a matter of simply checking the address and the date and quickly stamping an approval. It will be years before they all receive a decision.

And of course, that won't begin to be the end of it. Early patent decisions that go against the applicant inevitably lead to other actions. With the Chakrabarty patent, GE didn't just roll over when it heard "no" from the U.S. Patent and Trademark Office. And neither will these companies. In fact, the "reactive" actions have already started.

A case to watch is Novartis' cancer drug Glivec (which is sold under the brand name "Gleevec" in the United States). During the roll-up period to the new patent law, Novartis had been awarded exclusive marketing rights for its Glivec patent application and had immediately filed injunctions against six Indian companies that were manufacturing generic versions. Just like that, all the Indian generics were taken off the market. Novartis' annual price for Glivec? $26,000. The annual price for the Indian generics? $2,100. While Novartis was ordered by the Indian patent court to provide free product, no one believes that decision properly served the patient population. Cancer patients—specifically, leukemia patients—took the hit.

Now here's the interesting part: After the patent application mailbox was opened, the Novartis patent application for Glivec was rejected. In January 2006, the Indian patent office decided it was simply a new form of a pre-existing drug, and it didn't represent sufficient innovation to warrant a patent. (This reflected a specific provision of India's new patent law, which was intended to prevent "evergreening"—making a little change to your product to try to get twenty more years of patent protection.)

It was a bittersweet day for Indian leukemia patients, and Novartis didn't take the rejection well. It not only filed suit to overturn the rejection, it also filed a second suit saying that the 2005 Indian patent law was unconstitutional because it was out of compliance with . . . the TRIPS agreement! Obviously this is another legal mess, but the situation makes you wonder if the global pharmaceutical economy—as it is currently organized—is sustainable. Even the TRIPS agreement permits ignoring patents during social emergencies.

So let's try to mix the economic aspects of all this with the human ones.

o   o   o

INDIA'S GENERIC drugs industry has been supplying more than simply India's needs. Of great interest is the fact that it has become a major producer of generics *outside its borders*. India has been delivering its "process-patented drugs" for about 5 percent of what Western Europeans and Americans pay, and it's been delivering them throughout Africa, Asia and South America, to any country that does not have product-based patent laws. From anti-retrovirals to cancer drugs, from vaccines to blood pressure and heart medicines, we're talking about savings on the order of a factor of ten, a full order of magnitude. And the products have been going to the poorest of the poor. Many of the countries supplied by Indian generic companies can be found on the United Nations "least developed countries" list.

We've heard all the arguments from both sides of this issue until we're blue in the face.

Big Pharma has to pay for drug discovery, pay for all the clinical studies, pay for marketing, pay for all the drugs that *don't* work out. And the pharmaceutical companies have a legal right to the intellectual property they've created. The law is on their side.

In the other view, there are those who seek to help the sick and dying. They simply state: If we have the technology to alleviate human suffering and premature death, it's inhumane to deny it to any human. To their way of thinking, human justice is the issue.

There's simply no good way to spin it. In the Glivec case, rightful return on investment ran right into the health and welfare of leukemia patients.

That's not apples and oranges. That's apples and giraffes.

Of course, the curious fellow who keeps turning up in all this is Dr. Yusuf Hamied, the chair of Cipla, a leading Indian generics manufacturer. He's either a hero or a pirate—depending upon your viewpoint. Whatever he is, he's never boring. Cipla was founded by his father, and he has carried the torch passionately. Cipla, the company, is prolific. Dr. Hamied has remarked enthusiastically to more than one journalist, "We make everything Pfizer does!" And then some. Cipla produces more than 400 products, and Pfizer isn't the only place he trolls for potential meds. If he sees great medical technology anywhere . . . he goes for it.

There's also a real mistake in thinking that reverse engineering and subsequent manufacturing is easy to do. While this is undeniable theft of someone else's intellectual property, every pharmaceutical firm in the world could park its products with me, and I wouldn't be able to manufacture a single one. The entire process takes creativity, persistence, science, engineering . . . and the commitment of resources and time. Here, Dr. Hamied is no slouch. With a PhD in chemistry from Cambridge, it's clear that he makes significant and ongoing contributions to Cipla at every level.

Visions of Robin Hood are easy to come by, but Dr. Hamied—and his company—are more than capable of delivering innovative and original work. India's patent mailbox contained no fewer than 45 Cipla patent applications, and their work in the HIV treatment field is admirable. The Cipla products Triomune and Duovir-N combine three active AIDS drugs into a single pill that can be taken twice a day. Its latest breakthrough is Viraday—three drugs in a single pill, and it only needs to be taken once a day. That's progress. That's huge progress.

If you Google anything having to do with generics and the India patent mess, Dr. Hamied's name will pop up again and again. He's delighted to talk to the press. He's motivated to write articles and editorials. He's happy to get on the phone and give you a quote. He's excited to appear on television or give a public speech. He's indefatigable. And he's opinionated, which some say works against him. But how close "opinionated" is to a "refusal to back down from personal principles" is itself a matter of opinion. He's very clear: He's committed to continually driving down the price of all the generics in Cipla's corral. And he's uncompromising when it comes to AIDS drugs. They are to be manufactured and sold at cost. He claims that not making any money on a handful of drugs doesn't matter when Cipla has so many other profitable products.

Look closer, and you will find that he's also financially astute. In the late sixties, he lobbied Indira Gandhi extensively—and I'm sure everyone else he came across—to put the 1970 process patent law in place. This legislation worked to Cipla's own economic advantage.

Given that, there are those who argue he's walked on both sides of this street. So which is it? Social imperative? Economic return?

I, for one, believe Dr. Hamied's view of himself, which I detect is a businessman looking for a reasonable return on investment while serving the social good. And I have a very specific argument in his favor. He keeps the price of Cipla's generics down. Cipla sells drugs at 10 percent of what Big Pharma does. Would it be so bad to sell them at 15 percent? Or 20 percent? That would be clear profit. But Cipla doesn't. *And since Cipla doesn't, none of the other generics manufacturers can!* Fascinating. Is it true that this one man is almost single-handedly setting the price of Indian-made generic pharmaceuticals? It appears to be.

This is what is called a "utopian commercial enterprise." You make a profit, but that's not all you do. You make a reasonable profit, and you do good. What you don't do is maximize profit for profit's sake. You don't maximize your profits . . . just because you can.

Big Pharma on the other hand comes off as asking "Golly, how high a price can we charge for this?" Anyone who has walked away from the drug store with a huge and unexpected bill knows what I'm talking about. This image (whether real or perceived) is only bolstered by the undeniable record profits that Big Pharma is generating. In fact, some of the very same people who shake their heads at the cost of drugs also own stock in large pharmaceutical companies. Or their pension plans own such stock. It's a classic case of trying to have it both ways.

Independent of rhetoric, the drama of healthcare in India continues to play out against a backdrop of emerging intellectual property rights and climbing social need. Case in point: AIDS. According to the joint United Nations program on HIV/AIDS (UNAIDS), India is home to 5.7 million HIV-infected people, larger than any other known population globally. Far more conservative than Western societies in terms of pre-marital and extra-marital sex, India is still not protected. As Reuters correspondent Jonathan Allen reported from New Delhi on November 20, 2006: "The AIDS-causing virus is presently thought to be largely confined within a sexual triangle of poor, male migrant workers, the prostitutes they visit, and their wives back home." Yet the lack of HIV-transmission education is apparent at all levels of the population.

In the August 2006, Indian Prime Minister Manmohan Singh released a report entitled "Person-to-Person Advocacy with Parliamentarians on Populations Issues." It contained the results of a survey of 250 members of the Indian parliament, a body which is comprised of some 900 members in two houses. The survey revealed a striking picture of beliefs about HIV/AIDS. While nearly 80 percent understood that unprotected sex with multiple partners and the use of shared needles led to the transmission of HIV, far more worrisome were other responses. Fully half did not realize that HIV could be spread via blood transfusion or that mothers with HIV could transmit the virus to their infants. Over 60 percent thought that HIV could be transmitted by sharing the clothing of someone with HIV, over half thought that sharing food and utensils could spread the virus, and some 22 percent believed it could be transmitted via toilet seats. One wonders what kinds of anti-AIDS programs would be put together by such a group.

Ashok Alexander is the director of Avahan, the $258-million India AIDS Initiative of The Bill and Melinda Gates Foundation. He has been openly critical of the performance of Indian government agencies. Their mindset is clearly conveyed in Daniel Pepper's September 18, 2006 article, "Patently Unfair," in *Fortune* magazine: "Although at least 500,000 Indians have full-blown AIDS, enrollment in the free-drug program is fewer than 35,000. 'We have been going forward in a slow, guarded manner,' says A.K. Khera, who is in charge of AIDS drug therapy for India's Health Ministry. 'Now we are scaling up and going to expand in a very big way.'" One hopes so, but only time will tell.

Avahan—and Bill Gates—have been accused of fear-mongering and fomenting panic. It does not help that Avahan has documented far more widespread sexual activity throughout all levels of society than the social face of India would like to admit. This is a nation where in 2005, popular Indian actress Khushboo became the focus of widespread protests and was charged with over two dozen criminal lawsuits for remarking in a press interview that she saw no problem with young women having premarital sex, provided they were 18 years of age and followed safe sex practices to avoid pregnancy and sexually-transmitted diseases. She added further fuel to the fire by stating that no educated male could expect that his new bride be a virgin. Since criminal lawsuits may be filed by private individuals and private groups in India—as these were—it certainly dampens the idea of speaking your mind publicly against any popular mindset.

But at the end of the day, people with HIV need drugs.

Since the summer of 2006, much has happened. In August 2006, in the face of the public demonstrations and a coalition of HIV/AIDS organizations, GlaxoSmithKline withdrew its patent application for Combivir, a fixed dose combination of two essential AIDS drugs. Glaxo publicly floated that it did so in the public interest, but it was more popularly viewed as a triumph for activism.

In addition, a growing media campaign and public education effort are attempting to focus on the social stigma of HIV/AIDS in India. The hope is to reduce if not eliminate the marginalization of those who contract the virus, as many have been ostracized by their families. At the same time, India itself has recently increased its commitment to prevention and treatment with a five-year, $2.5 billion program.

Eventually new patents will be granted for Glaxo and other international pharmaceutical giants. What then? Under the new Indian patent law, three years after new drugs are issued patents, the patent-holding pharmaceutical company may permit Indian generics to produce the product under a royalty agreement. "May" is the operative word there. The law does not require the original patent holder to give its permission, nor are there guidelines to force them to. Permission is not a foregone conclusion. In the future, the first order of business for all advocacy groups will be to create public pressure to elicit these permissions and to ensure that they carry with them minimal royalties.

Even so, to the France-based organization Doctors Without Borders, the reality is grim: Under this new system, even in the best case, the latest drugs—humanity's best technology—will never be available to the vast swath of humanity on a timely basis, while the specter of developing drug resistance with prior medical technologies is ever-present. Three years is more than a lifetime for people with AIDS and cancer, tuberculosis and other diseases.

And so we live in two parallel worlds. In the world of business and investors—both large and small—reasonably trying to recover expenses and make a profit. And we live in the other world, the one in which the products we produce are not optional but mandatory for human existence. Do we have a moral obligation to provide humanity with the technology we create? Do we have a human imperative to get medicine to the people who need it?

○   ○   ○

THIS VERY conundrum weighed heavily on Dr. Chakrabarty, and he believes the solution lies in innovation and that we should encourage innovation in all countries—especially developing ones. He says:

> "Patents are only valuable when you make innovations. If there is no innovation, there is no patent. So, the most important thing that these countries—particularly developing countries—will have to adjust to now is how to bring innovative products into the market.
>
> There are many, many issues concerning intellectual property that divide the developing countries and the developed countries, so I think this is an exciting time in terms of actually understanding how intellectual property has helped developed countries. If you look at the United States, everybody admits that we are far ahead in terms of genetic innovations and the number of patents, things of that sort. I believe that that's partly because of the premise of the US Constitution. Thomas Jefferson, for example, and James Madison—more than 200 years ago, they came up with this document that actually said that the United States will encourage innovation in all its forms and help protect it. Now, it might be a little late for the developing countries, but it's never too late."

Perhaps he is right. The question we've been addressing is how companies can protect their rights to exclusively *sell* their products in all these countries. Which makes sense. After all, it's the World Trade Organization we're talking about. The subject is trade. But engendering global innovation —so there's a more level playing field of innovation, which could itself be traded—might be the better goal. No matter how poor a country is, it actually needs only a few innovators to make a huge difference.

Look at the difference Dr. Hamied's father made. The story of India might have played out much differently had he not been gripped with a unique vision and commitment to his country. If there was no pharmaceutical generics industry in India today, it would be a very different place, as would those other parts of the world where its medications make a dramatic impact. No one could have imagined when Cipla was founded in 1935, what it would become today.

Neither can anyone project what will happen if innovation suddenly breaks out in absolutely every country. Still, Chakrabarty is convinced that innovation can solve this economic/social puzzle.

To accomplish this, two elements are essential. First, there must be people with sufficient scientific, technical, and business background to address the challenges. And second, there's something a little harder to come by: There must be people who are natural innovators. They must be innovators every day of their lives, as if they wouldn't recognize life without it. They must *breathe* innovation.

That's right. It calls for people just like Dr. Chakrabarty. After he was awarded his gene patent, he could easily have rested on his laurels, but he didn't. In fact, I submit to you—he couldn't! He's an innovator.

His idea for using these genetically engineered bacteria for pollution clean-up was a good one, but there were concerns about unforeseen consequences. This made using his bacteria "in the wild" far too risky, so in the late 1980s/early 1990s, he started looking around for another research area. At that point he was working at a medical center, and he learned that the same kind of bacteria he had been working with—*Pseudomonas*—not only had a ravenous appetite for toxic chemicals, but also caused infections in humans—opportunistic human infections.

Some 80 percent to 90 percent of cystic fibrosis patients develop lung infections with *Pseudomonas aeruginosa,* as just one example, and by the time these children are ten years of age, most have this microorganism in their lungs. Once present, it stays there for the rest of their lives. Antibiotics and other drugs, as well as other therapies, work to keep it at bay, but it remains the major cause of death for people suffering from this genetic disorder.

Dr. C also noticed something else very interesting. "Pseudomonas aeruginosa," he told me, "seemed to secrete certain proteins that could enter preferentially into cancer cells . . . and not into normal cells . . . and kill such cancer cells by a number of mechanisms. This reminded me of the work of a surgeon named William Coley, who found out in the 1890s, when some of his patients got infected with certain bacteria, [that] the cancer would regress."

Dr. William Coley was a surgeon who worked at what is now Memorial Sloan-Kettering Cancer Center in New York City. In simple terms, he found that cancer surgery worked better *before* the introduction of antiseptics. How could that be? The key lies in the antiseptics themselves. What did antiseptics kill? Bacteria. Which was the point: killing the bacteria to prevent infection following the surgery. That was what was wanted, right? And yet . . . perhaps not. In the case of cancer patients, Dr. Coley noticed— as had various others over the centuries—that the patients with severe infections had a better chance of seeing their cancers go into remission.

Dr. Coley's early attempts to introduce bacteria directly into cancer patients met with some real success, but in others it was deadly. To avoid this downside, Coley turned to developing a "killed bacteria vaccine," which became known as "Coley's toxins." Dr. Coley passed away in 1936, yet interest in his approach has never died. Still, other cancer therapies have been considered more promising.

But Dr. Chakrabarty sees it this way: "[Coley's work] was more than 100 years ago. The technology for growing bacteria in pure culture . . . was not well-developed. What [Coley] found out was that if he could isolate the bacteria from his patients and grow them in the laboratory, and if he injected them, [in] 60 percent of the patients [their] cancer was either totally gone or significantly regressed." Coley did this with more than 300 patients. "His problem," said Dr. C, "was that he couldn't use dead bacteria. He found out that dead bacteria didn't work—only live bacteria did. But when you inject live bacteria into cancer patients, who are in an advanced state, or if the patients are old and not very healthy, then some of the patients would die. So it never took off because some of the patients died. You cannot have a treatment regimen when even a single patient dies."

In Dr. C's mind, William Coley's work was still promising:

"He did realize that bacteria, somehow, when entering the human body would allow cancer regression. They never give any credit to the bacteria in terms of their actively participating in the killing of cancer, because the concept that bacteria could kill cancer was not there, because you can't find a rationale as to why a bacterium could kill cancer. What we found out was that bacteria would actually produce certain proteins that have been studied in the laboratories for a long time, twenty-five to thirty years. A great deal is known about these proteins. Nobody ever thought that these proteins had anything to do with the killing of cancer.

So we are now isolating some of these proteins. We are characterizing the segments, called the 'domains' of the protein, that would either allow preferential entry into cancer cells [as in, they prefer to enter cancer cells], or allow killing of the cancer cells by various mechanisms. And we are trying to develop . . ."

Oh! I gotta stop here. We're headed straight for the biotechspeak rabbit hole. Suffice it to say that Dr. Chakrabarty is looking at critters even tinier than bacteria to "cross the blood brain barrier" and directly attack brain tumors.

You have to like the idea of using bacteria to work *for* us. He likens it to the development of antibiotics, where we develop microorganisms to kill other microorganisms. Remember the target for antibiotics is bacteria that make us sick. The target for potential anti-cancer drugs might also be to create bacteria, only these would attack our brain tumors and other cancerous regions.

Dr. Chakrabarty says, "This is a completely new way, I think, of attacking the problem of cancer. Whether it will actually work, we do not know." And then he got very excited. "But certainly the approach of using bacterial proteins is trying to tell you that bacteria do this purposefully. They don't *like* cancer."

And so you see, some thirty-five years after he started tinkering with genes using biotech, and some twenty-five years after he was issued the first gene patent, Dr. Chakrabarty is still on the job, a distinguished professor of microbiology and immunology at the University of Illinois College of Medicine. He's as involved as ever, relentless and constantly thinking. And he wants to do so much good in the world. He is truly the epitome of an innovator.

Which also brings to mind Dr. Hamied. I can't leave him out. You know that his mind is always working. And if Dr. Chakrabarty is right about balancing the scales by breeding innovators in every country, this just might be a job for Dr. H. He's the spoiler, right? And the hero as well. Why don't we see if *he* has any good ideas. . . .

So here's my pitch:

Yoo-hoo, Yuku!

(I hope you don't mind me calling you Yuku—I have solid sources who tell me that's what your friends call you!)

Yuku, I have this friend Chakrabarty. He's got a great idea. Why don't you dream up a way for all these developing countries to build their own pharmaceuticals industries? Not just bring the economics of pharmaceuticals manufacturing inside their borders. Find their innovators, and show these countries how to create a platform for innovation. I don't know exactly what I'm asking for here, but I have a feeling that you'll tell me.

Of all the people in the world, you—and maybe you alone—are the man for the job. Why not change the entire global economics of the pharmaceuticals industry? Why not find a way to combine economic imperative with social imperative?

Let me know how it's going, and of course, I'd be happy to help.
All the best!
Moira

This Is Dedicated to the One I Love

I'M TRYING to figure out how to tell this story without anyone knowing who I'm talking about.

"Oh, come on!" you say. "There are six billion people on the planet. Just tell the story!" Yes, but how many are chairman of global pharmaceuticals firms? They're all quite well known and obviously visible. You insist again. "You've been naming names this entire book!" Right again, but I haven't told quite this kind of story.

Perhaps I should call it "The Case of the Invisible Journalist." Not in the sense that members of the press lurk about, primed to jump out and report some embarrassing incident, relishing an opportunistic invasion of privacy at a time that would strategically do the most damage, political and otherwise. No, I'm talking about how a member of the media can be standing in full view, practically with a press card sticking out of his and her nose, and actually engaged in conversation with a very public and newsworthy person . . . and this person does something utterly inexplicable. It's as if he has totally forgotten that you are a member of the press. Or that a reasonable person who doesn't know him on an intimate basis is standing next to him. It's the you-are-

invisible-to-me phenomenon at its finest, and you really have to wonder what the person can possibly be thinking.

I actually wonder if the fella I'm talking about will recognize himself, even if he does read this chapter. Was he conscious of what he did? Or totally unaware? Will he suddenly recall it when he reads it in print? Or is it buried in the mists of yet another press interview. Who really knows at the end of the day? Well, it was the end of the day.

I found myself at the headquarters of an impressive pharmaceutical firm, in conversation with its chairman. Let me only give you a geographic clue . . . it wasn't in the U.S. I had been invited specifically by the chairman to come in and spend some time with him, because he had several issues he wanted to discuss with me, "Big picture" issues, he said, that had impact globally. I arrived, anxious to hear what he had to say, and he kept me in his office for the better part of an hour while an apparently important international sporting event played on the television behind him. All the while, he told me of multinational interests, bureaucratic intrigue, the good of the people, suspicious money trails, quiet resignations, national agendas, and his own role in the situation. It was all very interesting, even though it was interrupted frequently by a sharp 180-degree swivel of his chair, cued by excited crowds roaring from the TV. Or he might stop himself mid-sentence to shout out to one of his secretaries in the next room, imploring them to find this document or that. Or suddenly remember to make a phone call and ask a very specific question, like: Why are we buying supplies from this guy rather than that one? And when are those numbers going to come in?

He finally walked me out of his office with a big bag of documents that I should read and study. My head was spinning with all that he had been telling me, and here I was with a homework assignment, to boot. At that point, it was late in the day and the building had been slowly draining of people. There was no one left to walk me down to the lobby except his beleaguered staff. In an instant, he decided to take me himself, if only to give "his ladies" the opportunity to finish up whatever earlier assignments he had already handed out—before I presented myself and additional nonstop directives started flowing.

His enthusiasm had not waned, even once we got to the font lobby, and so he said, "Let me show you our conference room." It was impressive, indeed. A huge oval room, it had a big conference table smack in the middle, yet it was the walls that made it impressive. Floor-to-ceiling glass display cases were lit to a sparkle and filled with a wide selection of company products. He walked me step-by-step around the periphery, pointing up and down and missing no product, careful to comment on the economic landscape of one country and the intellectual property challenges of the next, the inexplicable popularity of one set of products in one part of the world as opposed to their rejection in another. After completing about two-thirds of the circuit, he pointed into the glass cabinet, and said, "That's our weekend Viagra." It took me a moment to realize that he was saying that it was a Viagra-like product whose effects lasted an entire weekend. Yikes! It took me that same time to realize he had stopped talking. He stood completely still. Then he tested the floor-to-ceiling glass door of the display, which had locks tastefully embedded in its design. The door opened silently, as if the genie owed him a favor.

He reached into the cabinet and pulled out the box of "weekend Viagra," opening the top. There were foil packets inside, each about the size and shape of a condom.... *Honestly, they looked like condoms! It wasn't that I was thinking about sex! Maybe the marketing division thought it was a handy subliminal suggestion to sell more product. You know, fits in the same space you keep your condoms. Come to think of it, that's not a bad marketing idea. Maybe I'm giving the whole thing away by telling you about the packaging. But I actually don't know that. I'm not that familiar with weekend Viagra . . . but I see that you are . . . (Note the press fedora which has suddenly appeared on my head) . . . And why is that? . . . Okay, you're off the hook . . .*

He turned the box over to scan the expiration date, and then he turned the box upright again. He scooped out a big handful of product and plunked them into his pocket. As quick as a bunny, he put the box back together, placed it precisely back on the shelf and re-closed the glass door. He waved his hand down the rest of glass cabinets, and said, "Well, you get the idea."

I got the idea, alright! What are you thinking?!? There was shouting going on inside my head. Don't you get that you just grabbed a handful of Viagra in front of a journalist? Like they were so many dinner mints? Did you forget it was you who invited me here? Did you forget why you were regaling me with—no, make that, subjecting me to—this whirlwind product tour of your company?

Let me be clear: There was no forthcoming explanation for his action. Hey, make up something, huh? *"There's not supposed to be real product in this room"* would work for starters. But, in his favor, there was also no—shall we say—unseemly vibe about it all. *I like to say I'm at that age where they pay you to keep your clothes on.* But what did happen was that the conversation lost its verve, even though I continued to ask him questions about the topic he found so compelling in his office. *Had all the blood rushed to his second brain? You guys! I swear you're all the same!* As fast as was polite, he escorted me to the front entrance and said to call or email him at any time. Before I could spit, I was out the door and on my way, being driven back to my digs in a city not my own.

I was certifiably puzzled. Could I ever tell anyone about this? Would I? What would be the point? After all, what really had happened? Nothing. Or was it something? Who would be interested in this funny little tale? And what good would it do in the world? Especially with the punch line being so perilously close to a statement about this man's . . . state of affairs? *He took them for a friend. Honest! . . . Or . . . He needed them for ballast!*

I didn't really know what to do with this story. Until right now. But now I know! Yes, I do!

Thinking about it, I realized I had truckloads of semen stories! Publishable ones! Where I could name names. I'd just lump all my semen stories together into one chapter! And this chapter I'd dedicate to men everywhere and how their brains get hijacked by Buddy, or Jack, or Thor, and even the one whose owner insists, "It doesn't have a name!" Okay . . . No-Name.

By some amazing twist of fate, all the names I'm actually going to name, who will tell us more than anyone would want to know about semen, belong to . . . women. Perhaps we are the only ones who can think straight. *Not funny.*

So let's get right to the biotech.

○   ○   ○

IF THE IDEA of weekend Viagra is all about fun and games, what isn't fun is a prostate exam. Now, I'm betting you guys are all pretty much up-to-date on the current state of things—no doubt, because it directly concerns you—but many women really don't know. So here's a quick primer.

Dr. Jenny Harry is the executive vice president for diagnostics at Proteome Systems. "Forty percent of men, by age 40, will have prostate cancer," she explains, "and over the course of their lifetimes, this [number] will increase linearly. By the time [they're] 80, the majority of men will have prostate cancer."

If you've never heard those statistics before, no matter what your gender, they are pretty shocking. The good news is that most prostate cancers are slow-growing, so playing the odds suggests it's best to leave them alone. You'll die before the cancer can get you. (Or at least that was true until biotech gave us all another ten, twenty, thirty years of life. We'd best keep an eye on that one . . .)

Still, "Three percent of men die from prostate cancer." That may seem like good odds—3 out of 100—but when you're one of the three . . . the game's up. Or it can be up. And while there are more treatment options than ever, if your destiny is aggressive surgery on the prostate and it miraculously saves your life, Buddy, Jack, Thor, and No-Name may never be up again.

That's why you better be right about what type of cancer it is in the first place. You want to detect it early, and you don't want to do any surgery you don't need to do. Early detection is key, both for minimizing deaths and maintaining the quality of life for those who survive. According to the American Cancer Society, in the U.S. alone, 230,000 men were diagnosed with prostate cancer in 2005, and 30,000 died. Part of that unfortunate statistic speaks to the less-than-optimal capability of current technology to detect it early.

For the present, we have this. The American Cancer Society recommends that all guys over age 50—and for high-risk types, all guys over age 40—take a two-prong approach. *Quit giggling.* Each year, they should take a PSA test, which is a simple blood test, and a DRE, also known as a "digital rectal exam." *Ladies, that's the part all the guys hate. The digit in question is actually the finger of a doctor, who is wearing a rubber glove. Of course, no one likes it. No, duh.*

It's bad enough that one of these two tests is certifiably unpleasant, but the fact is neither of these tests—either independently or acting together—really get the job done.

What they're looking for with the DRE are irregularities that the doctor can feel. Perhaps it's an aggressive cancer. Or simply a growth. Or something else is causing the prostate to change shape. But even an aggressive cancer may not be physically detectable by touch—what's called "palpated," or felt with your fingers. It's the doctor's call, and it's based on his experience and how sensitive his finger is.

The PSA test, on the other hand, is dependable, repeatable technology. It measures levels of "prostate specific antigen" in the blood. When it's elevated, this can mean that cancer is present in the prostate. *Can mean.* It can also mean that other not-so-great conditions exist, some of which are more annoying than life-threatening. But the PSA test is a foolproof screen. If you have cancer of the prostate, it will reflect it. Thank goodness for its existence. Unfortunately, somewhere around 75 percent of the time, it gives a false positive, which means that three out of four men who come up positive on the PSA test don't have cancer of any type.

So, the next steps to take can leave a doctor, a patient, and his family betwixt and between.

Generally, after a positive PSA, you get a biopsy. A doctor sticks a needle in the prostate to extract cells, which hopefully will tell the tale precisely. This is yet another less-than-appetizing step, and even so, a needle biopsy may leave some question. Were cells extracted from the right place or places? But if it's a direct hit for malignant cancer, then there's no doubt that it's time to act, and act fast. If it's the slow-moving kind, then there's some time to decide what to do. Even so, whenever surgery is on the line, it's troublesome. It's best not to mess with the prostate. You see, nerves essential to erection are present throughout.

A number of treatments have evolved, including a relatively new procedure called "nerve-sparing surgery." If the cancer—whether large or small—has not grown into the nerve bundles that control erection, the surgeon may be able to spare them. If they have, then I'm afraid you know the result. No nerves. No erection.

So detection at the earliest possible moment is what we all want to see. And that's what brought me to speaking with Jenny Harry. As she explained:

"What we're interested in doing is increasing the accuracy and specificity of [the PSA] test. What we want to be able to do is to determine if a person has prostate cancer or not, by very simple non-invasive means. *[Now, we're talking.]* We have partnered with a company that has intellectual property around a protein called 'human carcinoma antigen' [HCA]. Carcinoma means identification of cancer—not just a change in prostate condition. This protein actually is indicative of cancer in a number of organs. So ovarian, breast, lung and prostate tissue all can be positive for HCA.

"As a result, we have decided to develop a semen-based test, *[Yikes!]* because this will determine whether the HCA increase in expression is due to prostate cancer. The prostate contributes about 40 percent to semen, so this test would be pure for prostate cancer. In fact, the level of HCA in prostate is 400 times the level that one would observe in blood, so it's a much more sensitive test. This means we can detect an increase in HCA very readily. There's also no expression of HCA in a benign prostate change. Only when it's a malignant change. So it's purely specific to cancerous change."

These so-called HCA tests are still in trials, so let's be clear that at this writing, they haven't been released for general use. But the idea is a good one. Not only would it permit earlier and more specific detection, but men could say good-bye to the DREaded DRE. In Jenny's words,

"Hopefully you'd be able to identify [prostate cancer] much earlier, before you even see that change in size. If HCA is at a high level, then we know that we have the beginnings of cancer."

"The next step is to determine whether that cancer is going to be fatal, because as I said, only 3 percent of the time is this a problem. There's no need to put men through very unnecessary surgery—i.e., removal of the prostate, which has very ugly side effects—if this is not going to be a fatal disease."

This means they're working on being able to determine exactly which kind of cancer a fella might have . . . non-invasively. Perhaps from the level of HCA.

The public, in general, is beginning to get a sense of how prevalent prostate cancer is, especially now that we are well past the days when cancer could not be spoken of in private company, much less in the media. Phil Lesh, the longtime bassist with the Grateful Dead, came right out and announced publicly that he had prostate cancer. In reading the press release, you had to wonder about all the details that were revealed. Not because they were revelatory. But because they were so routine. He had an elevated PSA test, they did a biopsy, and it was determined to be small and slow-growing. When we look at the sheer numbers of men who will eventually all be positive for prostate cancer, you have to wonder when it will stop being called news. As in, nobody is interested in the fact that someone has slow-growing prostate cancer. Like . . . who doesn't?

On his website, PhilLesh.net, Lesh writes: "What do I have in common with Rudy Giuliani, John Kerry, Bob Dole, Joe Torre, Nelson

Mandela, Sean Connery, Archbishop Desmond Tutu, Emperor Akihito of Japan, General Norman Schwarzkopf, Colin Powell, Quincy Jones, Roger Moore, Sidney Poitier, and Robert De Niro?" The punch line is obviously prostate cancer. And lucky for Lesh, while his decision is surgery, the "slow-growing" part of the diagnosis lets him wait a month or so to work it into his busy schedule.

With the front end of the baby boomers marching rapidly into their sixties, there will be so many of these announcements that the only real news will be . . . when it turns out to be virulent. It would be interesting to know how early Lesh's cancer might have been detected with better technology. If this small, slow-growing cancer is involved with some of the nerve bundles . . . well, it can prove problematic.

One approach that Jenny Harry thinks would be helpful in the long run is to reset our thinking about testing for cancer of the prostate. Instead of seeking the once-a-year test, looking for a "yea" or "nay" answer, it may be more beneficial to track status throughout your adult life. Remember—if you are a man and you live long enough, you are going to get prostate cancer. "What we're anticipating," she said, "is that we will be able to determine increasing levels of HCA throughout life, throughout prostate development, and only when it gets to a certain stage, or is incredibly increased, would we then go in and do invasive work." And that's a good idea. Tracking HCA levels over time.

But then she threw me a curve.

"Initially, the test would be one that would be lab-based, until we had a thorough understanding of what those levels mean. But ultimately, I think it would be very similar to diabetics testing their insulin levels every day."

And now we get into interesting territory. You might test yourself? Well, after all, you have to produce the semen. Why not in your own home? *"Time for breakfast, dear!".* . . *"Be right in, honey! Just finishing up my test!"*

I went in for the kill.

"You know the million-dollar question here," I said. "Do you ship your kits with dirty magazines?"

She touched her hair. "How do we do this?" *You're asking me?*

I had her on the run. While she was thinking about how to answer, I threw in another challenge. "And you can never admit you couldn't take the test!"

Dr. Harry sidestepped it like the pro that she is. "It's an interesting question. Certainly, in terms of the general canvassing that we've already done in talking to people, everybody thinks it's a great idea. It brings a smile to the face, let's say, [rather] than the idea of having someone stick needles into your prostate. So, I think it's going to be a more favorable approach, and maybe we can get cues from fertility clinics or places like that to determine what is the most appropriate environment to create for this particular type of testing."

I let her off the hook. And why not. It's public radio, not Howard Stern. But I did wonder about how we would get semen as a man ages. I mean the older a fella gets . . . doesn't that mean the harder it is to produce semen?

o   o   o

THAT QUESTION was actually answered by Dr. Louann Brizendine, even though I hadn't really asked. She's a neuropsychiatrist at the UCSF Medical School, and she'd written a book called *The Female Brain*. During my *Tech Nation* interview with her, she talked about one study that arguably falls in the too-much-information category. It revealed that in nursing homes, some 25% of women ages 70 to 90 . . . masturbate. *NO! NO! I refuse to believe that. My mother was in a nursing home, and nothing was going on . . . ever! Could it be true? Twenty-five percent? Well, not my mother! And she was one feisty woman!*

"Well, their religious training is gone by then," Louann explained. "They've gotten over it, or whatever! I don't know. But observational studies by nursing staff have been done in different nursing homes [and] collated together in an interesting study." Then she tossed off an aside: "Of course, if you look at the number of males in the nursing home that masturbate, it's in the 80-90 percent range." *What?!?!?! What?!?!?! That's it! I'm never visiting Uncle Ted again!*

Of course, the presumption here is that we are getting voluntary semen samples.

Yeah. Go ahead. Re-read that last sentence. It bears re-reading.

That's right. They don't have to be voluntary. At least, I don't think they do. The very best person in the whole wide world I could ask about this is Dr. Betsy Dresser.

○   ○   ○

BETSY DRESSER is the Director of ACRES, the Audubon Center for Research on Endangered Species, just south of New Orleans. And she does many interesting things, including operating their Frozen Zoo. Ever heard of a frozen zoo?

"Well, the Frozen Zoo is a collection of cells," she explained. "They're either sperm cells or egg cells, which don't freeze real well yet, or embryos. There are also skin cells, now that we've gotten a little bit into cloning. And what we do is we freeze them, and we think we can keep them for hundreds, maybe thousands of years. They provide a safety net for a species if it gets so low in number and is threatened with extinction."

Did she say sperm? She said sperm, right? Yes, she said sperm.

"Okay, Betsy, what kind of animals are in your Frozen Zoo?"

"Many, many. We have gorillas and lions and tigers and rhinos, and we have frogs. We have aquatic species. All kinds of different bird cells. So [it's] quite a collection. We have over a thousand animals. Probably three or four hundred species are represented."

You have gorilla sperm? You have rhino sperm? I just blurted out my question. "How do you do that?"

For whatever reason, Betsy took it to mean I was interested in the science. "Cells are made up of around 80 percent water, and so what we do is we take that cellular water out of there because if you were to freeze it, [it would] form solid ice and fracture the membrane and destroy the cell. So what we do is replace that cellular water with something that's like an anti-freeze. It's called a 'cryoprotectant,' and as we slowly freeze . . . with a computer [controlling the process] . . . the cryoprotectant comes in, the water goes out and it forms a slush, so that when the cell is frozen it doesn't destroy the membrane.

"Once you get it to a certain temperature," she continued, "you can then take it and drop it directly into liquid nitrogen, which is minus-196 degrees Centigrade, or minus-383 degrees Fahrenheit. It's one of the coldest biological temperatures, and the cells just sit there. They slowly, veeerrryyy slowly metabolize, but other than that, they just sit there. It's a way of keeping cells alive, but keeping them so we can thaw them in the future. Maybe fifty [or a] hundred years from now."

Lions? Tigers? Sperm? I was just plain too embarrassed to ask the question. Would it be, "How did you get that gorilla to give you his sperm? And did you have to dance the hootchy-kootchy?" I decided to ask a different question, if only to buy time.

"Did you have to develop this technology yourself?" I asked.

"We had to develop a lot of the research that went into these wild animal species," she said. "Some of the basic research, of course, has been done with domestic animals—cows, cattle, sheep, pigs. We hired [for] our scientific team a cryobiologist, somebody who was renowned in his field in the area of domestic animals. He could then give us a base knowledge to build on, and each species you work with, whether it's a jaguar or a rhino, it's different. The cells act different. So, at least we have the base knowledge to build from, and that's a lot of the research—we handle all these cells."

Jaguar? You got a Jaguar to give you his sperm? Was his girlfriend there? I had other questions. I could use my other questions. While I was working up my nerve.

ACRES is south of New Orleans. It's hurricane country. (Little did we know, Katrina was just a few months away.) So I asked, "What are your plans if a hurricane hits?"

Betsy answered, "Well, picture a van goin' up the road with a frozen zoo. It's a mobile frozen zoo. The containers look like really large milk cans. There are huge liquid nitrogen freezers you can buy, that a lot of the domestic cattle industry uses, but we couldn't move those huge freezers, so we keep multiple milk cans, if you will. And we can easily get them into a van, and if we're threatened by a hurricane, we just move it."

And you take them all? Or just the important ones?

"It's really hard to choose," she said. "I mean, tigers are my favorite animal, so I'm going to say to you, that's pretty important, but in reality, there's some pretty important frogs, there's some pretty important gorillas, rhinos, or whatever. I think they're all important, and particularly if they were to drop to a very critically-low, endangered status. And you know we have a new insectarium that we're opening up here in New Orleans, so we're going to be freezing some insects."

You can get sperm from insects? You are GOOOOOOD!!!

It occurred to me that they could freeze all this stuff, but could they really bring it back to life? Some variant on *Jurassic Park* sprang to mind, so I asked Betsy to explain.

"Well, we've produced babies from these frozen thawed embryos, from frozen thawed sperm, so I think that's the ultimate outcome, because what we do is we don't want to just put everything in the Frozen Zoo and say 'Now we have it frozen. We're okay.' What we have to do is thaw them and produce babies to absolutely show that the technology works, and we've been doing that with just about every species that we've put in there. Still, we have a lot more babies to produce," she said.

As well as cloning?

On that point, Dr. Dresser said, "All the technology that we're talking about is called 'assisted reproduction technology,' and there's lots of tools in our toolbox of assisted reproduction technology. Everything from frozen sperm and frozen embryos. Cloning is just one of the tools that we're developing along with embryo transfer and *in vitro* fertilization for a test-tube baby. So it's really just one part of what we're doing, [although] it's probably some of the most recent technology, and that's why we're putting it in the toolkit. If you have a species like a rusty spotted cat, where there's only 17 of them in captivity or some Hawaiian birds that have dropped to a critically low number, we want to be able to bring them back. And that's where cloning would play a role. We wouldn't use it all the time. We would only use it in situations which are in crisis."

And just such a crisis presented itself . . .

"Take for example the cloned African wildcats," she said. "We have five females and three males. They're unrelated, because the females were all cloned from one female, while the males were all cloned from a male unrelated to that female. So, what we're going to do now is nurture, if you will, these babies until they're of breeding age, and then we're going to naturally breed them to show that cloning can work and these babies are normal. That's the first time that will have been done in these cats. I think we need to study these animals and work with them while we have them, because when they drop so low in number and you don't have enough to work with . . . (silence) . . . extinction."

As interesting as the Frozen Zoo was, there is plenty more going on at ACRES. Betsy lives there and she even invited me to come by for cocktails on her terrace next time I was in town. "We can hear the lions roar." *Huh?* Okay, so you're in the United States, on someone's terrace, and lions are roaring nearby. Think about it. *Yes, I'll have another cocktail. Better make it a strong one, okay?* You see, I had actually seen the lions earlier that day. They have their own clearing in the middle of the lush Southern Louisiana woods. They were in a big enclosure, simply surrounded by a high chain link fence. We journalists had scrambled out of the van and walked right up to the fence without a second thought. It was just like a fence in someone's back yard. A little higher, but that's all. The kind that Fido from next door sticks his nose through so you can rub it and hopefully be moved to give him a treat. But here, on the other side was a lion. A real lion. I mean a real lion. That close. *Hey, buddy? Can I have some sperm? Or did you already give at the office?*

The BBC's Matthew Wells became intent on recording a real lion's roar. And I have the close-up to prove it. The lion pretty much lay on the fence, just as your cat might lay against you seeking warmth. He had already stood up on his hind legs and put his front paws all the way up on the fence—which was impressive, because he was a lot bigger than we were—but now he was down again. Resting, so to speak. Eyeing us. Out came the handheld microphone, and the BBC guy started inching in. He was crouching down and holding it at the level of the lion's face. Moving slowing in. This huge lion's head just stared at him. His mouth was parted. We could hear him breathing. A light pant. In-out. In-out. As the microphone came within inches of the lion, I snapped my pic and the lion roared! Whoa! Yes. I have a lot of respect for lions. Even more now. Especially this lion. Fortunately, I didn't shake the camera. It was a shot for the ages. Destined for the journalist hall of fame, should there ever be one.

We were then informed he is a "teaser lion." A *teaser lion?* "Yes, for those female lions over there," our van driver casually remarked.

Sure enough. There are three or four lionesses, each in their own chain link condos. *Are they separated from each other? From him? Did they draw straws to see who got which one? And why does the lion get to have the big field all to himself?* It must be a lion thing, because we'd been told that they want all the animals at ACRES to live in situations that are "more like they would find in the wild."

Wait a minute. There are "teaser lions" in the wild? There can't be teaser lions in the wild! We would have heard of them. Later on, I asked Betsy.

"Well, that's true, but the lionesses don't know."

They don't know he's a teaser lion? So, that makes it alright?

"We vasectomized him because we didn't want to produce more lions," Betsy said, by way of explanation. "Females are induced to ovulate. In other words, when they copulate, that's what causes them to ovulate. So he's more than a teaser. He acts, gets to breed, but no fertilization occurs. No babies. That way we can use the [lionesses] hopefully for surrogates. For tigers, we're trying now."

So the female lions are now ready to accept an embryo?

"Yeah."

And you put a tiger inside?

"Yeah. Well, that's what we're trying now."

If I were to come back in a year? Possibly . . . we could have a tiger from a lion?

"Maybe, yeah," Betsy said.

You know that old thing about apples and oranges, and lions and tigers? Forget it. It all means something new at Betsy's house.

And in biotech.

○   ○   ○

THE OUTSTANDING question remains the same: Just exactly how does Betsy get all that semen? From lions and tigers. Rhinos and gorillas.

Eventually, I found out. Let me just say, boys, you're better off giving it to us voluntarily.

And so we close our little riff on semen and how it gets you guys into trouble, about how important semen seems to be, and how it may become even more important in the years to come. But you should be made aware of something for your future planning needs: As of January 1, 2007, Medicare no longer pays for Viagra, weekend or otherwise.

In addition, there may be other bad news from the lionesses in your life.

Now, we're back to the topic of prostate cancer.

For many men, prostate surgery—if it comes at all—comes later in life. I know of one long-married couple with many grown children and grown grandchildren besides. They had enjoyed a long and full life together and were inseparable. It was then that he received the dreaded positive on his PSA test, and after a series of medical decisions, it was decided that he should go forward with surgery.

His wife waited anxiously outside the operating room, and before long the surgeon came out, and he looked relieved. "I have good news for you. We found what we were looking for, and it's not cancer."

"Thank goodness!" she exclaimed. "Thank you very much, doctor."

But he wasn't done. "And in further good news, I want you to know that he will return to full sexual functioning."

Without blinking, she looked him straight in the eye and said, "Well, whatever you do, don't tell Bob."

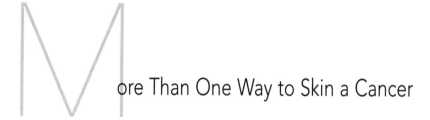

ore Than One Way to Skin a Cancer

IT WAS A sweatbox. A roaring sweatbox.

There I sat with Bob Alls, who just may well have had every technical engineering job at WHYY, the local public radio station in Philadelphia that most NPR listeners associate with Terry Gross and *Fresh Air.* He was at that particular moment being one heck of a sport inside this dark, low-ceilinged, wildly hot and extremely loud makeshift studio, smack dab in the middle of the exhibit floor at the Philadelphia Convention Center. It was BIO 2005, and this time we thought we had figured it all out.

We were wrong.

The previous January I had gone to scope out the local scene and met Ted Martin, who works with the State of Pennsylvania. A great guy, he had introduced me to any number of biotech people in both Philadelphia and Pittsburgh, and he got on board with *BioTech Nation* right away. Shortly thereafter, Ted came up with a terrific idea. Would we like to set up a recording studio in the middle of the Pennsylvania pavilion, the focal point of the BIO 2005 exhibits?

Would we? You bet we would!

No more convincing people to come over to an off-site studio, like we had to do at BIO 2004. No pleading with WHYY to suck out a bunch of their studio time. We could record to our heart's content, and it would be easy for our guests.

Not only that, I'd call WHYY to see if they could send over the equipment and an engineer, to boot. The person I ended up speaking with was Bob Alls, and we had such a great time on the phone, he decided to do the engineering himself. In fact, he brought their gear *and* his gear, just to make sure we got the job done.

Only now we were in a fix and, truth be told, I pretty much brought it on myself. The specifications I sent read "as quiet as possible" and "the smaller the room the better." I was thinking that the larger the room, the more noise it would generate. And the quiet part? I was thinking quiet like a hotel room. Hardly a professional recording studio, but a decently quiet room.

These specifications were turned over to the folks who build exhibits. They build little rooms all the time. We arrived the day they were setting up, *and it looked great!* One wall was floor-to-ceiling Plexiglas, so people could look in at us. Two modernistic tables were provided—one for the engineer and one for me and my guest. There was low lighting for effect and our own air conditioning unit. *But wait a minute? An air conditioning unit? Are you kidding? That makes noise! Big time noise! Hey, let's check this out.*

We went inside our spiffy booth, and inside . . . it roared. ROARED! It was a wind tunnel! What was going on? Was it the Plexiglas windows? Was it the giant air-conditioning outside for the entire exhibit floor?

The construction team went to Home Depot and came back with heavy drapes. We silver-taped the drapes over the Plexiglas, covering every hole. It was a little better . . . but not much. How could that be? And then I looked up. Yes, there were acoustic tiles in the ceilings. Each white tile nestled sweetly into its two-foot by two-foot frame. Only . . . only . . . not snuggly. I could look up and see daylight. They just loosely fit into the frame. I pointed up. The foreman looked up. I gave him a quick lesson in acoustics. "Oh," he said.

Another hour went by, and now they started layering foam on top of our little studio. It was better. Yes, it was better. Nowhere near the quality we needed, but maybe we could fix it with technology. I called Bob Alls on his cell, and he said he'd bring a selection of equipment with him. Maybe it would be alright.

Sure enough, the next day he rolled in at o'dark-thirty, only to be refused at the loading dock. One obstacle after another presented itself, until we all finally rendezvoused at the Pennsylvania Pavilion, and in front of the *BioTech Nation* recording studio. Yesterday it looked uptown. Today it looked like a homeless encampment.

I unlocked the door, and Bob went inside, wheeling the hugest load of recording equipment I'd ever seen mobile. Especially these days, since technology has gotten so tiny. He said, "I didn't want to take any chances. Whatever audio there is, I'm going to get it."

I had just been informed that this was all they were going to do for us. The exhibit hall was opening, and we had to work with what we had. We could turn the air-conditioning off while we were recording so we wouldn't hear the whoosh of the fan and the hum of the compressor, but that was about it. We couldn't make it any quieter than it already was. So we decided we could live with it.

I took a quick run to the press room before the exhibit floor opened, and on my return, I spied the foreman on a ladder next to our booth. He had a sharp razor in his hand and he was trimming the foam on top of the booth, so it would look nice and fit in the original frame. I stopped and motioned for him to come down off the ladder. I took him in the booth and pointed up. The foreman looked up and saw light. "Oh," he said. He told me that the set-up was complete, so he couldn't even put it back the way it was before he started cutting the foam.

Bob threw up his hands. "I doubt we can tell the difference with all the noise in here any way! Let's just do it." And we did.

Three solid days of the roar of the crowd—the constant, relentless roar of the crowd.

Mark was out there drumming up interviews, while Bob and I worked the studio. I swear he brought in a new set of microphones every day. He had me move this way and pushed the tables that way. He never did give up. But we both knew we were making the best of a bad situation, and God only knows what Monty would say when I got back to San Francisco, when he listened to the quality of the audio.

Monty Carlos is my longtime honcho of all things technical on *Tech Nation* and *BioTech Nation*, and the head of operations at KQED-FM. It don't go until Monty says it goes, and I knew this was going to be a tough sell. He was all over quality of audio. If anyone other than Bob Alls had been doing the engineering, not a single second of any of our interviews would have made it to air. But it *was* Bob, and thank goodness. My only other concern was the interviews.

Before I left San Francisco, I knew there was one person, for sure, I wanted to get into the BIO booth for a *BioTech Nation* segment—Dr. Paul Hallenbeck, the founder and chief scientific officer of Neotropix, Inc. I had plenty to thank Ted Martin for, but introducing me to this guy is definitely one of them.

I remember the first time I met him. It was over lunch the previous January, a freezing day in Philadelphia. I asked him one question when we ordered our meal, and he was so gripped telling me his own story, he didn't have time to eat. I told him he was definitely on the charts for our return visit.

Dr. Chakrabarty had told us that bacteria could be a very good thing, and as far as Paul Hallenbeck was concerned, viruses could be a very good thing, too, as he explained:

"They can be a *very good* thing. Actually, the field of virotherapy, utilizing viruses to treat cancer, has been around for about a hundred years now. It was noticed about 1888 by several physicians that people that had cancer had their cancer spontaneously regress if they also had a viral disease."

Sound familiar? Didn't we hear this same sort of thing from Dr. Chakrabarty, only he was talking bacteria? Following surgery without sterile preparations and without antibiotics, those patients did better if they had a bacterial infection. Hmmm.

"That's actually the first notice that viruses may actually, specifically infect and kill cancer cells," Hallenbeck continued. "And then, about the 1950s, several physicians started to inject patient's tumors with crude viral preparations. It turned out that while some efficacy [was] seen, there was still too much toxicity, because they were using known human pathogens, such as herpes and measles and other types of viruses. It was actually about the early 1990s that myself and several other investigators in the field discovered that we could either engineer viruses to make them very specific for cancer cells, or discover viruses that are very specific for cancer cells."

Hmmm. Sounds familiar again, but this time we're talking viruses. We all know that viruses are different from bacteria. We go to the doctor with a cold, and ask for antibiotics, hoping it will knock it out of us. I hate when the doc says, "You have a virus. Antibiotics work on bacteria. They don't work on viruses." No matter what else you and I might know, we all know this.

Paul Hallenbeck looks at this as taking advantage of the wisdom of viruses themselves. "It's just like natural products, which have been of interest to the pharmaceutical industry for years. Some of the best products that we have, have really come from natural products that you find in the ocean, the rain forest, or from a variety of great places.

"Viruses are kind of the same way," he said. "There's actually quite a diversity of viruses, and it turns out they have evolved over millions of years to do just what we want to do in cancer. They have evolved to kill cells very, very specifically, and some viruses will kill tumor cells very, very specifically, including the one that Neotropix was actually founded on."

Now the story gets interesting.

"The virus that we found turns out to be an animal virus, so that's actually one good feature right there. Humans don't have neutralizing antibodies, so you can systemically deliver this product."

What he means there is that our immune system hasn't developed antibodies to deal with this virus. It would be new to anyone that takes it, and we wouldn't ramp up our existing antibodies to fight it. As Paul explained:

"This has been a big problem in the viral therapy field, that viruses can't be systemically delivered, because we all have antibodies to actually prevent the virus. As soon as you deliver them, [the viruses] actually become neutralized.

"We found this virus that will infect cancers that have 'neuroendocrine' properties very specifically. This turns out to be some of the worst, most aggressive cancers known to man—such as, small cell lung cancer. Unfortunately, small cell lung cancer patients, if untreated, only live about twelve weeks—treated, at best, twelve months. There's less than a 5 percent survival rate in this kind of cancer. It's a really serious type of cancer, that we're utilizing this virus for, and we found that this virus is extremely specific for these type of cancer cells.

"Typical chemotherapeutics, which are commonly used in oncology, have a specificity ratio of approximately ten-to-one—meaning that for every ten tumor cells that are killed, one normal cell is [also killed]. And that's why they're so toxic. This is why when you take chemotherapy, you lose your hair and you get sick. It's because those cells are actually being killed by the chemotherapeutic. This is why people don't tolerate them very well. That one [cell] is a big thing. Typically, what ends up happening is you push a patient to the limit of what they can take with chemotherapy, and then quite often they have to back off and they actually have to stop taking the chemotherapeutic. And I think everybody knows, it's an unpleasant thing to go through, even though it's helped people to live a few more months [in these types of cases]. There haven't been significant breakthroughs with traditional chemotherapeutics.

"However, this viral therapy—the virus we're working on—has a specificity of a million-to-one. So, we're actually killing a million tumor cells to a normal cell. That's how much better this [therapy] is than a traditional chemotherapeutic. We don't see any toxicity in any of the models that we use for this virus. So, we anticipate that this virus will not only be much, much less toxic, but it's actually much more potent to cancer cells as well. Again, its natural propensity is to kill these type of tumor cells, and not normal cells."

Animal viruses? I wondered how he would deliver this drug.

"It's actually pretty simple. Just a simple systemic administration."

English, please!

"It's a one-hour IV administration. When you actually deliver a virus like that, it doesn't infect normal cells. It only infects tumor cells, so it will be cleared from the body pretty rapidly, except for in the tumor cells," Paul explained. "In the tumor cells, what will happen is [the virus] will continue to replicate and spread in the tumor cell mass that's infected until there's no tumor cells left. And then it gets cleared from the body."

Replicate!?! Spread?!? Not trying to provide one viral cell for each tumor cell? And the virus replicates like viruses always do? And continues to replicate as long as there are cancer cells?

He answered by saying, "This is actually what we observe in our models. They will continue to eat tumor cells. They will continue to replicate and spread through a tumor cell mass, until there is no tumor cell mass left. We see complete eradications of pre-established cancers in our models from a single systemic administration.

"This is another difference that Neotropix, I think, has compared to a lot of other companies in this area. We can systemically deliver this virus. That's really the only thing that makes any sense for cancer therapeutics, because cancer is a problem when it's metastatic and when you can't see the cancers. That's where the real issues come in. If you can see a cancer, you can usually surgically remove it, or treat it with radiation."

So, the dosage is really about getting enough in there to get things going?

"That's right," he said. "I think that's one of the significant advantages." Then he elaborated.

"Think about a drug like Herceptin, which is a monoclonal antibody—that's an antibody that specifically binds to a receptor on breast cancer cells and about a third of breast cancers have that receptor expressed. If you look at a drug like that, it's very promising, but part of the issue . . . is that not only does the antibody have to bind into a receptor expressed on cancer cells very specifically, but it also needs to be able to kill those cells. Otherwise, there's no therapeutic benefit.

"Viral therapy—and the virus that Neotropix is working on—not only binds very specifically to receptors expressed on these neuroendocrine cancer cells, but it also will enter the cell and kill those cells. Not only will it do that, which monoclonal antibodies don't do, but it's the only drug that I know of where you actually get amplification of your therapeutic at the pharmacologically desired site, and that's the tumor.

"So your actual therapeutic will continue to replicate and spread throughout the tumor. We think that's a significant advantage."

And every person who has ever had a cold knows about viruses. They get in there and they grow and grow and grow and then they peter out.

"Yeah. That's right. That's absolutely right."

I wondered what Paul Hallenbeck's and Neotropix's next cancer target was. His response was immediate.

"We're actually coming up with a technology to derivatize this particular virus for other cancer indications. We're actually working on that right now. We haven't quite decided. Sometimes we kind of let the technology lead us toward what is the best cancer indication. Kind of what's happened here— we definitely are fortunate that small cell lung cancer is a very unmet medical need, and we're certainly hoping to make an impact in that field. And we're hopeful that a similar situation will occur with our new therapeutics. But I do want to make the point that it's not just for small cell lung cancer.

"For other neuroendocrine cancers, which I think people have heard of, there's a variety of pediatric oncologies that have this target. These include cancers such as neuroblastoma, medulloblastoma, retinoblastoma, and Wilms. They actually are all a very good target for this particular virus, and we have several collaborators that are very interested in testing this virus on those types of cancer models—investigators at the National Cancer Institute, the Children's Hospital of Philadelphia, the Baylor College of Medicine and St. Jude Children's Research Hospital in Memphis."

I wondered how these kinds of cancers differed in children versus adults. According to Hallenbeck: "There's not so much a difference in the biology of the cancer. I think we know a lot about the biology of the cancer and [a little about] how cancer is caused. I think emotionally it's a much more difficult issue, dealing with kids who have cancer. [The fact that they are growing and their cells divide rapidly] makes pediatric oncology even more complicated. We certainly think this is potentially a terrific product for kids, and we certainly would like to get it tested."

Then it was time for the tough question. How many humans had Neotropix tried this on so far? Paul responded: "Humans? We anticipate being in clinical trials [in early 2006]. It hasn't been in humans yet, but it's been in a variety of models that we feel comfortable will predict how well it should work in humans. We really won't know until we get into clinical trials. At this point we have a Phase I-IIa trial planned, and we're on track to start those trials the beginning of next year."

Asked whether they had tried the virus on animals, he said:

"Yes, we have actually tried it on a variety of animal models. Unfortunately, that's really the only way that you can test this new, novel therapy to be really confident that you can enter human clinical trials with a certain degree of safety. We've been able to demonstrate that not only are mice a relevant model, but that we can actually deliver this virus in a million-fold the dose it takes to eradicate pre-established small cell lung cancers in mice. That's one [example]. It's also been [used] in preliminary primate studies, and viruses that are very similar have already been in pigs. There's been a lot of animal model development that's already been accomplished."

"All the tumor studies were done in mice. We actually see very good results in mice. We've tested five different neuroendocrine tumors in mice, and in all five we see significant efficacy with a single systemic administration dose.

"It's exciting. We couldn't be happier."

Actually, they could.

On May 17th, 2006, Neotropix announced that the FDA has approved proceeding with a Phase I study. They will be checking for safety in patients with certain types of neuroendocrine cancers, including small cell lung cancer. They'll also look at where the virus goes in the body, the elimination of the virus from the body, the immune response to the virus, and its impact on tumors. Neotropix will also be figuring out the optimal dose to be used in their next study.

On the human side, they've also given their virus a name—the Seneca Valley Virus. And while I like that name, I'd already named it after our studio. I call it "The Virus That Roared."

CHAPTER TEN

Dead Ends... or New Beginnings?

"I WOULDN'T hire you, even if I could."

That was a bit of shock. I looked up at my escort. She was taking me from the main building of Bush House, London—famed home of the BBC World Service—to the wing adjacent.

A bit of cold water, that was. Especially as I wasn't looking to get hired, but the rejection registered all the same. It was like meeting a married man in a business context and having him declare: "I wouldn't date you, even if I could." Who said anything about dating? And who said anything about hiring?

Still, I might have expected a friendlier reception.

The grand entrance to Bush House features two impressive statues, representing Great Britain and the United States, respectively, and ostensibly on very good terms. In a gesture of interchange, these two statues and four gigantic columns in close proximity were fashioned out of stone blocks quarried from, of all places, Indiana! The very place I had toiled for four long years earning my graduate degrees in science and engineering. Another sign of welcome was extended by the inscription above the entrance: To the Friendship of English-Speaking Peoples.

Did my escort think I was speaking in a foreign tongue? Perhaps she was unfamiliar with Indiana. Did she not know they spoke English there? Perhaps she was always looking down when she walked into the building each morning and had missed the grand idea. I wasn't getting the feeling that she was ruling out employment to better set her sights on friendship. Which left us standing awkwardly in front of the near-ancient elevators.

I managed to mumble something along the lines of "No, no! That's okay. That's not why I'm here. Ah...Um..." and thought I'd try to change the subject fast.

In truth, I was in London on other business, and had by happenstance met a higher-up in the BBC Worldwide organization at a public radio conference a few weeks earlier. We thought there might be some mutual benefit, as the BBC was looking to revamp one of its technology programs and was also very interested in expanding their biotech coverage. Since the BBC works regularly through the KQED studios, this was a natural. And it was how I came to meet this person for whom I shall never work.

I had just been introduced to her in a meeting, where she had been asked if it were possible for me to sit in on a taping that very afternoon. She had been quite alarmed. "No. It won't do at all. I have a new announcer. No. It would make her too nervous. No." *Did she say "announcer"? Or "presenter"? Or what title? I don't know. The meaning was the same.* Which was a bit strange. The person in whose office we were meeting was equally puzzled. He repeated himself, apparently thinking she had simply misunderstood. She repeated "No" quite firmly, and there was no doubt she wasn't going to change her mind, even though his division paid the bills for a hefty chunk of the programming her unit produced, and indeed paid the bill for the very show in question. The answer was "No."

He eventually pressed her to at least bring me over and introduce me around, certainly to the producer of the show with the new and wildly sensitive host. To this, she had finally agreed, and that was how we came to that location where she had found the perfect opportunity to make her proclamation: "I wouldn't hire you, even if I could."

As she stared in silence at the elevator doors, an idea came to me. *I know! I'll ask her about her background!*

This is always a good thing with a science/tech journalist. We find out where we each are coming from, our favorite topics, our depth of understanding in particular areas of science, and our personal challenges addressing others. In truth, we all come from different backgrounds and that gives us varied insight. Some of us start with English or journalism degrees, while others hail from the sciences, engineering, technology, or medicine. Some have business expertise, while others studied law, education, communications, psychology, or ethics. It brings a richness to science journalism that each of us appreciates, while we each meet the challenge of understanding and then explaining, placing the subject within a broader context, uncovering the issues, pointing out the impact. We share in the act of making the previously unknown, known—the previously misunderstood, understood. And our respective backgrounds are always grist for the mill of conversation. *This* was a surefire bet.

"Tell me about your background. What did you study? Where did you go to school?"

"Oh, you wouldn't know the university," she said immediately, shaking her head and throwing a quick glance in my direction.

I was puzzled. Thinking I had misheard her, I said, "I'm sorry. Which university?"

She was resolute. "You wouldn't know the university," not even bothering to look up this time.

"Okay," I said, ever-chipper, "What did you study?"

She kept staring at the closed elevator doors. "It doesn't matter."

A small crowd was starting to gather, waiting for the recalcitrant lifts.

"No," I said. "I'd really like to hear. What did you study?"

Inside my head a banner ad had started to flash: *Don't we know all the universities? Don't we know all the universities?*

Perhaps she felt pressure from the crowd, imagining they would notice that I was talking to her and she wasn't talking to me. After frowning for a bit, she said, "I like to hire people with non-science background. I just hired someone with a graphics design background. I really find that they explain science far more effectively than people with science backgrounds." *Yes! It's so easy to explain it when you haven't a clue!* Uh-oh! She was getting to me. So, my PhD in engineering was a curse? My masters in computer science best forgotten? Should I rue the day I started work at NASA? Chuck my software patent that extended scientific research? Could she possibly mean this?

Whatever her background was—and she could well have had an advanced degree in nanomicrosuperduperastrospacebiochemistry—she wasn't giving up where she went to school or what she had studied. Could it be that she had no actual background in science? Is that why she felt this way?

Perhaps . . . perhaps . . . I was overanalyzing this. Maybe she just didn't like me. Or I didn't understand some Brit take on things and had inadvertently done something to offend her. Or maybe it was something else altogether.

The conversation was now past icy. She had frozen out the small talk while executing to the letter what she had agreed to do. I should have bolted on the spot, but no—I'm a journalist. Persistent, if nothing else.

I later discovered that the BBC receives some 80,000 queries each year regarding jobs in broadcasting, yet they are able to offer positions to a relatively few people. This adds up to a mountain of rejection letters, each of which has got to be pretty discouraging for the person on the receiving end. Toughened journalists like myself are used to being thrown out on their keisters. (This is the flip side to being wined and dined. Think Mr. X.) But the point is: Discouraging people may be part of this woman's job! She's likely developed a whole knapsack of tactics for keeping would-be BBC-ers at bay, especially the wildly challenging ones who somehow make it past the Indiana stone columns and physically into the building. Such a threat would need to be handled forthwith, and arguably, it compelled her to whip out her best stuff. Unfortunately, that realization came later. At the time, I was simply confounded.

$$\circ \quad \circ \quad \circ$$

WE MADE it into her "unit," a sea of cubicles, and she introduced me to the producer in question. She told him she'd be in her office and not to forget about the recording session which would start shortly. Then she turned and walked away. Both her producer and I stared at her back as she plodded down the corridor. She didn't say good-bye, but what did I expect? Another proclamation? "Even if I could, I wouldn't say good-bye!"

The producer must have taken her cue, for he only half-turned away from his desk to speak to me and I was sitting somewhat behind him. The result was that most of our conversation was conducted over his left shoulder. *Did I have a big "L" on my forehead and couldn't see it when I looked in the mirror?* We'd had several on-air guests in common, and I explained the upcoming opportunity that I had with a globally influential person in the tech field who any journalist would consider "hot stuff." As I had discussed with my original BBC contacts, I was happy to carve out a portion of this interview time to make it work for their programming. Professional courtesy. To see how we might work together in the future. After all, the number-two place for biotech was the U.K., and for my part, I could easily connect them with everyone who came through my studio. I was sitting right smack in the middle of both Silicon Valley and the largest biotech cluster in the world. I also had a string of national people flowing through my doors.

The BBC people I had originally come to see were as gracious, energetic and visionary, as my escort and her producer were disinterested and cold. If only that was the extent of it. The producer took up where she had left off.

Right away, everything I said was misconstrued. He said their program could have no part of this opportunity. I wasn't doing a journalistic interview.

Why would you say that?

It's really some internal corporate gig.

No, it's not. It's the public event of a non-profit group.

Then it must be some paid infomercial set-up.

What part of non-profit are you missing? And I'm not getting paid. This is a public event.

Oh, not that? Hmmm.

Look, I'm meeting their corporate communications folks next week. Maybe we could . . .

He interrupts me: "We don't pass our questions past public relations people. Out of the question."

Look, if you want to talk to the Pope, you've got to talk to his publicist. Journalists speak with publicists all the time. We tell them what we want to talk about—so that at the very least, the guest is prepared. None of that "If I knew you were going to ask" waffling dance that you get. And sometimes we can get some inside dope that's really good or additional documentation that's very helpful. We all know the rules. If they tell us some subject is off the table, we can always walk away. If we say we're unwilling to take on a particular subject, or we *must* talk about something, *they* can always walk away. Everybody knows that. We keep it on the up-and-up. And we're tough. Why am I being misinterpreted at every turn? People like this are impossible to get to agree to do interviews. And they invited me. And it's a public event. He can't get out of whatever he says. We have a free walk here.

Still, the producer was focused on an interview the show had done with another executive from the very same company, whose president and CEO

I was about to interview for the public event. Apparently, the executive had either been unprepared to answer their questions or had given completely unacceptable answers as far as they were concerned, or both. The producer felt the BBC interview had been quite a success, a real feather in their caps. He told me the segment had gotten quite a bit of international attention in the press when it was aired. (He reiterated this in a subsequent e-mail. The "interview was picked up by many news sites and caused some embarassment (sic) to the company." The audio was still on their website, and I should go out and listen to it, he urged me again and again.)

Finally—in all likelihood because of my hosts in the main building—he agreed to e-mail back and forth and explore the possibilities further. Then he said he had to go. Very busy, you know. About to record this week's show, you know. *I'll show myself out!* I volunteered. *Not a problem!* He thought that was a great idea, and turned back to his desk.

o   o   o

INSTANTLY, I knew I was wrong. This *had* to be a problem. No media outlet ever let's anyone walk around unescorted. Certainly not the BBC. But the producer either had forgotten that, or didn't care, or just wanted me to leave, and the idea of spending another few minutes escorting me from the building was simply too much to bear.

Later on, I got an e-mail from one of my original contacts, the very person who had introduced me to my escort and, through her, to the show's producer. The e-mail had been sent that very afternoon and said, "It was a pleasure to chat, and I am dead certain that [the producer], once he is on the case, will be really keen to talk and develop links . . . I will chat with him next week . . . have a safe journey home."

If you could only spend optimism.

Try as I might to listen to the interview the producer had so proudly referred to, the BBC website would link me only to the previous week's show. No matter how many e-mails I sent to the producer, he couldn't get this problem through his head. And so, I couldn't listen to it. No one could listen to it. The website pointed to the wrong audio. *It was not to be heard.* And as for it being "picked up by many news sites," I could find no reference to it anywhere on the Internet. What could he possibly have been talking about? No matter what I typed into Google to refer to the interview—the program name, the guest's name, the interviewer's name, the company's name, the purported content, the date—there was no Google trail. There's *always* a Google trail. *What could he possibly be talking about?!?!!!*

Undaunted, I was able to get a strong sense of what the interview was all about, because the regular tech commentator on the show wrote about it on his blog. (The BBC has links to the websites of various people who appear regularly on its programming. It covers itself by citing, next to any links posted, that "the BBC is not responsible for the content of external Internet sites.") It was through this mechanism that I figured out what all the shoutin' was about. Needless to say, I didn't agree with the interview's basic premise—what a surprise! Remember the bit about speaking or not speaking with publicists beforehand? The guest had come on to talk about one subject, and the BBC fellows hit him with another.

This surprise line of inquiry expected the guest to know about an obscure specification for a computer designed by a tiny group of engineers, who wanted to build a low-cost computer for the poor in India. They ran into problems getting it funded, and while they were waiting around, the guest's company had eliminated the product line that were called for in the specs. As you might imagine, the guest was completely unprepared. The tone taken by the producer and the guest tech commentator suggested a lack of concern for the poor and for fledging entrepreneurs, and they finished it off with a nice dusting of corporate greed, since only a relatively few units would be sold in any event. Muddying the waters even further was the fact that it was unclear that the BBC folks understood typical tech life cycles, the economics of high-tech production lines, or that when engineering specs experience delays in getting built, they quite naturally need to be updated to newer technologies. Happens all the time in Silicon Valley. Happens all the time in building technology. Which may answer the question as to why references to the interview couldn't be found all over the Internet, as had been suggested to me by the producer. Initial reaction would have been withdrawn, when the situation was reconsidered in the fullness of time. And for the conspiracy theorists among us, there's always the curious case of the missing online audio. As for ambush journalism . . . well, that happens enough of the time for the press in general to earn a bad reputation.

Amazingly, my turn in the hot seat was not yet over

My e-mail interchange with the producer played out over several months, and went circular several times, as in: Go to the website to get the audio. Oh! Can't do this! It is a paid company event! Oh, it's not? Go to the website! Oh! We don't run questions past PR departments! Oh, you're not? You need to go to the website and listen to the audio! Eventually, I gave up.

It did occur to me at one point that they were deliberately playing dumb. It could be positively Monty Python-esque in stature, and I could see them having a real chuckle over it. It would be great fun to think up ridiculous and unresponsive e-mails to send back to me, as I earnestly tried to catch every mud pie they threw my way. But realistically, there were no mixed signals. They expressed their disinterest from the start. First, in the meeting, when my escort insisted it would be completely unworkable for me to go to the taping of the show. Then, by the elevator, right before I learned of the existence of the "secret university." And straight on through to the e-mail runaround. While my primary contacts at the BBC couldn't have been more wonderful, these working journalists should have been my natural allies. But they were not. 1 down. 79,999 to go.

○   ○   ○

I NEVER thought I'd be writing about this experience. Primarily, it's a story of failure. But then I ran into Mark Thompson, and I knew there was every reason to write about it. You see, we're from Silicon Valley. We eat failure for breakfast.

Mark Thompson is now a visiting scholar at Stanford University, after a long career in venture investing and as the executive producer of Schwab.com, the innovative discount stock brokerage. He even chaired such Silicon Valley start-ups as VMAX and Rioport. You might remember the Rio. It was the first MP3 player that actually looked like one, an early aspirant in the mobile music scene whose technical embodiment wouldn't come to fruition for another decade in the familiar form of the Apple iPod. While Thompson gives major kudos to the utter brilliance of the iPod itself, the Rioport was underfunded and too early to catch the right wave, the opportune convergence of essential technologies. And to be truthful, this reflects just one short period in his long and illustrious career. More recently, Mark had interviewed some 200 people from various walks of life about success and failure. He and his co-authors, Jerry Porras and Stewart Emery, had just published *Success Built to Last*.

"The first failure is something that you wear like a badge of honor here in Silicon Valley," he says. "It's one of the powers of the place, and thank goodness. It's attracting talent from all over the world; all of these dyslexic, backward, revolutionary folks are all coming here to make their dream happen."

To Mark Thompson's way of thinking, embracing failure is part of the key to success:

> "It's almost a matter of looking to failure for some of your best insights, and then harvesting failure, because you've paid the awful tuition anyway—in money, time, and effort. 'I'm sorry! You blew it!' Are you really going to just 'think positive'? This is where that whole idea of just choosing your attitude actually doesn't work.
>
> What often appears to be an imperviousness to pain, or an abnormal sort of strength of resilience is a dedication to some idea that really matters so much that 'Dammit!' They're not gonna let it be hijacked by this overwhelming current of emotion that they're feeling right now. They're just so dedicated to it. They use all they have, and part of what they have is their weaknesses, their set-backs, the mistakes that they've made. These are all great data.
>
> It's interesting looking at these people, looking at a large population of them. If you took away the outcomes, if you took away what you knew about the story that came out, you'd actually think that they were a bunch of losers, because they have such a strong relationship with failure. They talk about it a lot. They talk about being so unfinished on their way to doing what they think is really important to do.
>
> Ed Penhoet, the biotechnologist who became a professor and then went on to create Chiron, the biotechnology company, talked about trying to go out and talk to entrepreneurs to see really what they had learned, and he was amazed at how many had fundamentally gilded the lily. They wanted him to believe that they'd always had it figured out, that they had no failures, that they really were prescient, that they were able to predict the future. Of course, when he got into his job, there were so many days that he was [so] concerned about his people that he had to throw up in the gutter on the way to the office, because he was so stressed out about it. That's when he really came to the conclusion that you can't dismiss

your failures, or you're doomed to repeat them. You better get really good at learning from them, and you can't just try to think positive either, because you won't go back and harvest them. This is an *and*, rather than an *or*. [It's not] I'm gonna think positive *or* I'm gonna harvest my failure. No, you gotta do both.

As Esther Dyson says, 'Always make new mistakes.' You've got to have a way to really objectively do that."

How to handle failure became a part of what Thompson would ask the successful people he would interview. How did they learn from their failures? What did they learn? It seemed that failure might be accepted—if not honored—in Silicon Valley. That didn't necessarily mean you learned from the experience.

He told me this story: "I was talking to Quincy Jones, and I said, 'You know, everybody says yadda-yadda-yadda. You gotta learn from your mistakes. Here you are saying it again.' And he said, 'But when was the last time that you really did that? That you stopped and took the lesson?' *And* didn't learn the wrong lesson, which is, 'I'm never gonna love again' or 'I'm never gonna try another start-up.' Take the right lesson, and realize that [what] you're trying to do is more important than that one failure."

I pressed him, not even thinking about my BBC experience at the time. What about when people tell you that you or your idea is really screwed up? According to Thompson:

"That's a wonderful paradox in being successful for the long term. The people who isolate themselves, because they're so damn right that they can't hear anything or any input, don't get very far. And [then there are] the folks that cave every time someone comes along and says, 'You know, that really is a stupid idea. I mean, just don't do it that way.' Both equally are going to be devastated and not be able to move forward.

There's also a deeper level that I thought was fascinating and subtle. You can learn from your failure, but there also might be the seeds of your genius *in that failure*. This is not something that was obvious to me until I went to work for Charles Schwab and was involved with Schwab.com. I was executive producer there and working with Chuck Schwab. He's very dyslexic. It turns out he has a very difficult time reading anything that's in a written form. And I'm also dyslexic."

"So you thought you'd write a book?" I asked. "Great idea!" He acknowledged this with a laugh and said that it even gets better.

"I also thought I'd do communications programs and CEO series and all these things that require reading! But here's the weird thing about having a so-called handicap. It just might be that your coping mechanism, or the difference that you have at looking at something, might actually be a point of differentiation for that technology or for that idea that you have.

Now [Schwab] was always passionate about investing. I mean, the guy was selling fertilizer and chickens at thirteen. And then walnuts. [Then] business after business that succeeded or failed, and most of them failed until he got Charles Schwab started. So six or seven failures later, he's succeeding in a business that he's really passionate about—investing.

Part of the key was . . . every single day when you're dyslexic, you have to break things down to simple parts. You cannot live with complexity. So you have this skill that you use to replace what is a handicap at actually breaking things down to their component parts. Well, as it turns out, the public really appreciates [it] if you can break down this overly sophisticated complex world. [Schwab] basically invented the discount brokerage, and then he invented one-stop shopping for mutual funds and the online services that went with that—things that everybody thinks are natural now, but something that he invented only because simplicity for him is a *requirement*. It's not an option. He could see it.

He also did something else. He recruited a team to this dream. If you've spent time with many technologists or scientists or people that care about the ventures that they're creating, it can often be the case where they're the smartest person in the room. They assume that it's hard to get good help today, [hard to] get people who are up to your standards. So, [Charlie Schwab] recruited a team—without that arrogance.

When you talk to venture capitalists, they have two exit strategies always in their mind. How am I going to make my money on this [venture]? My ten or twenty [times my investment] or greater. And they're also thinking, How am I gonna get rid of [the original founder], because often they can't scale. They can't recruit the team that can subsidize the areas where they're weak and then grow the business beyond that one individual's vision of it. So the strength of the entrepreneur becomes their vice later. It usually works against them as they try to build the business.

But there can be a seed of your genius in this wound . . . or this handicap . . . or this failure that you've had, besides just learning from the explicit data that's presented from it."

o   o   o

A SEED of genius in this wound . . .

Whatever could that be?

These words brought me back to thinking about the 80,000 people who make their hopeful queries to the BBC each year. Are 78,000 of them terribly discouraged by the response? *"Dear John, Thank you for your inquiry. Even if we could, we wouldn't hire you. . ."*? Do these 78,000 know to keep on going? To shrug it off? To take the proper lesson? To continue on despite the odds, no matter what was said? Do they know that there are more media opportunities emerging now than ever before? And that what the media looks like today is nothing compared to what it will look like tomorrow?

The BBC World Service moved into Bush House in 1940. What media was like then is nothing like it is today. In the interim, the world of media has changed many times over, as each new wave of technology crashed upon a receding one. And it will change even faster still in the years to come.

No doubt, the BBC has been a defining entity throughout their lives. But did they know this? The BBC does not own Bush House. Its lease runs out in 2008, and it will have to move. Even the mighty BBC cannot control its own destiny.

It's hard to remember such things when you have been summarily dismissed. It's hard to remind yourself that the rejection does not define your possibilities, your worth, your aspirations, or the difference that you can make in the world. The blessing is that today—with technology—anyone can be a member of the media. Anyone can reach and touch just about anyone else on the planet, and you don't need to be a part of a global media empire to do it. You can have an idea about a program that only you can see. That only you can do. And you can do it on your own. That would not be possible if you went to work at a company that had a very specific job in mind. So, yes, rejection—and failure—can sometimes be just the thing to let a seed of your genius sprout.

But what about me? What should I take away? What of the BBC-ers who wanted to lose me so fast, you'd think I was yet another ugly blind date set up by Auntie Edna. I'm surely off their radar screen as they blissfully go forth. And should my name be mentioned, they can truthfully answer, "Who?"

Well, I'm not quite sure, but while I'm figuring it out, I know exactly what I'll do! I'll send them copies of my book! Personally autographed! I'm sure they'll be thrilled!

The kinny on Genes

"**OBESITY IS** a huge problem in this country, and these people need to learn to exercise some self-control! It's all about self-discipline."

I was shocked.

The message was delivered with a touch of annoyance. And there was so much wrong with this statement that I didn't know where to begin. Especially because it was delivered by a well-known economist from a prestigious university with a long and highly celebrated career. He said it while recording an interview in my KQED studio. It wasn't some casual remark in a social setting. He wanted to make this point publicly.

Mental note to self: *Thank goodness we're not live radio. This statement has to be cut.*

Second mental note arriving on top of the first one: *This man will never again be on* Tech Nation.

I let him talk a bit more about his opinion on obesity, and then we wrapped up the interview. Other parts were usable and relevant to his expertise. But this? What was this all about? Frankly, I didn't want to know. There was so much wrong with it—even without considering the science—that I didn't care to waste my energy following this particular rabbit down this particular rabbit hole.

But there you have it. The bald prejudice against obesity, a prejudice that is well-documented, but seldom verbalized publicly. We "hear" that people have such prejudice. We are told about its consequences, about how it feels to be on the receiving end. Yet in polite conversation, people generally reach into the denial bucket, claiming that some of their most beloved friends are obese. In America, that's not exactly a stretch. According to the National Center for Health Statistics, a part of the Centers for Disease Control (CDC), one out of three adult Americans are obese, and another one of those three adults is overweight. Friends would be hard enough to come by if you only restricted yourself to thin ones.

And yet . . . prejudice runs thick in the air, make no mistake about it. How it presents itself and its impact is well covered in other venues, but what can science tell us about the origins of obesity and the tendency to be lean? Are there genetic components—the nature and not the nurture part—that cannot be ignored?

Good question. Especially because we're under constant assault to eat right, exercise and get our weight inside a particular range located on some table and published by *who*? And if we don't, *it says something about our character*?

We're told it's all about self-discipline, and that's why the character question comes up. Which makes it all so important to ask the question: Can we see skinny on genes? How about obese? How about a little chunky? Can we spot who's gonna be a chunky monkey from day one?

I was thinking about these very questions while I was talking to science journalist David Ewing Duncan, our chief correspondent for *BioTech Nation*. I should explain that in the two-plus years since we started *BTN*, the biotech segment has become more and more popular. (And why not? Who doesn't have DNA?) We added some new parts, including the *BioTechSpeak Word-of-the-Day*, as well as the *BioIssue of the Week*, where David and I discuss biotech topics that are unfolding. These topics have ranged from the back-story on the Michael J. Fox political ad that ran in Missouri—and was so famously criticized by Rush Limbaugh—to the outcome of the Global Climate Change Conference, the results of environmental toxin tests on David (which he did for National Geographic), and "Frankenbunnies" (which are chimeras, a mix of two animals). These particular chimeras are rabbits genetically modified to produce human proteins, animal factories, so to speak. David and I jawbone each week, and I knew that he had done a lot of investigative work around obesity, including a segment that aired on PBS *Nova ScienceNow.*

When we were sitting in the studio, having just finished another edition of *BioIssue of the Week,* I asked him flat out, "Can we blame it on our ancestors if we're fat?" He answered straightaway:

"Partly. Probably the way to start is to ask the question: Is obesity genetic? Or not?

Do we just sit and chow down on Big Macs all day? And that's what this epidemic is all about, or are we just eating up to what our genes are telling us to. It's a huge controversy, and I even have friends in the scientific community that debate this with me, because I've done a couple of these stories.

It's an interesting cultural controversy and argument. Obviously, there's a food industry that, for the last twenty to thirty years plus, has been producing stuff that we all love to eat. Junk food and fast foods that taste better and better and have all kinds of salt and sugar and carbs and stuff, which we love because our ancestors didn't get enough of it. And we get too much. Is that a plot by the food industry to make us all fat and them all rich? There's a whole contingent of scientists, nutritionists, and others who blame most of [the trend towards obesity] on our society and the food industry, [giving] us all this junk food and [making] us fat. They don't like the idea that this may be genetic.

They're not wrong. They're probably both right—as usual."

If we wanted to study obesity genes, I asked him, would we have to find populations that didn't have the junk food present? He answered:

"Or you could find populations where the modern diet has been introduced recently, and you have both overweight and thin people. And that's exactly what I did for an *MIT Technology Review* article. They sent me to Micronesia, which is way, way, way, way west of Hawaii. It's north of Fiji, actually directly north of New Zealand. It's a scattering of islands, the Federated States of Micronesia, and I went to one called Kosrae [pronounced 'co-shry']. It's a beautiful island. It's like something out of someone's *South Pacific* fantasy. Beautiful bay and a mountain, and the people there are basically

Polynesian, and about thirty years ago, it transitioned from being a U.S. protectorate to its own nation.

Somewhere along the line, the U.S. started shipping in modern food, and especially in the last thirty years or so, there's a ship that literally comes in every month. There are about two or three thousand people who live on the island, and this big ship comes in full of stuff like Spam, white bread, hamburger meat, and Sugar Frosted Flakes—it's kind of an old diet for the United States. What we were eating maybe fifteen or twenty years ago. High-carb, high-sugar kind of foods. For any number of reasons, they buy it and eat it. It's subsidized so it's relatively cheap. They think they're being modern and eating modern food. And look, it was a lot of work to chase down coconuts and fish, because that's what they ate before.

The reason we think about Kosrae is, there was a scientist named Jeff Friedman at Rockefeller University and he's famous for discovering a hormone called leptin, which we'll get back to in a minute. But his other work is trying to figure out why 80 percent of the people on Kosrae on this modern diet are overweight or obese. They're huge. It's even higher levels than in the U.S., which actually is pretty high. But there's a small element of the population—about 20 percent—that are lean and who eat the same diet. So, he went: 'Aha! There's some genetic component going on here.'

He went there and he had certain theories, because the Polynesians have been mixing in with European populations for centuries, ever since the first whaler discovered the islands. Caucasians tend to be leaner than these Asian-Pacific peoples. He thought maybe there was an inter-mixing there, and you were getting these Caucasian leaner genes with the Polynesian larger genes, if you want to call them that.

It turns out that's actually not the case, but he's still convinced that there's a genetic component. Since then, there's been a lot of work done on how genes may impact obesity, and he believes that obesity has about the same genetic component as, say, height. And that's about 60 percent or 70 percent genetics. Obviously, your height works until you reach your full height. But your size, your girth, so to speak . . ."

"Is the gift of a lifetime?" I said. Agreeing, he went on to explain more:

"Yeah. We sort of intuit this. Friedman and the other scientists who believe these genetic theories—that obesity is largely caused by genetics—that's what they say the genetic component contributes. Of course, that has been just a raging controversy.

One example is the 'thrifty gene' theory, which is a counter-intuitive name for it. The 'thrifty gene' is something that makes you fat, because it's using food in a thrifty way, when you [don't] have enough food. It was developed by geneticist James Neel back in the sixties. He came up with this notion that for peoples who were hunter-gatherers, it was an evolutionary advantage for them to actually get fat fast. You didn't know when you were going to get food next. You killed a wooly mammoth back in the day, and you gorged on that for several days. Our system is actually designed to be able to handle huge influxes of food, and the fat system in mammals is basically there as storage for when you don't have food. So, there's some intuitive proof for this thrifty gene theory.

The idea is that those who got fat fast and who could eat a lot of food and could absorb it and create fat, that was a thrifty thing to do. If they survived and those who were skinny didn't, then the skinny ones died off, and their genes weren't passed on.

There's another theory that's sort of the cousin of that theory, which is the 'Fertile Crescent' theory. The Fertile Crescent, of course, is that area in Mesopotamia that goes from modern Syria through Iraq and into Iran. That was one of the cradles of civilization, and it's one of the places where agriculture was developed and people became settled.

You don't want to have the thrifty gene if you're sitting there chomping on agricultural products like wheat, which are always there. You'll gain weight and get all the diseases we know today, like diabetes and everything else. [Now according to] the Fertile Crescent theory, those people who had a leaner propensity were the ones who survived, and the people who gained all the weight didn't.

Both these theories are somewhat controversial, as you can imagine, but that's the general idea, and it does tend to fit the pattern. Europeans—where agriculture moved in pretty early—and people in that Fertile Crescent area . . . tend to be lean. They can eat and eat and eat, but they don't get as fat, whereas some other areas—like say, in Latin America, Asia-Pacific, and parts of Asia—you look at a cookie and you gain weight.

It's curious how patterns [emerge based on] general ethnic [background] and the locale where your ancestors come from. If Caucasians get a little bit fat, they tend to get the weight-related diseases, whereas Africans—who tend to have the thrifty gene and can get large more easily—they don't get diabetes until they have seriously increased their weight, on a comparable scale, recognizing that obesity is a major cause of diabetes. So you don't get as high an incidence of diabetes and other weight-related diseases among African-Americans, even though they have more obesity. These [diseases] don't kick in until they are really large.

To make it even more interesting, people of South Asian ancestry have a higher percentage of body fat than say, Caucasians or Africans or others, and they can actually appear to be fairly lean or be slightly overweight, but since they've got a higher percentage of body fat, they can actually get diabetes more quickly."

That obesity and leanness might not be uniform across the human population speaks again to the "single table" approach to what any of us ought to weigh. On this point, David said:

"Humans are unbelievably adaptive, and there are all these studies coming out saying how we can adapt, even in a matter of centuries, to different diets and to different climates. The people of Kosrae for centuries ate fish, a couple of local plants, and coconuts, and that's pretty much it. They're going to have a pretty different physiology, because they adapted to that diet.

One of the problems with Friedman's notion is that it's hard to find what's going on genetically. There's been a search for a 'fat gene' or a 'skinny gene,' and there are profiles, but there's still work that needs to be done. Remember the hormone called leptin, which Jeff Friedman discovered over a decade ago now? Well, now that comes back into play, along with a gene that has been discovered. We just did a *Nova* show on it.

What happens in the body when you eat food is that it turns into sugar, it goes into your bloodstream, and your body uses what it needs. If you have a propensity to gain weight, it creates fat with the surplus. For other people, it's flushed through. There are lots of places where it goes, but what regulates that is not down in your gut, it's actually up in your brain.

When the blood sugar in your system reaches a certain level, or in other cases, when your fat cells reach a certain size, they throw off hormones. These hormones go off in your bloodstream, and they go up through the blood-brain barrier, and they go to your hypothalamus in the back of your head. It's a very old and ancient center of your brain, which controls appetite, and that's really the defining factor here.

It's not so much your metabolism, as people think, it's actually the hunger drive that makes you eat more and makes you gain weight. What happens is, leptin is one of those hormones, and it's one of the major ones that controls appetite. It comes out of the fat cells. When your particular genes say 'Okay, you've enough food onboard, you've got enough fat onboard,' it injects this leptin out into your blood-stream, it swims up to your brain, and it hits two different neurons in your hypothalamus, one which turns up appetite and one which turns it down. So you have a kind of balancing act going on between these two neurons.

That's one of the things that Jeff Friedman studies in his lab . . . using brain cells, and he's developed all sorts of technology to study these things outside of the body, obviously. This is human tissue. He gets very excited when he gets a shipment of brain cells from some cadaver somewhere. That's what his source usually is."

It's fine to talk about the potential for a genetic link to obesity, but I asked David if we had actually put our finger on anything.

"What we looked into in the *Nova* show is: Is there a gene that definitely causes people to be fat? We looked all over the place, and we were having trouble finding one until we were told about a researcher in Britain named Stephen O'Rahilly. Dr. O'Rahilly is the head of the Department of Clinical Biochemistry and Medicine at the University of Cambridge, and he practices at Addenbrooke's Hospital in Cambridge. He has followed Friedman's work and done some other work similar to Friedman, but what happened was he was combing through the genetic databases being created in Great Britain called Biobank. They have several hundred thousand Brits that are giving their genetic data. They're doing genomes and doing a library of genes related to diseases in this British population. It's still not finished. It's got several more years to go, but [O'Rahilly] was muckin' around in the database, looking to see if there were correlated genes for getting fat.

And he found one. It is called the MC4 receptor gene. Now this is pretty cool."

The pace of David's speech slowed to a crawl, as if science was my second language. Which, let's face it, it is. "The MC4 receptor gene is the gene that normally allows the neurons that have to do with appetite to grow receptors that are able to receive the leptin and other hormones that tell them, 'Okay. You're full.' . . . And so what happens with people with a mutation in their MC4 receptor genes is that their MC4 receptors are either malformed, or they're not formed at all."

I reacted. "So your body could throw leptin at them all day long, and you're not gonna feel full?"

"Nothing's going to happen," he replied. "Cell surfaces are filled with thousands of receptors receiving instructions, meaning that all kinds of proteins are coming in and delivering messages. This message—the leptin message—needs to have a plug."

The proteins are delivering messages to receptors? And for a specific message to get through—like leptin—there's got to be a matching receptor? David continued at length.

"That's right. You've got the little leptin coming in, and it's gotta look for this receptor. For people who are normal size, they've got those little receptors and the leptin comes in, and they've been chowin' down, and they suddenly say, 'I cannot eat another bite!' That's the way it's supposed to work.

"But in people with mutations in their MC4 receptor genes, their MC4 receptors never grow. So the leptin just keeps pounding away. Eventually they do stop eating. There are other things that tell them [to stop], but this causes these people to be *voraciously hungry all the time*. You know what it's like to be incredibly hungry. There are people that feel like this all the time. Even after they've had a huge meal. And they just keep eating and eating and eating.

We actually found a patient. Her name was Teresa Godfrey, and she agreed to have us film her. She was a patient of Stephen O'Rahilly and another physician there, Sadaf Farooqi. Dr. Farooqi came and introduced us to Teresa, and Teresa—she's definitely large, but she's been much larger. She has this malformation on this MC4 receptor. They were able to take genetic material from her, put it into a Petri dish—basically, isolate the mutation—then put that mutation into the tissue of one of these neuron cells . . . and watch it *not* grow. It was an incredibly cool experiment."

I had to ask him to explain that again.

"Basically, they took some tissue—probably blood—from Teresa, and they isolated the MC4 receptor gene. They took the gene out and they inserted it into a neuron that was in a Petri dish. Just this little cell sitting in a Petri dish. They were able to tweak the cell machinery of the neuron to accept her gene and then *not grow* the MC4 receptor—which you would expect the neuron to do under normal circumstances.

They did another test with her ,,, where they put her in this room in the hospital. They give her all the food she could possibly want, like this whole table filled with food, and just told her to keep eating. And she did. She could just continue to keep eating and eating and eating, and they could actually predict, using that test in the Petri dish, what her appetite level would be and when she would stop.

She's one of the worst cases, because she doesn't have the receptor at all. Some people will have a partial receptor. They have some of the hormone getting through, telling them to stop eating. And you can predict how long that will take.

But this is profound. According to the [U.K.] Biobank data, almost 1 in 200 Brits have this mutation, either the full-blown one or a partial mutation. And that's a pretty large number for a disease."

I kept thinking of all the people who have this mutation and have spent their whole lives not only feeling ravenously hungry all the time, but feeling all the judgments of society around excessive weight. Feeling so out of control and like such failures. It's not that there's anything wrong with them as people; it's their genes! It's just reality. It's like being upset that you've got brown hair instead of blond hair. It's a genetic roll of the dice. David added these thoughts:

"Again, your size is not your fault. It's genetically determined. And this was what was so great about doing the *Nova* show with someone like Teresa Godfrey on camera. She told us how it had changed her life . . . to know it wasn't her fault.

She also has a son named Jake, who also has inherited the mutation, and we saw pictures of the two of them. They've lost weight. They're actually both quite healthy now. You know, you can be overweight but healthy.

This is where the 30 percent to 40 percent which is not genetic comes in, because you do need to combine your [food] intake with exercise. One of Friedman and other's points is that you have a range. Everybody has their own range of what size they are, and you can have the healthy range or the unhealthy range. Theresa Godfrey is now in the healthy range, even though if you looked at her without knowing anything else, you would say, 'That person is overweight.' But she's healthy within her own particular genetics. Friedman calls it the 'set point.' Everybody has their own set point, where basically their appetite and their need for calories equals the amount of calories that they get. You can overshoot that, and that's where eating too many Big Macs can get you in trouble. You can also eat within your set point incredibly unhealthy food, and even still be at the good end of your calorie intake. Of course, this has other problems, like heart disease and other conditions. So what you eat is also important."

While we all want the lean gene, it just may be that it's the absence of obese genes that is really the ticket.

According to David, "One thing that some of these scientists are really adamant about—and I think we have to agree with—is we do have an obsession with really abnormal thinness. Almost nobody's as thin as these models and these people that we see in magazines and on television. And even they have a hard time keeping that weight. The reality is that people come in different sizes."

Then there's the issue of weight and aging. A subject near and dear to my heart. David had an answer for that, too.

"There was a study that said that being slightly overweight looks like it's the healthiest. For women, yes. And for men, too, having a little paunch or something is actually healthier for things like heart disease and diabetes than being really skinny. Of course, then you get into the caloric restriction issue. If you're super skinny, getting too few calories but getting enough nutrition, that extends life span because it triggers defense mechanisms in your cells.

And here's yet another example. Our brain is divided up physically into three [centers that correspond to] evolutionary periods of development. The reptilian brain is the really old one. It's where the appetite center is. The limbic brain, which is the mammalian, makes us all want to work together. And then [there's] the neocortical, which is our rational, logical brain. These three [parts of our] brains are not particularly well-connected, especially the neocortical.

When you talk about willing yourself to diet, for instance, there's some fascinating studies going on [related to] the wiring of the brain and how it is a fairly minor influence on appetite, using your neocortical to make yourself do something.

This has some interesting implications for free will. Philosophical implications. Jeff Friedman makes the point that you can will yourself not to eat for a while. People go on hunger strikes. You can go without food for many days. . . . He says, 'If you see a rancid piece of meat there, your reaction is yech! You don't want to eat it. But if you go five days without eating, that [meat is] going to look better and better all the time, and after ten or twelve days of not eating, you're probably going to go ahead and try to eat it, because you're starving and that's taking over.

There are a couple of post-docs in Friedman's lab who are trying to figure out the wiring—literally the pathways—for the neurons connecting the neocortical to the appetite centers, and seeing how connected they are. They're discovering that they are *not very*.

And there was another student who was figuring out that when you see food, you have a reaction. Especially when you're hungry, part of it is a saliva reaction. You actually produce a little bit of extra saliva, and that seems to be one of the triggers that gets your brain going. 'Oh! I must be hungry!' And this guy was figuring out the neural pathway—both the input and output of the saliva going into the appetite center of the brain and then back out again.

Very cool stuff. But it is all really, really in the beginning stages."

Still, knowledge is power. Sure would be nice to know the skinny on our genes.

CHAPTER TWELVE

A Sheep in Sheep's Clothing

SOME PEOPLE walk through the door, and you just know they're good news.

Thus it was with Steen Riisgaard. He looked like a typical CEO. An executive's gray suit. Closely trimmed, graying hair. Nondescript tie. Lace-up shoes. He sure looked like a CEO . . . but somehow . . . he *didn't* look like a CEO. No elite markings discernible to the naked eye. No giveaways in his demeanor, his dress, his vibe—as we like to say in California.

There was nothing dark from his childhood being obviously played out in his presentation, and he lacked that "Don't you know? I'm at the helm of a huge corporation" expression, which tends to spray the room the same way that oil spits up on the windscreen of a British sports car. *(If it's a British sports car, it's a "windscreen" and not a "windshield." I have an old British sports car, so I've been spit upon.)* The man doesn't look remotely like the type who has to buy a luxury racing machine to bear witness to his money, power and self-set importance, ego monsters requiring feeding of addict-level proportions. You'd be surprised how often and how easy it is to spot these things once you start seeing these fellas in the flesh. Just looking at him, I'd have guessed he didn't have much of a story . . . and I'd be wrong. Very wrong.

Steen Riisgaard is the President and CEO of Novozymes. It's a pretty big company. Once a part of pharmaceutical giant Novo Nordisk, it split off and is now publicly traded on the Copenhagen Stock Exchange with 2005 annual revenues coming in at around $1 billion. Nothing to sneeze at, that's for sure.

I looked down at my notes. This was Jorgen Thorball's boss. Jorgen kept telling me I should talk to him. It had been two years since I had laid eyes on Jorgen for my first intentional biotech interview, and I . . . well, frankly, I hoped no one at Novozymes held it against me. Is it possible they forgot? Turns out they didn't. Their American publicist, Roger Friedensen, was still all smiles. Everyone seemed thrilled. Go figure. In the interim, I had somehow sussed out that Steen had started out his career as a "radical environmental chemist." Having met my share of folks staunchly self-elected to the radical train, to me he didn't seem like one. So I asked Steen his opinion of himself.

"I think there's a certain element of truth to that. I actually started the Danish version of Greenpeace. It's called NOAH. I started our local section of NOAH outside Copenhagen where I lived when I was a student."

Well, certainly Greenpeace knows all about being radical. But even Greenpeace drop-outs still have that signature spark of anger, that way of making searingly harsh accusations about a complex issue, to which no one could possibly be prepared to respond with a quick and ready answer. Frequently, the accusation sports an underlying unspoken premise that we all should have been paying attention and haven't been, and as a service, the accusation embeds the identification of the evil powers-that-be, who no doubt are continuing to perpetrate the social harm. It's a real art, it is. And I write "even Greenpeace drop-outs" for a reason. I'm thinking of Patrick Moore, a co-founder of Greenpeace and its one-time president. Some twenty years ago, he had a falling out with his compatriots and, instead of either mellowing out or becoming even more radical, he did an about-face. He spun around 180 degrees and now advocates nuclear energy, farmed salmon, genetically modified food, and a whole selection of things he formerly abhorred. By all reports, the only thing that hasn't changed is his personality.

When I had Moore in the studio, he actually got mad at me when I started questioning him about the scientific reasons behind his various positions. He was offended. I was supposed to take his word for his con-clusions without question. I was supposed to accept his person as a suf-ficient credential that he was competent to talk about everything he had an opinion on. The only problem is that I have this little policy about my airspace. I only let people talk about what—through education and/or experience—they are qualified to talk about.

This policy wasn't just for him. It's for *everybody*. Including me. It's why I was so wigged out about trying to do a radio show about biotech. *What the heck was biotech? And what did I know about it?* How could I possibly do an adequate job reporting on something I didn't understand? It's my job to make sure that what the listeners hear is accurate and trustworthy.

Even if I thought I could pull a fast one, they're not passive listeners. *They're really* listening! They'll tell you if you blow it. Thank goodness for me, in all these years of broadcasting, I've only made one error. And it was a doozy. "Go big or go home!" I always say, and I didn't disappoint myself that time. It was just plain wrong. Within three hours of satellite uplink I had received 1,300 e-mails. Some people politely pointed out the mis-take. These e-mails were in the minority. Others were condescending: "You *do* know the difference, don't you? I would have thought better of you." Others were outraged, or even insulted: "How could you waste my time, filling my brain with misinformation? What else have you gotten wrong? How can I trust you again?" Signed, "Longtime listener, now reconsidering" and "Previous listener." I guess you want to know what the big mistake was. Well, I confused Roseanne Roseannadanna with Emily Litella. *No doubt some of you are reeling in horror at this very moment!* For the rest of you, these were two characters, both played by Gilda Radner in skits on *Saturday Night Live* in the 1970s. Yep. Listeners will not be trifled with. Clearly, whatever a person is talking about on-air, I have to make sure it's right.

According to various published materials and the ones provided to me by his public relations folks, Patrick Moore was coming up short. According to the resume on Moore's website, he had a bachelor's degree in forest biology and a PhD in ecology, both from the University of British Columbia. But nothing in his career, from Greenpeace on, suggested that he had particular experience to be addressing some of the issues he wanted to talk about. Still, he *could* quote others—individuals with obvi-ous credentials or reports from relevant organizations or public records. He *could* talk about what other, more qualified people and groups did, said or wrote. *That* I could work with. But not Dr. Moore. He just wanted me to take his word for the conclusions he reached.

It also didn't help that this stance was further undermined by the fact that he now had a consulting firm "focusing on environmental policy and communications in natural resources, biodiversity, energy, and climate change." So . . . *who was paying him?* Not only had he made an almost alarming switch of position on a number of issues, but he's now getting paid to voice them? A search of the Internet revealed a client here and a client there, but many of his issues are simply his own personal advocacy for the public good, which he does at his own expense. I believe that Patrick Moore believes in what he is doing. I believe he believes he has sound reasons. It just can't fly on the radio. At least, my radio, that is.

To be honest, I didn't give him any more of a hard time than I give any-one else. And I'm sure he can find others who would be more than happy to sympathize with him or to swap stories of the hard time I gave them as well. He's not the only one who didn't get air time, although I try to be as polite as possible. I can always edit out that part of an interview that I feel is without sufficient grounds to bring to air.

Perhaps Dr. Moore didn't know that I wasn't singling him out. Perhaps he thought I didn't agree with his position. Or maybe he didn't like the fact that I had made a judgment about his credentials. Whatever his reasons, his face went red. His posture became rigid. He literally threw off heat. Quick to anger might be a good description. At the time, it was a bit of a surprise. His website touts that "Dr. Moore believes strongly in the multi-stakeholder, consensus-based approach to resolving conflicts involving environmental, social, and economic issues." You gotta hope that he's got someone on staff who can facilitate consensus. I can't imagine he could begin to know how to make it happen, left to his own devices.

Still, Patrick Moore, even with his about-face and public falling out with the Greenpeace folks, is more typical than not of my interviews with *some* people from *some* radical groups. (I'm already anticipating the e-mails here.) And it was also apparent that nothing I just described about Patrick Moore applied to Steen Riisgaard, the so-called "radical environmental chemist."

Like Patrick Moore, Steen Riisgaard felt strongly enough to found an environmental advocacy organization. But Riisgaard was able to move on, to evolve to another level. While keeping his values, he didn't run away from industry. He ran toward it.

He said, "I decided that to really make an impact for a better environment and more sustainable future, then I better join the action, so I joined the industry. Since then I've had the good fortune that I can work as an environmental activist and secure that my company makes money in the process."

And that he does very well through Novozymes, the "world's largest producer of enzymes for industrial use."

o   o   o

ENZYMES SCHMENZYMES! Who knew what an enzyme was?!?!! Mark, my biotech-patent-attorney producer, wasn't always around for me to get a dose of New Orleans science, so I would ask the passing scientist I happened to chance on. It was like asking a missionary about his religion. Information would burst forth with full passion and energy. The result was akin to the old saw of being told how to build a watch when you had only asked for the time.

That's why I actually liked Steen Riisgaard's description of an enzyme better than most. Besides, if Steen didn't know what an enzyme was, Novozymes was sunk, and the board of Directors would never let that happen.

"Enzymes are nature's catalyst," he explained. "Enzymes are what makes any living being alive."

Yes! I like this!

"You, for example, will have in you about 30,000 different enzymes."

Well, I used to like it. Up until the 30,000.

"And that's why you're alive," he said, nodding confidently.

Then I guess I better get used to it . . .

I realized I had better remember everything I already knew pronto . . . we've got these enzymes inside of us, inside of our cells—and so does everything organic—and these enzymes "make things happen." They're the "catalyst," the energizer that gets things going. Or sometimes they make whatever's happening in the cell, happen faster.

The next question is traditional, but the answer is always boring: What kinds of things do enzymes make happen?

I couldn't bear it.

The first example that everyone always rolls out is laundry detergent. All laundry detergents contain enzymes. You pour the liquid or the powder you bought at the store into your washing machine, and then the enzymes in the laundry liquid or powder go to work. They find and meet up with whatever is making the stains and smells on your clothes, and these enzymes break them down. That's why you need to have enough laundry detergent in any load. Don't get cheap here. And don't think that overdoing it is going to do you any good. There's got to be enough enzymes to match up with everything you want to break down, that you want to get out of your clothes or your tablecloth or your towels or whatever it is you are washing. The dirtier they are, the more laundry detergent. The less dirty, the less detergent.

This may seem obvious to you, but there are all kinds of laundry detergent people in this mad world we live in. There are "the box says to put in a half-cup, and that's exactly what I'll measure" types. There are the "I'm going to be economical and use a quarter-cup in every wash" folks. There are the "I'm going to put in extra and make sure every load is good and clean" kids. And then there's my personal favorite, the "Just dump some in and let's get on with it" contingent.

But stop! We're all wrong! This is science, folks! The only amount that's effective is a one-to-one match of enzymes with the crud that's in the load you've just shoved into your washing machine. (Can't you just guess which type I am?) Of course, there's no way to know precisely what amount of detergent you need. So I don't recommend that anyone change his or her approach. Then again, you might re-think your strategy. Once you know a little washing machine science.

The truly committed can get into an academic discussion as to the length of the washing cycle itself. One of my sons—who shall remain nameless—thought he would save time by putting all his stinky sports clothes into the washer and setting the wash part of the cycle, but not for eight minutes or for six minutes or for even four. He had figured out how to set the dial so the washer spent the tiniest of moments in the wash cycle. He did this all in the interests of speeding up the time it took to do the laundry. Science needed to step in here and straighten things out. The enzymes have to get into the liquid and make their way all around and into your crud (and, in my son's case, industrial-strength teenager crud). They have to find and interact with all this stuff and have enough time to break down the spots, smells, and whatever it is you're trying to remove by washing them in the first place. He couldn't figure out why his clothes still smelled and the spots didn't come out, no matter how much detergent he poured in. *Mom, will you wash my clothes? I can't seem to do it right.*

And water temperature? Read the bottle. Or the box. The enzymes may—*or may not*—need heat to get the job done. No guessing here. It's just a fact.

Which leads us to the next popular example of enzyme use—stonewashed jeans. There's a part of me that hopes they'll go so far out of fashion that we can't use this example anymore, because no one will remember what they are. But right now, I think we're stuck with them. Stonewashing was originally just that—washing the jeans with stones in a revolving tub. This stonewashing technique battered and broke down the jeans so they looked lived in and cool. But it used a lot of water and was a big mess, besides taking a lot of time. Today, using special enzymes—presumably different from the ones you use in laundry detergent, since those are supposed to preserve the colors of your clothes as well as the fabric's integrity—these enzymes actually fade the denim and break down the fibers of the jeans in a suitably restrained manner. Manufacturers could now produce a pair of stonewashed jeans in fairly short order and far less expensively, dispensing with having to deal with all the stones and all the other rigmarole.

Now we could go on and on, for apparently the list of applications never ends, so my advice to you is to never broach the subject with an enzyme person. The next example is likely to do with something you might eat—or worse yet, have already eaten, consciously or otherwise. Think about the enzymes in meat tenderizers—yes, there are enzymes there. Dump tenderizer onto a tough piece of meat, and the enzymes break down the long proteins in the meat. The end result is a much more tender steak. *Yum, Yum! Wanna come over for barbecue? We're having enzymes tonight!*

But back to the action with the guy who sells all these enzymes to industry. What could I ask him that would be enlightening—and comprehensible to the average listener—and didn't involve stupid questions about laundry detergent and stonewashed jeans?

Okay, these enzymes have got to be really tiny. *Really tiny.* They're proteins, for heaven's sake. I know what question I'll ask him! If I were to buy a bunch of your enzymes, would that be a test-tube-full? A cupful? A boxful? A tankful? How big would the order be? (For all I knew, they shipped them around in FedEx envelopes.)

According to Steen Riisgaard, "Usually when our customers buy enzymes, they very often will buy several tons at a time, and we ship them in big bags—one ton in each bag." *You can buy a ton of enzymes???* "Liquid enzymes we also sell—from ten to twenty cubic meter truckloads of liquid enzymes." *That would be maybe a nine-foot by nine-foot by nine-foot container. Of liquid enzymes. That's a lot of enzymes.*

Then Steen took it upon himself to jump in and help me out here. Answer a question I hadn't even asked him. *What good fortune!*

"The most hot topic right now is the application of enzymes to produce fuel ethanol."

Fabulous! Thanks! People can really get into fuel ethanol. Almost everyone drives cars or rides in them. We can talk about biofuel. That would work. Everyone including the president has given speeches about getting off fossil fuels. The federal government has stepped up with subsidies for the production of ethanol on our farms. California has mandated a 6 percent ethanol mix in the gasoline we pump to meet federal requirements. For whatever political (or financial or environmental) reasons all this happened . . . it's happening. Both in the U.S. and globally. In the last several years, ethanol production has skyrocketed. Now we had a great topic!

In 2004—the last year for which there are numbers, as of this writing—Brazil produced roughly 4 billion gallons of ethanol, with the United States in second place at 3.5 billion gallons. And just so you know, Brazil has been hovering at production levels of 3 billion to 4 billion gallons for the better part of a decade. This output meets about 25 percent of Brazil's energy needs, and FYI, it makes its ethanol from sugarcane. The United States only really began to wake up a few years back, so over the next few years, we can expect the numbers to change, as well as how everyone makes ethanol and what they make it from. To be sure, we can expect change as the future unfolds.

The good news for me and this interview? You need enzymes to make it all work! Now, Steen wasn't talking about how we do it now. He was talking about the big news of a breakthrough, which will make an impact in the future. So we better start with today.

Up until now, American farmers built "biorefineries" and used the corn kernels themselves to make ethanol. The process went something like this: Harvest your kernels of corn and then grind it up and add water to create a "mash." Now the idea is to release the sugars, which will then be converted to ethanol. To make that conversion happen, you need to *add enzymes to the mix* and cook it all up, which I'm told gets rid of all the bacteria but might play some other role as well. Then you add yeast, so it can start fermenting. After about four days, the sugars turn into ethanol. Next you distill the whole batch to separate the ethanol from whatever is left in the mash, and you've got something with plenty of alcohol in it.

How close this process is to grandpappy's moonshine still, you'll have to ask grandpappy, but just to make sure nobody drinks it, the farmers then add something called a "denaturant" (also called "the spoiler" by the local teenagers). Afterward, it's undrinkable, and what you have now . . . is ethanol. Also called "fuel ethanol" or "bioethanol," different names for the very same thing. Bottom line—you put your corn in, and you get your ethanol out.

Now what about what's left in the field? The stalks and all that? To date, it's all been waste. Biowaste. Why can't it be used to produce ethanol? Here's where Steen's big news fits in.

I think you would get an inkling if you've ever seen a stalk of corn in the field or decorating someone's front stoop at Halloween. They're dry, dry, dry. Contrast that with eating corn-on-the-cob. The kernels of corn are all juicy and sweet. Filled with sugar. You can even eat them raw if you want. (That's a California organic hippie thing, but you should try it some time. Cut the kernels off the cob and throw some raw into a salad— another California thing—or slice off the kernels, put some butter, pepper and salt on them, and barely heat them up in the microwave. Really great. Much better than my enzyme barbecue.) The point is . . . if you're human, you can eat the kernels. But the stalks? Those dried up leaves and such. And the husks? You could boil the husks for days and you wouldn't get anything edible. And that's why they became biowaste.

The official name for this stuff is "corn stover," which is easy to forget. Doesn't seem to relate to anything else any of us knows. The people I've spoken with—well, some call it "stover" (singular) and others call it "stovers" (plural). Even my Microsoft WORD application doesn't think it's a real word. It underlines it in red every time I type it. As far as I'm concerned, the closest living relative to the word stover in the post-industrial age is arguably Stove Top Stuffing, Cornbread Flavor, which has got to contain something genetically modified in it somewhere. But I diverge. Let's get back to the science.

The scientific reason that the corn stover isn't edible is that it's got high quantities of cellulose. There is plenty of sugar in the stalk and the leaves and the husk, but it's *trapped by the cellulose*. Aha! Now we have a job for biotech!

Suddenly, everyone has jumped on the bandwagon of springing the sugars. Even Richard Branson of Virgin Everything fame has promised to invest $3 billion over the next ten years in biofuel and other alternative energies. But he's a newbie. Five years ago, the U.S. Department of Energy (DOE) laid down a challenge to the biotech industry to drive down the cost of ethanol made from cellulose to the same price point as gasoline. The DOE even put cold hard cash behind the challenge. Two enzyme companies each received around $17 million to come up with the enzymes to make the ethanol-from-cellulose value proposition work. The two companies? Novozymes and Genencor International, with 44 percent and 18 percent of the global enzymes market, respectively.

Steen leaped in, explaining:

"The real trick is that this research is very similar to the research you do when you do pharmaceutical research to develop new [drugs]. But here we have to translate the science from a test tube to a huge-scale industrial use. We have to figure out, from readings in a lab in tiny test tubes, what is going to happen in a huge factory where people produce fuel ethanol, so this translation is quite a difficult task.

Today, there's a different route to bio-ethanol—where we use the corn as such, and the starch from that corn is transformed into fermentable sugars using an advanced set of industrial enzymes that we provide, and the sugar in turn is fermented into fuel ethanol. In the future we believe that we can use agricultural waste—the stovers, for example, or the husks from corn. This is technically a more challenging task because now we have to break down cellulose—rather than starch—and cellulose is inherently much more difficult to break down to fermentable sugars. But once you break it down, it will be the same type of fermentable sugars, and then you can again ferment the sugars into fuel ethanol, and here you go."

Converting the corn stover into bio-ethanol *cheaply* wasn't a slam dunk. Steen continued:

"When we started out working with these enzymes, the cost of conversion to produce one gallon of fuel ethanol was about $5 per gallon for the enzyme part, which of course was way too high. We were then granted between $17 million and $18 million by the Department of Energy in the United States, and we managed with that funding to bring down the cost by a factor of thirty, so we are now between 10 cents and 18 cents per gallon for the enzyme costs. Now we are pretty close to the price that will make this process possible."

Unbelievably, there's an additional benefit produced in this cellulose-to-ethanol process. Contained in the mash is something called "lignin," which is not fermentable. It's there after the fermentation of the cellulose-rich mash has been broken down. And . . . the lignin can be burned! It apparently has about the same energy value as coal. Therefore, as you take out the lignin produced from one batch of ethanol, you can burn it to heat up a subsequent batch. A pay-it-forward kind of approach, which is always a neat idea. With the contribution of lignin, the cellulose-to-ethanol process becomes even more economically attractive. That puts lignin into a whole other category. Since the lignin contributes positively to the economic proposition, they call it a "value-added chemical." *Ain't that attractive! Just remember that if you should happen upon the term "value-added chemical," it means there's money in it somewhere.*

Another consideration when someone is talking about ethanol is that one gallon of ethanol does not equal one gallon of gasoline. Oh, the volume is the same—remember, a gallon is a volume measure. A gallon of ethanol is the *same size* as a gallon of gas, which is the *same size* as a gallon of milk. Believe me, we don't want to talk about the physics of it, but it takes about one and a half gallons of ethanol to drive your car the same distance as it goes on one gallon of gasoline. So we can't just look at how much a gallon of each type of fuel costs to figure out if we've got the costs in line.

This explains, in part, why it's so confusing to understand the big picture. Lots and lots has been written about whether ethanol production is really worth it. Is it really cost-efficient? Is it hurting the availability of our food supply? Will it drive up the price of food as corn is diverted from the food supply to produce fuel? Are too many natural resources being used to grow the corn and produce the ethanol? Is it really worth it?

What I know is this . . .

Every detailed analysis I've read to date has been based on the economics of the **first biorefineries,** which are in place today across many of our corn states.

If we are talking about the first popular wave of biorefineries, then we need to know:

- They only use the edible corn kernels.

- Yes, those edible corn kernels, in fact, are removed from the available food supply (if those fields were growing corn orginally destined for your table).

- The stover is biowaste and is not used in the process.

- 1½ gallons of ethanol lets you drive your car as far as 1 gallon of gasoline.

The **imminent and emergent biorefineries** can also break down cellulose, and they present a different economic picture:

- They *do or don't use* the edible corn kernels *at the biorefiner's option.*

- The edible corn kernels *may or may not* be removed from the available food supply, *at the biorefiner's option.*

- The stover *is also converted* to ethanol.

- Part of the remaining biowaste, which is lignin, can be burned to heat a subsequent batch of mash, *resulting in lower production costs.*

- There is less remaining biowaste.

- 1½ gallons of ethanol still lets you drive your car as far as 1 gallon of gasoline.

So where does that get us? It gets us to two other important points . . .

1. All analyses of ethanol production that you have come into contact with to date *may no longer be accurate.*

2. *Every analyses* of ethanol that you come into contact with in the future must be questioned as to:

○ *Which biorefinery process are they talking about?*

○ *What parts of which crops does the process use?*

○ *Are there any value-added chemicals in the process, and what part do they play in the economics of ethanol production?*

○ *Are there any other factors that contribute to the total economic proposition?*

You might wonder why I'm pushing you to analyze, analyze, analyze. Part of the reason is that on the subject of ethanol production, there's a healthy dose of activist rhetoric in the wind, a similar dose of national and state political positioning, the demands of social conscience and widespread economic interests. Times like these require you to be at the top of your game.

Case in point: the price of tortillas in Mexico.

This is a multifaceted theme park for spin if ever there was one.

For those who like to follow the money, they see a plot of greedy cornmeal distributors, forcing an artificial rise in the price of white corn, the very type used to make the tortillas consumed at every table in Mexico.

For those who mistrust the free market system, they can pine again for the year 1999, when Mexico eliminated its tortilla subsidy. To their way of thinking, the free market doesn't care about the little guy, while those who love the free market can get all worked up about the new price controls recently instigated by President Felipe Calderon. In this particular case, there's something in it for both sides.

The socially conscious tend to see the 50 million Mexicans who live on $4 or less per day, and know that raising the price of their staple food 50 percent and more—in some arenas, several hundred percent over three years—will obviously cause suffering.

If you're into blaming big business for everything, you need only point a single finger at a single player—the food megapower GRUMA, which controls some 70 percent of Mexico's tortilla and cornmeal market.

And finally, there are those who tie the price rise in Mexican tortillas into a much bigger picture. They believe that the American corn crop is being hijacked and turned into ethanol, literally taking corn from the mouths of Mexicans to put fuel in American gas tanks. A stunning accusation . . . if only it were true.

Let's look at a few facts. The United States is the world's largest grower of corn, as well as the world's largest exporter. Certainly, growing corn simply for the purpose of producing ethanol has been on the rise in the past years, as has the price of corn. We all know that demand creates markets—that's simple economics. However, in parallel, a fear has been floated that this will take food out of the food supply. And that the basic price of the corn that we eat and our corn-derived food products will rise . . . alarmingly. The dramatic change in the price of tortillas in Mexico has been touted as the first hard evidence.

But it's not.

In the January 13, 2007, edition of the *San Francisco Chronicle,* staff writer Carolyn Said describes the situation succinctly: "The production of the gasoline additive ethanol has taken off in the past year, consuming millions of bushels of corn. But Mexico grows most of its own corn for consumption. And the yellow corn used for ethanol and livestock feed is different from the sweet white corn that's ground into masa for handmade tortillas, although some mass-produced tortillas are made from yellow corn."

So there you have it. Mexico has been growing its own corn to eat. It's not importing American corn for this actual purpose, and Mexico is not reporting that it's growing any less sweet white corn. So what's the story? My vote is for market manipulation by GRUMA and friends. Wouldn't be the first time the financial types got greedy. But whatever the reason, the price of Mexican tortillas is not about the price of corn in Iowa.

What about this persistent rumor that we are going to compromise our own food supply? It seems an obvious equation. If we convert fields that were growing corn for consumption into corn for ethanol, the corn available to consumers will decrease and the price of corn will increase. (If this alone reduced the vast amounts of high-fructose corn syrup we produce and consume, it might be a hidden blessing.) But economics gets tricky. Push on one part of the equation, and another part jumps. The price of corn might hold steady at a slightly elevated level, and that would seem okay to us as consumers. But have you ever heard of corn-fed beef? Beef prices might rise. Even dairy prices could rise. It would be a matter of which specialty corn crops got planted and which got replaced. All corn is not created equal. If the price of corn for livestock rose, we consumers might never be aware of it.

Whatever's happening economically is always more complicated than the classic "guns and butter" example of introductory economics, but the good news is that if you look hard enough at any situation, you can always connect the dots. And I mean you—you can connect the dots.

But never forget the impact of technology. And innovation.

When humans put their minds to anything, all manner of amazing things start to happen. Scientists and engineers are now working on even better biorefining processes. They are working on genetically modifying corn and other crops to make them better candidates for biorefining. Not only are they looking at more cost-effective strategies, they are looking at the environmental equation. Is this sustainable? If not, can we make it so? Can we make it even better so that we can pay back some of the environmental debt we have created elsewhere and/or earlier?

Better yet, there's no such thing as a cellulose-poor nation. Cellulose is available everywhere and in numerous plant forms. No matter what your climate or growing conditions, biotech is working on a cellulose-plentiful plant for you, if nature hasn't already served one up on its own. Yes, technology—and biotechnology—has turned its gaze on biorefining, and that means change. Much more will be coming forth from this sector, and that's why every time you hear anything about biorefining and ethanol and the like, you need to question it. And even when the information is absolutely correct, it may only be valid for . . . six months? A year? Times are a-changin'. Tech is a-changin'. And that includes biotech.

o   o   o

WITHOUT A DOUBT, technology is gearing up to support the production of all biofuels, including ethanol, and here's but one example: Jim Greenwood, the President and CEO of the Biotechnology Industry Organization (BIO), told me about some interesting tech developed by John Deere, the farm equipment manufacturer. (If you want to see some real he-man technology, mosey on out to www.deere.com. You will be amazed!) Well, John Deere is working on farm machinery to harvest the biomass from corn and separate out the edible kernels . . . automatically. Send the kernels to market, and send the rest to the biorefinery. When you think about the ethanol processes which work on cellulose, why we could have our corn and eat it, too! And it makes us, once again, reconsider the economics of ethanol and the impact of ethanol production on the food supply.

The main reason there is all this activity is that it's big business. Just look at the California numbers. The ethanol we've been talking about is exactly what gets mixed in with old-fashioned gasoline and gets pumped out of all the service stations in California. Today, California uses in excess of one billion gallons of ethanol, and they buy outright a good chunk of whatever the Midwest can produce. The Midwest farmers should be warned, though—the Californians are looking to cook up some ethanol of their own. For such is the free marketplace.

And don't make the mistake that our energy needs will—or even can be—fossil-free anytime soon. The United States burns through 140 *billion* gallons of gasoline each year. Only 3 percent of it is currently ethanol. The Department of Energy hopes to move that figure up to 30 percent of our fuel supply by the year 2030. *What? Ethanol would only be 30 percent of our fuel supply? And it will take twenty-five years to get there?* Well, that's the studied goal, given all the farmland and everything else that goes into it.

But this is technology . . . biotechnology. Anything can happen. Who would have predicted that Novozymes could get a 98 percent reduction in the cost of the enzymes with just a five-year effort? I would say that particular government contract has to be right up there with some of the best-spent $17 million contracts the federal government has ever let out.

And just to be clear, while Novozymes is the largest enzymes company, there are others out there, and they're all wildly dedicated to making a dent in this situation.

In addition, biorefining corn and other crops are not the only alternative fuel sources our Department of Energy is looking at. One potential source is animal manure. The United States alone produces more than 150 million tons of animal manure each year. And that's a lot of . . . a great, great deal of . . . *potential?* . . . for value-added chemicals.

While the story of finding enzymes to make the cellulose process work is compelling indeed, for me there's another compelling story here. For that, we return to Steen Riisgaard and his commitment to the environment. If you read the Novozymes annual report, you will notice that it reports more than financials, market outlooks, and economic predictions. An essential part of the annual report is environmental sustainability. According to Steen:

"We must be one of the first companies in the world to combine our annual report with our sustainability report. Not only is it combined, it's also audited. It's audited by our auditors, Price-WaterhouseCoopers.

We operate really much the same as for the financial part. In the financial part you say we have this goal—next year our profit will be up by 10 percent, sales will be up—I don't know—by 11 percent, and this and that. In exactly the same way we set goals for our environmental performance. So we say next year we will be using energy this much more efficiently, we'll use less water per ton of product produced, and so on. We set up the same type of goals.

I have found by doing that it's much easier to make sure that it actually happens, because then we are in the routines that companies know how to operate under. If we set targets, then they are broken down into individual targets, and so on, and we meet the targets. And this is now done for our environmental targets, as well as for our social targets.

What we have done—and I think any company would have to do when they start—is to figure out exactly where is your environmental footprint. [Then] what is really important for you in terms of your environmental footprint? For us, it's the use of resources, it's the use of energy, and the use of clear water, and the way we purify that water. So, these are the main contributions, the main environmental footprint. What we do is . . . set goals for better and better use-per-ton of products of these inputs, and reduction of the outputs. Last year, for example, we could show that we improved the efficiency of our energy usage by 16 percent, and the efficiency by which we used water by a similar amount. If you go back and track that down in the ten year period that we have been following this, it's actually very, very significant savings of the environmental footprint that we have been able to show."

Of course, Novozymes' enzymes are intentionally used to reduce the energy load in manufacturing processes worldwide. On that point, Steen said:

"That is essentially much more important. When we do our sustainability report, it's really because we want—when we sell our products—to emphasize the environmental benefits that they bring to our customer's processes. To do that in a credible way, of course, our own performance has to be impeccable. The most important part of our business is that whenever we introduce a new enzyme and change an industrial process to an enzymatic process, we invariably end up replacing a polluting process with a much less polluting process. We have shown that with very careful life cycle analysis [LCA] in every single case.

The effect of what I'm talking about can be calculated in many ways. If you take a very conservative estimate for the CO_2 savings that is coming from our little business, if you extrapolate the results from those LCAs to the rest of our product range, and use a very, very conservative estimate, you can say how much CO_2 we save per kilo of enzyme. It actually turns out—using such a measure—[that] we saved the planet from the liberation of 14 million tons of CO_2 last year. That happens to be what Denmark must save to bring down Denmark's emission, so that Denmark can meet the Kyoto protocol goals. It's not a trivial amount. It's a huge amount. Enough to save little Denmark at least, so that we can ensure that Denmark meets its environmental goals."

So, I ask, Novozymes is singlehandedly meeting Denmark's environmental goals?

He laughs. "Yeah, yeah. That's correct."

It's not so surprising, then, that Novozymes has been awarded the Presidential Green Chemistry Challenge Award from the United States Environmental Protection Agency—not once, but twice. Or is it three times? I can only find two, but Steen seemed to think three. With all the ways companies merge and split and buy each other out these days, it's hard to keep track. In any event, EPA's Green Chemistry Challenge Award acknowledges "outstanding chemical technologies that incorporate the principles of green chemistry into chemical design, manufacture, and use, and have been or can be utilized by industry to achieve its pollution prevention goals." It couldn't have been a tough call for the awards jury.

Still, I wondered what had shaped this man, his thinking and his approach. He was a radical environmentalist in his youth. Could he continue to be a radical environmentalist—in his own way—today? I decided to research NOAH, the environmental organization that Riisgaard had founded a local chapter for, so many years ago. Surprisingly, I found it to be much like the man himself. The opening sentence of NOAH's biotech subgroup speaks directly to the kind of actions we see at Novozymes today.

We work towards ensuring that biotechnology is developed, used and applied in an environmentally conscious way.

While clearly committed to an environmental agenda, NOAH members didn't seem to be out boarding a lot of vessels at sea. There wasn't a lot of getting arrested, making noisy protests, breaking up public meetings, and engaging in inflammatory rhetoric. Its goal is "to be achieved through producing information materials, encouraging debate in the public and the media, participating in relevant meetings and hearings, and more." The words had clarity instead of argument, commitment in place of anger or rage.

Succinct and straightforward, the biotech subgroup discussion of NOAH provided perhaps the best (and shortest) description I've read of many activists' concerns about biotech—with the determination, but without the drama.

To be sure, it would be difficult for Steen Riisgaard and Novozymes to remain in absolute alignment with NOAH, but I wondered how close they actually remained. When you read the following excerpt, which is taken from the Gene-technology section of the NOAH website, you can see that the enzyme business—with proper safeguards—could work. If you'd like, go out and read it directly for yourself at www.noah.dk. Be sure to click on the "English version" button, unless you'd prefer to read it in Danish.

The issue
The existing knowledge concerning the environmental aspects of production and use of genetically modified organisms (GMOs) is limited. Uncertainty is great, in that the risk evaluation is often built upon scientific estimations and guesswork rather than concrete knowledge. Researchers at Risø National Laboratory have shown that resistant genes (resistant to certain herbicides such as Roundup) spliced into agricultural crops can be transferred to weeds and thereby make the weeds resistant - possibly creating so-called "super-weeds". Similarly, many experiments have shown that antibiotic resistance can be passed with ease onto other natural bacterial strains. This could possibly result in bacteria that cause sickness, such as Salmonella, to be resistant to available antibiotics.

Our policy

Our group differentiates between GMOs used in "closed" and "open" systems. One example where GMOs are used in closed systems is the production of enzymes or medicine using genetically modified micro-organisms in a laboratory or factory where a procedure for killing the organisms (boiling/chemical) is used before they are released into the open environment. An example where GMOs are used in an open system is the cultivation of transgenic (genespliced) crops in agriculture. We are principally against the use of GMOs in open systems, in other words, the release of GMOs into nature. Why we are against it is because we consider that this form of biological pollution could potentially be catastrophic in the long-term for the environment and the consequences wouldn't be balanced by any benefits.

NOAH's Gene-technology group is against the release, whether deliberately or accidentally, of genetically modified organisms (GMOs) into the environment.

What to consider

The term biotechnology covers a wide spectrum of techniques involving genetics e.g. from enzyme production by genetically modified bacteria to the cloning of animals. Therefore the environmental concerns differ greatly depending on which area one focuses upon. To evaluate whether a given form of biotechnology is environmentally sound or not, we think the following questions should be considered:

○ Is the system open or closed?

○ Is there a risk to the environment or nature, even unintentionally?

○ Is there a risk to human health and/or animals?

○ Is it ethically acceptable?

○ Is it truly needed?

An example: Are there any unwanted long-term effects of the cultivation of genetically modified corn on the environment (is it open or closed)? Could the consumption of GM-corn be detrimental to human health? Is there actually a need for GM-corn other than to make money? Is it ethically acceptable to manipulate the plants genetic makeup?

○   ○   ○

GOOD QUESTIONS. All. And as anyone can see, everything in biotech is related to everything else. The corn in the genetically modified food fight is related to the corn in our biorefineries is related to the enzymes in our laundry detergents, which is related to the bacteria that Dr. Chakrabarty so handily sliced-and-diced so many years ago.

And while we are mulling right from wrong—and what we really know from what we really don't know—the one definitive take-away for me—as Steen Riisgaard's life definitely illustrates—is that it is possible to live our professional lives in alignment with our personal beliefs. Still, it's a bit surprising to learn this powerful executive rides his bike to work every day.

"I do. Yes. Well, this is quite common to do in Denmark," he pointed out.

Even in the winter?

"Also in the winter. That's when you really feel this sense of accomplishment, when you come to work, when it's been snowing and the wind was against you. I drive fourteen kilos each way."

Stunning.

Presidential by Any Other Name

THE SCIENTIST/EXECUTIVE was clearly shaken.

Flanked by two young and pretty PR flackettes, he was wringing his hands, his eyes darted from side to side, anxiety writ large across his face. The flackettes were trying to calm him down, their hands hovering at his elbows, their concerned looks frozen in place. He simply wasn't calming down. Here he had come to BIO 2006 in Chicago, and somehow he had been tapped to do this interview.

You would think he'd been asked to jump from a plane at 30,000 feet for the good of the company. But this was only a radio interview. *How could he possibly be so frantic?*

I walked up and shook his sweaty hand, and he immediately realized he was all asweat. He stared down at his hands, as if they had betrayed him. He shook his head in combination frustration and apology, and let off yet another wave of anxiety, this time palpably mixed with impending doom.

I, too, tried to talk him down off the precipice, which is an exercise expected of talk show hosts faced with nervous guests. But the very height of the precipice should have been a tip-off. Never had anyone been quite so agitated. But that was a determination I only assessed in retrospect.

It usually worked to simply go over what the guest was going to tell me, and somewhere along the line, the person's mind would re-engage. It's as if they are finally able to say to themselves, "Oh, yeah. That's right. I remember now. I know what I'm talking about." But this time it didn't work. Oh, he was articulate, but he kept getting his points out of order and having to backtrack. This simply doesn't work when you're talking biotech—or any kind of science—on the radio or anywhere else for that matter. And for some reason, he just wasn't calming down. If anything, his terror was escalating.

It was time to pull out trick number two in the pre-interview batting line-up. Get him to talk about anything *except* what he was supposed to talk about in the interview.

Okay, I thought, looking down at his business card. *Let's give that a try.*

o   o   o

THE FELLOW in question was a wonderful guy—Dr. Mahendra Rao, the vice president of research in regenerative medicine and stem cell technologies for Invitrogen Corporation.

Invitrogen's a big player in biotech, and generous, too. The last time I went out to their website they offered "Our Way of Saying Thanks! Receive a $10 coffee gift card when you purchase 10 or more tubes of DNA Oligos through November." It was almost like I was out at Amazon and about to be rewarded with free shipping! I had to click through on the Order Now! button. Was there a trick? The next page revealed more detail: ". . . a $10 premium coffee gift card every time you order 10 or more tubes of desalted DNA oligos (25 or 50 nmol size) . . ."

You see the trick now, don't you! They have to be "desalted" and either the 25 or 50 "nmol" size. Live and learn, hey? If you're totally lost, "oligos" are short for "oligonucleotides," and now you should be even more lost. That's all I'm going to tell you. That's more than most anyone needs to know.

Suffice it to say, Invitrogen is a California company located in Carlsbad, which is Southern California and outside the great San Francisco biotech nexus. Still, it's a very innovative company. Publicly traded, Invitrogen has revenues in excess of $1 billion, employs some 5,000 people worldwide, and sells some 20,000 products. You'd be hard-pressed to find a scientific laboratory or a biotech enterprise that doesn't use some product from Invitrogen.

Whoever Dr. Rao was, he had a big job with a big company that sold well-respected products. This was no PR snow job. He wasn't hoping to convince me, and the world, that they had something incredibly fabulous to offer, when they were just wishin' and hopin' for big results. *But why is this man so nervous?*

The only thing that I knew about the interview was that we were supposed to be talking about something new Invitrogen had come up with. Or, at least, new to Invitrogen. They'd bought plenty of companies and technologies in their day. The focus had presumably been settled when Mark had scheduled the interview, but at this point, the PR flackettes would settle for getting the name of the company right, and they didn't care whether I said it, or Dr. Rao did.

"You in charge of all the stem cell lines?" I ventured. (Easy guess. Look at the title on his business card.)

He stopped, suddenly motionless. "Yes."

Well, at least he was beginning to look focused.

"What does that mean?" I asked, as casually as I could.

He responded with an actual sentence. To be precise, three. Among other things, it was Dr. Rao's job to make sure all the stem cell lines that they used for their research at Invitrogen were properly maintained and thriving. Hmmmm. Maybe I was getting somewhere. So I asked him a flippant question, hoping to get him to laugh.

"Would those be Presidential stem cell lines? Or less prestigious ones?"

He stopped, completely froze again. *What had I said? Was there an insult here I didn't fathom? Was he a Republican?*

"Both."

"Both?"

"Both."

I knew I had my interview. It was a question I hadn't asked before, since it was a question I had never thought to ask. *Why would a private company use Presidential stem cell lines?*

Every time Presidential stem cell lines were in the news, it was always about federal funding. Federal research funds for stem cell research had been restricted exclusively to scientific studies using the Presidential stem cell lines. And no other stem cell lines could come near them. Ask any researcher. Not a pencil, not a paper clip, not a molecule from non-Presidential stem cell lines—and any associated research—may cross into the physical space that receives federal funding for stem cell research.

It's a major hassle, too. Many researchers have given up on it. They find funding elsewhere. And they find their stem cells elsewhere too. But this company shouldn't care about federal funding. Commercial concerns are well funded either by revenues or by the well-heeled venture capital community. Invitrogen was a full-fledged, money-making proposition. They weren't looking to the feds to give them money. They had all the money they could possibly want. *What were they doing with Presidential stem cell lines?*

If you're late to this whole story, let me recap: Around the turn of the millennium, the science and technology of stem cell research were really beginning to make strides, as you already know having read Brooke's baby chapter (Chapter 5), about *in vitro* fertilization. Properly cultivated, these embryos could be developed into stem cell lines, which—in the best scientific scenario—could produce identical cells. Then, any scientific studies that used these stem cells all had a common basis. Oh, happy day!

The folks in Washington were really hip to that beat. So much so that they realized they had concerns—bioethical concerns. Possibly even religious concerns, but it doesn't really matter. There were objections. It sure looked like the scientists were planning to have a field day with all the embryos they could get their hands on.

To make a long story short, on August 9, 2001, President George W. Bush issued an executive order. (We've already been through how effective these executive orders can be. Here is yet another one.) The White House web site provides this quote from the President:

> As a result of private research, more than 60 genetically diverse stem cell lines already exist. I have concluded that we should allow federal funds to be used for research on these existing stem cell lines, where the life and death decision has already been made. This allows us to explore the promise and potential of stem cell research without crossing a fundamental moral line by providing taxpayer funding that would sanction or encourage further destruction of human embryos that have at least the potential for life.

At the time, there weren't anywhere near the 400,000 frozen embryos created by enthusiastic would-be parents, but there were those who realized there was a storm-a-brewing. And here is where President Bush made his stand.

He didn't/couldn't make stem cell research illegal. He didn't/couldn't make the creation of stem cell lines illegal. But he did and could—by executive order—limit how federal funding was spent on stem cell research, and that is where—and how—he took his stand.

It was a tricky argument, at best. These stem cells had already lost the potential to become human beings. If you really believe that it was wrong to create stem cell lines in this manner in the first place, one might think that using these already-existing lines would be disrespectful, if not just plain unethical.

Be that as it may, that's what the President did.

King Solomon split the baby, and then asked who wanted which part.

Many argued that the private sector would be unaffected by this decree, but we shall see that that's not true. Many also argued that university and non-profit research was essentially gutted. Well . . . that might be true. There was no doubt he threw a spanner in the works.

For one thing, just as every person is different, so is every embryo, and the stem cell line that might be created from it. If none of the so-called Presidential stem cell lines had the right kind of DNA that you were trying to study, you had nothing to work with. Let's say you got all excited about the absence of that MC4 receptor that regulates appetite and feeling full. If none of the Presidential stem cell lines had that mutation, you were out of luck. There was no reason to even seek federal funds. You didn't have the raw material to do the science.

It's been five years now, and the original Presidential stem cell lines are five years older. I had Dr. Mahendra Rao in front of me, and it was his job to keep them healthy for Invitrogen. In fact, he had been so concerned about the state of the Presidential stem cell lines, he'd written a paper about it. This, I knew, he could talk about. This subject he knew. Even if he still looked like he'd rather be anywhere else on the face of the earth.

We went into the studio, I settled him down, and I asked him why Invitrogen uses Presidential stem cell lines, and when it does not. He said:

"We use whatever is best. Right now we don't think that we can use only Presidential stem cell lines, because many of them have aged after they've been kept in culture, and some of them have been lost. We need more than the lines that are available from pre-August 9, 2001, and so we use both. We use cell lines which have been derived more recently as well.

There's one very important fact. Presidential lines are the oldest or the first derived lines, and many, many researchers have used them. They have published results with them. And so there's a lot of information available with these lines. We use them because we need that kind of information, because we can't do all those experiments all over again. We use the new lines to get additional information, which is not available with those lines. Even though we're not funded to use the Presidential lines, we still use them because of the information that's around."

Ah! That's it! There's a great body of published scientific information around the Presidential stem cell lines. If you want to check out your own research, you had better do it on these same lines, *whether or not you have federal funding.* And that's science. Try and keep everything that you can the same. Then introduce one or two variables. With luck, you may be able to tease out the precise effect you are looking for. You can't just do the same experiment on another stem cell line. The results won't make any sense. It would be like studying the effects of a new drug, and halfway through your study, you changed human subjects. You'd have to start all over again. This is part of what scientists mean when they say they "stand on the shoulders of giants." It means they take advantage of the work that has come before. You go to the literature, you duplicate the experiments to prove you have the same environment, and then you go forth from there—tinkering, hypothesizing, testing. And it all relates back to the research that has gone before.

I wondered, "If there were some sixty-plus Presidential stem cell lines to begin with, how many are there now?"

"The stem cell task force, which was organized by the NIH [National Institutes of Health] in response to the Presidential directive, identified 75 stem cell lines, which had been derived worldwide before August 9, 2001. The NIH made a strong effort to see how many of them could be available to federally-funded investigators, and they managed to obtain only about 25 or 27 of them. Out of those 25 or 27, so far about 10 are currently shipping from providers. An additional 5 or 6 may become available in a subsequent time period. At the same time, some subset of lines have been lost. And so I think overall there are between 10 to 17 lines which one may access now from the stem cell banks that have been funded, and that's about it. The number that might come out of the remaining 75 or so is quite small."

I had heard words to the effect that the Presidential stem cell lines were "dying," and I didn't know what it meant. Alternatively, I had also heard terminology that suggested some of these lines would be "lost." I asked Dr. Rao to explain what it all meant.

"It's really important to understand that stem cells were not designed to just grow forever in a culture dish," he said. "That's not their function when they are present in the normal body and play a role in normal development. So there's naturally some stress on these cells. And every time you put cells in stress, they can change. That's normal to happen with all cell types."

I interrupted. "And by 'growing,' you mean those cells dividing and dividing again—replicating themselves, again and again?"

"Exactly," he said, "because you need a whole lot of them for any kind of therapy [and because of] that kind of stress, we cell-select—to try to grow the best in these cultures. And one of the ways they do it is just like a cancer cell. A cancer cell grows well in culture because it's changed itself so that it can grow well. So stem cells can also change themselves so that they now grow well. And the one change that can take place, which allows them to grow well, is to change or lose some genes which suppress growth, or acquire additional copies of genes which will push them to grow better. That's what's happened with some of the cell lines which have been grown in culture. The older they are, the higher the chance that some of this will happen because they've divided so many more times in culture."

Adaptive critters, no? That would be us human beings right on down to our genes. But that wasn't my next question. What I wanted to know now was, "Does the change in the cells, which enables them to grow better in culture, change the effective nature of the cell?"

Dr. Rao answered, "Exactly. So just like . . . any change that's occurred in cancer, it's changed the cell so that now it doesn't respond to appropriate signals, or it behaves in a way you wouldn't really quite like it to behave. That's what can happen with the cells that have changed in culture."

I needed clarity. "So," I said, "there's plenty of live cells in the dish. They're just not the same, identical cells. They're not cells that we 'want.' We say, therefore, the line is lost, because we don't have the appropriate make-up of the DNA in the cell?"

"That's right.," said Dr. Rao. "The way we look at it is by looking at the chromosomes that are present and making sure they all look normal. These cells have become 'karyotypically' abnormal, meaning the number of chromosomes or the pattern of chromosomes has changed such that they don't look like the normal cells would."

Wow! So, how many lines might we lose?"

Dr. Rao was explicit. "In time, we might lose all of them, but it's already pretty clear that we have lost some. And we've tried some relatively heroic measures to try and rescue them by trying to identify the few normal cells that have been left in a dish, and that's been pretty hard. We've been successful in rescuing one line—it was a separate group—but it hasn't happened with the others. So, I think it is something you have to constantly monitor, and we always have to worry that we may lose some."

Dr. Rao had explained to me that they would remove a small number of cells and perform tests on them to determine if the stem cell line was continuing to prosper without changes to the basic DNA. So I asked him: "We have a concept in engineering called non-destructive testing. Can we look at the cell and figure out that it's okay without destroying the cell?" In his words:

"That's sort of the holy grail for this sort of testing that we want to do. Right now we don't have an easy way to look at how normal they are, in terms of their gene structure, without destroying the cell. So the trick we use is to take advantage of the fact that cells can grow a whole lot. We just take a little piece of them out and then destroy those, but the rest of the cells keep growing.

"We take the little subset of cells that we've taken, and we [do] some equivalent of non-destructive testing in that we stress them a whole lot more than we would the rest of the population. [From there,] we can make some predictions, like this is normal and it seems to be quite stable, because when we stress it a whole lot it doesn't go bad, while another cell line is normal right now, but when we stress it, it seems like it's much [easier] for it to go bad."

In a sense, they're not checking the current status. They are checking their future likely status. They're super-stressing them, and seeing if they're going to change.

"Yes, and we stress it a lot more than it would normally be stressed in culture," he said.

With 400,000 frozen embryos in the U.S. alone, and with Dr. Carolyn Givens' patients alone donating somewhere between 400 and 800 frozen embryos each year, I had to wonder how many stem lines were out there today.

According to Dr. Rao, "We don't have a precise number, but we certainly have a minimum number, and that minimum number is at least another 150 or 200 lines. There's a big group, based out of Chicago, which published that they have derived at least another 100 lines, and that's just one group. What we know, from internal . . . polling, is that there are at least 150 or 200 lines derived after August 9, 2001. So that number is at least ten times the number of lines that are shipping from pre-August 9, 2001—the Presidential lines."

Anyone can do the math—the Presidential lines are dwindling down. They're aging. At the same time, scientists—both the public and private sector—are doing more and more research. All that research would accelerate the demand and increase the stress even more on the existing stem cell lines. Wait a minute! "Does the executive order need to be revisited," I asked, "if federally-funded science is to go forward?"

"I think you have absolutely stated it very accurately," said Dr. Rao. "It's inevitable. I worked for the NIH before I left and joined Invitrogen, and I made this point when we had this sort of result. Everybody agrees that it's a matter of time. Nobody's quite willing to say how long that time period will be and when that decision will be made. But scientifically, it's very clear. It's going to be soon that we will need new lines, at least to replace those that have been lost."

o   o   o

ALL THIS got me to thinking.

Was President Bush's declaration an ethical dilemma? Or more to the point, a religious dilemma? Whatever it was, it's doubtful that it was a political decision . . . or he would have played his cards much differently.

Five years after the issuance of the executive order that limited federally funded research to the stem cell lines already in existence, both houses of Congress approved a law that would lift that restriction. Since the Republicans controlled both houses at the time the bill was approved, it's clear that political sentiment had not only shifted, it had actually broken traditional party lines, and by a sizable margin. Even then Senate Majority Leader Bill Frist from Tennessee said it plainly: "I am pro-life, but I disagree."

Still, President Bush stayed his course. On July 20, 2006, he vetoed the bill outright, and it was the first veto of his two terms as president. Many thought they would never see this day. His party controlled Congress. Surely, they would be voting in alignment. The two-third's vote that each house needed to override the veto could not be mustered, and so the president's veto stood. Yet more and more, he seemed to stand alone.

That's why I think he stood his ground for religious reasons. Politically, he could have said: "The representatives of the people have spoken." Even the polls showed that the majority of Americans supported stem cell research. But he didn't come up with a political rationalization. He didn't offer a single new argument, but he did offer a new option: The idea of adopting frozen embryos. And he had a number of these so-called "snowflake babies" born from IVF embryos wreaking a modest amount of havoc at his press conference. Of course, at that point only 128 snowflake adoptees had been born, so he was still in need of recruiting several hundred thousand more "gestational carriers" to begin to make it all work.

The bottom line was that he repeated his former stance, as steadfast as his position on Iraq, and he suffered for it. As did his party—in the 2006 midterm elections a scant four months away.

Things fell apart in a single day. Never before in the history of the United States had both houses switched majorities at a midterm election. The last two years of the Bush administration would be nothing like its first six.

Political analysts tell us that in this midterm election, the nation voted locally, but the issue was national. Iraq, Iraq, Iraq. It was an implicit vote for or against Bush himself.

In that national referendum of sorts, the nation's pulse regarding stem cells might be missed, except for that bastion of conservatism: Missouri.

Days before the election there was a now-infamous dust-up that reached new pre-election media heights. Popular film and television star—and Parkinson's sufferer—Michael J. Fox had recorded a television spot for the Democratic Senate candidate Claire McCaskill. Conservative radio talk show host Rush Limbaugh accused Fox of "exaggerating the effects of the disease" and "either he didn't take his medication or he's acting, one of the two." Rush apologized, and Claire McCaskill won, although it was likely that she was going to win in any event. What got missed was that there was more to the stem cell issue in Missouri than the vote for the Senate seat.

Missouri is not one of those places that sways according to the latest breeze. Missouri is the "Show Me" state. Conservative, yes, but more importantly, clearheaded. Missouri moves in its own determined way. Labeling it "Midwest conservative" underrates perhaps the greatest characteristic of its citizens. They don't move as a group; they move as individuals. It's not the "Show Us" state. It's the "Show Me" state, one person at a time.

When Missouri goes to the polls, you need to do more than simply count the votes. You need to pay attention to where the votes came from. And this time around, the vote showed us something rather surprising.

Yes, the media focused on the Michael J. Fox political spot on behalf of a particular candidate, and the presumption on the national talk show circuit was that a vote for that candidate was a vote for stem cell research. This was an obvious mistake to make, since the issue clearly divided the two candidates and split them predictably along party lines. Yet sentiments in the state were far more nuanced when you take a closer look.

Whether or not a particular voter cared for one Senate candidate or another, there was also a state referendum asking the voters to affirm that stem cell research would continue under existing federal guidelines. This affirmation of federal policy may seem unusual at first glance, but it was designed to protect and support the private donations to stem cell research already under way in Missouri.

Key here is knowing Jim and Virginia Stowers, founders of the American Century Investments empire. Both cancer survivors, they've donated $1.5 billion to fund the Stowers Institute for Medical Research, a prestigious St. Louis stem cell research facility. The work that the institute does would be jeopardized should the state—within its rights—decide that it wanted a narrower interpretation of federal policy. As a result, the Stowers donated $29 million to run the media campaign supporting the initiative. You might call it "insurance" in its simplest form. Or smart thinking. Whatever you call it, it was historic in proportion. This amount was larger that the campaigns of the combined candidates in any race in the state's history.

Massive campaign backing for biotech issues has been mustered before, in other states, and that experience tells us it's no guarantee that the votes will be forthcoming. In spring of 2004, a coalition of biotech concerns funded an assertive $700,000 campaign in the sleepy little county of Mendocino in Northern California. On their ballot was a measure to ban the growth of genetically modified (GM) products within the county's borders. Usually, you can count on the activists squaring off against agribusiness and a good deal of middle-of-the-road voting. But in Mendocino, everyone from local growers to health professionals and community governments came together, and Measure H passed with 57 percent of the vote. In the end, the GM folks spent about $60 for every losing vote, while a few dollars here and a few dollars there were spent on the winning side. Mendocino became the first American community to ban growing genetically modified crops by popular vote. It proves that sometimes no amount of money can make a difference. Look below the surface clash of politics and economics and what you generally find is the will of the people. And I'm not talking about democracy, per se. I'm talking about what happens when a whole lot of humans decide to move in a particular direction.

And that gets us back to Missouri. The state's 2006 stem cell initiative passed in favor of stem cell research, 51 percent to 49 percent . . . and it turns out the vote did not break down along party lines. In rough terms, about one-third of the Republican voters supported the measure, and about one-third of Democrats didn't. Of independent voters—a signature in Missouri, as you might imagine—they split roughly 50-50.

All this is a complicated way of saying—that how each vote was cast on stem cell research was individual, not tied to party ideologies or partisan voting. For some, it was a matter of personal experience with horrific disease, or an expression of hope for a better tomorrow. For others, it was a matter of faith. But even for people of strong religious faith, it would be a mistake to think you know how they voted.

Ask any person of faith, and they will tell you—faith sometimes asks you to continue on in the face of challenge, while at other times, challenge itself leads the way. For who can escape the fact of our human bodies? Who can live a life in opposition to his or her own quiet logic?

And even faith itself comes in many flavors. There are those with a faith solely in the amazing mystery of life, while others have a faith in the essential rightness of man's quest to pursue science, taking to heart the biblical directive: "Know thyself."

In the end, each of us makes decisions in his or her own way and for his or her own reasons, consciously and sometimes otherwise.

How today's science will be viewed fifty years from now—independent of the results it will bring—we can't begin to guess. With or without Missouri, with or without the funding of the United States government, this science will indeed move forward.

At the same time, it would be a mistake to dismiss what happened in Missouri. Especially because it *was* Missouri, a state of independent thinkers and also a place where people have strong religious convictions. Perhaps not unlike President Bush's convictions. If a great number of conservative, clear-headed individuals in a state like Missouri could all stand up together, all at once, and say, "Okay, show us," this tells me that the tide is turning in the United States. The water level is rising. It's going to happen. Stem cell research will not be denied. It's simply a matter of time. Nevertheless, the religious and ethical objections will likely never go away.

Still, we might take a page out of the United Kingdom's book here. The U.K. has been addressing all things embryonic, ever since the birth of Louise Brown, the first test-tube baby back in 1978. In 1991, it created the Human Fertilisation and Embryology Authority (HFEA), which oversees anything you can think of, including stem cell research, *in vitro* fertilization clinics, egg and sperm donation, stem cell line creation and scientific research. All these areas are regulated and licensed. Thus, there is no question of how many frozen embryos there are, how many stem cell lines there are, or who is doing what with them. It is at once more free and more controlled—all at the same time.

○   ○   ○

EVERY INTERVIEW comes to an end, and finally I had run out of questions for Dr. Mahendra Rao. He was so nervous that somehow I knew there would be no "post-interview euphoria." In fact, he didn't even show relief. I thanked him and tried to encourage him at the same time.

"You were great! Now, that wasn't so bad, was it?"

He responded without hesitation. "Yes, it was. I never want to do that again for the rest of my life."

What luck! I have an exclusive!

CHAPTER FOURTEEN

Destined for Diabetes?

"**THERE'S NO** geographic monopoly on a good idea."

The person before me was Dr. Neville McClenaghan, the COO of Diabetica Limited, a biotech firm originating from of all places . . . Northern Ireland.

It just so happened I was looking for a good idea. Actually, I was looking for a number of good ideas. Partially because I'd been swamped with diabetes data, and I was beginning to get confused.

Were there 200 million or 300 million people with diabetes worldwide? Were there 300 million or 500 million "pre-diabetics" worldwide? The numbers were exploding, I was told over and over again, and yet the numbers were different depending on who I spoke with and which sources I checked. Perhaps I would try to get a fix solely on the United States.

The American Diabetes Association projects that 21 million Americans have diabetes, whether they know it or not—and some one-third don't even know it.

Then we have the pre-diabetics. Some 54 million Americans are projected to be pre-diabetic, and an even larger percentage of these people don't have a clue. And why don't they? Most have no symptoms at all.

Side-by-side with these numbers come the escalating statistics on obesity. As obesity rapidly increases, so does the incidence of diabetes, which is why the diabetes statistics are hard to latch onto. We need to count people who don't even know they have the condition, and we have a circumstance (the rapid increase in obesity) that is accelerating the whole situation as a backdrop. It's like Typhoid Mary is still at large while the typhoid cases have started pouring in. No wonder it's difficult to get a fix on what's really happening.

What's also a bit disconcerting is getting an answer to why this situation doesn't seem to be turning around. The "Eat right—Watch your weight—Exercise regularly" mantra is being repeated by everyone, including Dr. Phil, but few are heeding the call.

Could it be because tens of millions of Americans don't know their status?

Remember that old expression "fat, dumb, and happy?" If you're dumb—meaning you don't know you are pre-diabetic—then you have no reason to work on not being fat. What's a little fat if you're happy?

And perhaps you look like everyone in your family. Maybe your ancestors were chunky and you just inherited their genes. You may be overweight according to the population standards, and *not be* pre-diabetic. Why put yourself through all this worry, if you have no reason to?

Of course, your ancestors may never have lived long enough to become pre-diabetic, and beyond.

And then you might be thinking: So what, if I'm pre-diabetic? It's not diabetes. How bad could that be?

Bad.

At least, bad enough.

According the American Diabetes Association, "People with pre-diabetes have a 1.5-fold risk of cardiovascular disease compared to people with normal blood glucose. People with diabetes have a 2- to 4-fold increased risk of cardiovascular disease."

And what's cardiovascular disease? It's a whole range of conditions, which include our old friends, heart disease and stroke.

You could think: What's the big deal? Maybe I'm permanently pre-diabetic. Maybe it's in my genes. Is a 50 percent higher increase in the risk of heart disease or stroke all that much to get worked up over?

The answer is yes. If untreated, pre-diabetes is a ten-year waiting room on the road to full-blown type 2 diabetes. And during that time? That's when you move from the "1.5-fold" risk to the "2- to 4-fold" risk of cardiovascular disease. And you do increasing damage done to your body all along the way.

If we believe the numbers offered by the American Diabetes Association, perhaps 25 million Americans are walking around with pre-diabetes and don't even know it.

Is there some good news in all this? Yes.

○   ○   ○

THE CENTERS for Disease Control tell us: "Studies have shown that most people with pre-diabetes go on to develop type 2 diabetes within 10 years, *unless they lose weight through modest changes in diet and physical activity.*"

So, it's a two-part answer:

1. "Most people with pre-diabetes go on to develop type 2 diabetes within 10 years." This is bad. The odds are against you spending a lifetime being pre-diabetic. If you're pre-diabetic, you want to get off that list. That's why you want to concentrate on the rest of the sentence.

2. ". . . unless they lose weight through modest changes in diet and physical activity." Many people can get off the pre-diabetic train, just by watching what they're doing. Their tests will show it. But some people can't. Oh, they can lose weight and exercise, but they are still pre-diabetic. And here's where you really want to be watching what you're doing to stave off the effects of simply being pre-diabetic. When people are finally diagnosed with diabetes, they frequently arrive with damage that cannot be reversed.

So what I'm talking about here is *having a reason* to actually do the "Eat right—Watch your weight—Exercise regularly" regimen. Without a reason, it's a lot like "Just say 'No.'" Except. . . nobody's saying "no." And the obesity statistics prove it.

The next question is, How tough is it to get tested for pre-diabetes? Isn't there a test?

Of course, there's a test for it! And it's pretty straightforward and not unlike a lot of other blood tests you take. But it is a blood test.

Let's start with what they're testing for. They need to test your body's ability to tolerate glucose. Diabetes is simply the body's inability to produce the insulin needed to convert sugars, starches and other food into energy. Or the inability to use the insulin you do have to do that conversion. If the test shows you've got too much glucose, you're either not producing enough insulin or you're not able to use the insulin that you do produce. Too much glucose in the blood tells the tale.

And now the test: To be tested for pre-diabetes today, you would likely either take the fasting plasma glucose test (FPG) or the oral glucose tolerance test (OGTT). While one test makes you fast overnight, in both cases, you've got to get your blood drawn. Then it's off to the lab.

What we're talking about here is technology, and it's in the nature of technology to get smaller-faster-cheaper. It's also in the nature of technology to blast onto the scene and change everything.

Here's one example: VeraLight, Inc., a company based in Albuquerque, New Mexico, has announced a new non-invasive test. Their technology takes about a minute to scan human skin under a fluorescent light, and it looks for indicators of damage from high glucose levels. They've been working on various age groups, since youthful skin is much different from aging skin, and they've also been working on various skin tones. What they've been able to identify are various biomarkers that are produced in higher concentrations in the presence of high glucose levels. In fact, these biomarkers accumulate over time, and so the extent of damage can also be estimated. VeraLight anticipates commercial introduction of this test in the U.S. in early 2008, and believe me, they're not alone in the quest to improve detection.

But here's the problem. You can have all the technology in the world, but unless you use it, it's of no use. So I think we need another good idea.

The most recent information available from the CDC about the cost of medical expenditures due to diabetes in the United States was from the year 2002. That number was $132 *billion*. Clearly, it's more than that today, and it's projected to continue to climb sharply.

But that's not what really sticks in my craw. How is it—in this technological age—we don't leap up and say, "People don't know they are diabetic!?! People don't know they are pre-diabetic!?! What do you mean we're not testing everyone six ways to Sunday?" Well, for one thing, we have many people who have no medical insurance whatsoever, and no money, to boot. But even people with private medical insurance aren't tested. Unless they go for a regular physical and fall into a particular group at risk, it's not recommended (and therefore, not paid for). To be fair, we're also seeing major evidence of over-testing across the board, so tests are generally only recommended for people who appear to be in a group with a good chance of having the condition.

Still, if everything the government is telling us is true, *this is a major public health crisis.* And that calls for bold societal moves.

It seems to me that massive and continual funding of pre-diabetes tests *on a nationwide basis,* would be better than a good idea. Perhaps, even a *great idea.*

Fund everyone to come in and get tested. *Know your glucose level!* That would make a handy campaign slogan. And make it free. Encourage employers to give people time off, or have the tests done on-site. And keep it going. Year after year. Send units out to polling places. Test anyone who shows up, not just voters. And how much would that cost? That has to be worked out. But anyone can do the math. The cost of tests will increase, but the cost of long-term, chronic care will decrease.

There's also the social math. Preventing a person from developing diabetes, pushing off its onset, minimizing its effect—these are all good things for every person and society in general. With new technology coming along all the time, all it really takes is *the will to do it.*

What would happen if such a program came into being? Well, we'd definitely have a better grip on the numbers, that's for sure. And I have no doubt that many people would begin to take action on their own behalf. And why? Knowledge is power. Just so they know where they stand. Even if they're a normal weight. Even if they're young. Even if they think they're just fine. They may not have any symptoms, but if they are pre-diabetic, they could already be doing damage to their systems. This is the kind of nationwide public health initiative that technology supports perfectly.

○　　○　　○

THE "EAT-WEIGH-Exercise" mantra works better when being overweight brings on a known problem specific to the individual. As we discussed in Chapter 11, for some people, simply being a bit overweight brings on the problem, while for others, there is no obesity link. All obese people are not diabetic, and all diabetics are not obese. Therein lies some confusion.

Are some of us destined for diabetes from day one? Are some of us destined for diabetes only if we put on weight? And others, not at all?

This was the perfect question to ask Dr. Kari Stefansson, CEO of deCODE Genetics in Reykjavik, Iceland. deCODE is a biopharmaceutical firm with a very unique approach. According to Dr. Stefansson:

"It is unique in that it uses human genetics throughout the whole process of drug discovery and development. We use gene isolation to find the target, and the target is basically the protein that that drug manipulates. So we begin by finding out what is the weakness in the person who is predisposed to a disease. What is the genetic variant that causes the disease or increases the risk of the disease. We find that, and that is the beginning of the process, and then we use genetics the entire way from the target to a drug to a clinical trial.

For example, we use genetics to help us to find individuals who are at the greatest risk of a disease, to try to recruit them into our clinical trials. We are characterized by the use of genetics."

Before founding deCODE genetics, Kari Stefansson was a professor of neurology, neuropathology, and neuroscience at Harvard University, and director of neuropathology at Beth Israel Hospital in Boston. And before that he was on the faculty at the University of Chicago.

One would think that the United States would be a much better place to start a business in genetics, as opposed to back in his native Iceland. But Kari says:

"Our population has a wealth of information on its genealogy. And remember that the study of genetics is the study of the information that goes into the making of man, and how that information goes from one generation to the next. The genealogy gives you the avenues by which the information flows. We are also a relatively homogeneous population . . . and then," he adds laughing, "let's just face it, we have great scientists! We have the best."

But what I was most interested in was the genetic basis for diabetes. And I was not disappointed. Kari continued.

"What we have discovered is a genetic variant that has great impact on the risk of developing type 2 diabetes. Type 2 diabetes is a fairly common disease. It is a disease that is on the rise. It is one of the diseases of the affluent society, where there is an abundance of food. What we have discovered is a variant in a gene, and if you have one copy of it, you have about a 40 percent increase in the risk of developing type 2 diabetes. Thirty-eight percent of Americans have one copy of this [gene variant]; 7 percent of Americans have two copies, and they have basically a 140 percent chance increase in probability of developing diabetes."

At last! Here is something we might begin to identify at any time! A predilection for the condition. A reason to be vigilant. Kari wasn't finished on this point.

"Type 2 diabetes has turned out to be a very, very difficult disease for the geneticists to crack. But in this case, we have found the variant—just one snip . . . a single nucleotide change that increases so dramatically the risk of this bad disease.

If you look at the total population of patients with type 2 diabetes in America, if you would take out this one snip, 20 percent of them would not have the disease. So this is a variant that has a very significant impact.

Another interesting aspect . . . is the patients who have developed diabetes, and have this genetic variant, are younger than the average patient with type 2 diabetes. They are thinner than the average patient with diabetes. Another very, very interesting aspect of all of this is that these diseases—the common diseases that we are studying, and that certainly applies to type 2 diabetes— they are diseases that happen at the interface between genes and environment.

So you have a genetic component to risk. You have an environmental component to risk. And you could actually argue that all of these diseases, particularly type 2 diabetes, are diseases that basically reflect the way in which man interacts with his environment. Which is exciting.

What is beginning to emerge out of our work is that the role of this interaction of man and the environment, and the parthenogenesis of the disease, basically is reflected in the distribution of these variants."

But diabetes is a worldwide epidemic, which Dr. Stefansson also addressed.

"You have people living in Africa, and you have people living in Iceland—living in totally different environments. It is very likely that many—I'm not actually saying more—that many of the disease-associated variants will differ when it comes to the distribution in Africa and . . . in Iceland. So, basically, we will see ethnic and geographical differences in the distribution of this variant. For example, we have found a variant in this diabetes gene that only increases the risk in African-Americans."

Out at the CDC web site, you can readily see that black Americans are more inclined to develop diabetes, followed by Hispanics, and then white Americans. But what Kari is saying is that White and Hispanic Americans may have the gene, but that other genetic "settings" could come into play. The risk of diabetes is not increased by these genes alone.

I also began pondering the centuries-old efforts to erase racial prejudice, but Kari wasn't finished. "And that is similar to a discovery that we announced when we found a variant that increases the risk of heart attack in African-Americans by 250 percent, and in White Americans only by 15 percent."

At that moment, I remembered what Dr. Bryan Sykes told me. He's a professor of human genetics at Oxford University, and chairman and founder of Oxford Ancestors. His work in tracing the genetic roots of humanity led him to create the company, which in turn performs genetic tests and provides a background of where you came from. He made two points that I thought were important. First, he said that they received numerous requests from the States, and that a very large percentage of Americans were surprised to find that they had Indian blood. In fact, there had been quite a lot of mixing of genes in America all around, and the descendants were generally unaware of it until they received their individual analyses.

But it was his second point that I think is important now. He said that when two people meet and he tells them that way, way back they share a joint ancestor, you can see that they immediately begin to bond, to have an affinity for each other. "They straighten up, and look at each other," he said. They realize that they are truly related. He thought it was quite remarkable.

Which brings me hope. Along with the genetic differences we may now be discovering along ethnic and racial lines, trend wise, there is hope that this new information may not be as divisive as it appears at first blush. We can only hope that when we finally discover how related we all are, a natural inclination toward affinity will begin to come forth.

After all, genetics research is a study of humanity itself. Kari continued:

> "The genetics of common diseases seems in most instances, basically, to be the genetics of the spectrum of [normal] function, and the [normal] function is always open to selection by evolution. We are beginning to see that number one, the incidence and severity of these diseases reflect very much our interaction with our environment, where we are, what our population history is. And that's exciting to look at in the context of our work in genetics and the intent to develop drugs. That is very much in keeping with the concept of personalized medicine. Medicine that will be developed for people—not necessarily just for disease, but [for] the match of the disease and the person."

○   ○   ○

IN THE END, it's not group medicine, but individualized medicine.

Could it be that the best social good will be served by decoding everyone's DNA, so that they can have the best medical treatment possible?

That's way in the future at this point. It would be good to hear another idea—with a shorter time horizon. One about treatment. One that says there might be hope for those who are pre-diabetic or diabetic already. I wanted to be assured that this wasn't just a case of simply trying to avoid diabetes by making lifestyle changes, and then being resigned to it once it arrived, perhaps, even having to endure a lifetime of constant glucose monitoring and daily, multiple insulin injections.

Two examples immediately presented themselves.

The first came from Bob Curry, the Chairman and CEO of Sensys Medical in Chandler, Arizona. Sensys looks to be the first company who will gain FDA approval for a non-invasive glucose testing product. In plain language—no more having to draw blood to stick in your glucose monitor three or four times a day. You hold this new device to your arm, and through the magic of infrared spectroscopy, some 30 seconds later you get your reading.

It is hoped that this technology will lead to more frequent testing during the day for better diabetes management, and that there will be a more accurate measurement as to how much insulin a person should inject at any one time. With over 90 patents in place and about to undergo clinical trials, Sensys' GTS (Glucose Tracking System) will likely be released in Europe in mid-2008 and in the United States in the second quarter of 2009.

The other example came from Neville McClenaghan, who earlier declared "There's no geographic monopoly on a good idea."

He got right down to it. "We're involved with diabetes therapeutics. We've got a drug platform that's based on a molecule, and this molecule is realized from the gut when you feed."

Realized? Feed? Oh, he means that when you eat, after the food hits your stomach, it eventually makes it way down to your intestines. It's at this point that this molecule is normally released. I get it. They've isolated this molecule.

"It naturally lowers blood glucose, and it does this by increasing insulin secretion from the pancreatic beta cells, and doing other fancy things around the body," he said.

Ah! Their molecule gets your pancreas to put out more insulin! Then your blood glucose level goes down! (That is, if what you need is more insulin, and your body can use it appropriately.) He explained further:

"What we [at Diabetica Limited] have done is stabilize that molecule, as it is rapidly degraded in the body. It can be given as a therapeutic to stimulate insulin secretion in [people with] type 2 diabetes.

Certainly this drug would also be effective in obesity. When you are obese—particularly when you are extremely obese—you're in a situation where there is a really serious demand on the various body tissues, on the demand for hormones, like insulin, to work. What you're really doing is supplementing that effect.

We've licensed our drug to Amylin Pharmaceuticals, to help the body cope with the lack of insulin per gram of body weight, if you like.

We also have another drug, which has come from the same platform, and which enhances the way insulin works within the body. The other drug actually suppresses the action subsequently of that molecule, and this may be helpful for secondary reactions. There may be some people that would produce too much insulin.

It's a very interesting molecule. When it's released in its intact form, it goes around and stimulates insulin secretion. The body then has different enzymes that chop it up. Once it gets chopped up, then it works in a very different way.

So, we've developed two different types of drugs. One that's based on the intact molecule, and one that's based on the fragment molecule. One molecule works by stimulating insulin secretion—that's the intact molecule. The other one is a fragment molecule, and it enhances insulin action. This is a natural physiological thing that happens in the body. What we're doing is replicating the action of this molecule naturally within the body, both in its intact form and in its shortened form."

I asked Neville if this drug would have to be injected—given that so many people are trying to avoid needles.

"I think in the first instance this would be an injectable," he said. "Saying that, what is clear now is that there's emerging technologies where you can deliver them as a 'depot.' So you deliver them once a week or once a month. It would be kind of a slow-release idea, so that you've constantly got the molecule there doing its job."

To be sure, there's an enormous amount of work going on out there in the area of diabetes and obesity. For some of us, it's our genetic destiny.

But knowledge is power. Knowing it's our destiny is one thing. Changing our destinies is exactly what we humans do so well with the technologies we build.

All we need is a few more good ideas.

onkey Business

"I GUARANTEE you, you'd get a baboon."

A baboon?

I had just posed a hypothetical question to Dr. Sean Carroll, a genetics professor from the University of Wisconsin. Certainly, he had enormous professional credentials, such as also being an investigator at the Howard Hughes Medical Institute, which funds (in part, if not entirely) his genetics lab. Closer to home, he'd been a guest on *Tech Nation* discussing his previous book, *Endless Forms Most Beautiful: The New Science of Evo Devo*. Now he was back with another: *The Making of the Fittest . . . DNA and the Ultimate Forensic Record of Evolution*.

What I had learned from his first visit was that he was a plain speaker, a natural teacher. And as real teachers do, he didn't shy away from a direct question, even a hypothetical one. Great teachers tell you what they know and what they don't, if you are on the right logical path . . . or the wrong one. If you are being realistic . . . or not. And so it is with Sean.

I guessed he would answer my hypothetical question—but first, I should tell you why I asked him about the baboon.

○   ○   ○

SINCE THE completion of the Human Genome Project in 2003, scientists have sequenced a number of human beings, along with a complement of animals, plants and bacteria. In truth, *any living thing* was—and is—up for grabs. Scientists around the globe are now sequencing everything in sight. It's new data about ourselves—new data for a new millennium. I asked him to bring me up to date.

"It's one of each for now," Sean said. "Sort of a standard. For humans, we actually have lots of human genomes. We've covered more humans so that we can get a sense of variation in human populations. But really, as we go through the list of mammals, I think there's a dolphin. Certainly there's a rat. There's a mouse. There's the chimpanzee. They're working on the gorilla. Dog is definitely done. I think [there's] an opossum, so that we have a marsupial. And the list is a little bit longer than that. And then things like some fish and a chicken and a cow. And now the technology has changed so much, and the tools have changed so much, that our ambition has changed."

And how has that ambition changed? Well, the technology yields up more than simply the DNA itself. Just as the scar on my leg belies a decades-old knee operation, DNA can also give up evidence of what's happened to humans in the past—and every living thing and its past—as they descended one generation to the next.

"It's written in the DNA of every species," he said. "It's an incredibly rich record of who they descended from, and how they came to be, and the lifestyles of their ancestors, and of all the adaptations that have helped them live the lifestyle that they live today."

I asked, "So, now that we've decoded a number of humans, how do we look as a whole? How different are we, one from the other?"

According to Sean, "Humans are not that different from each other, but humans are fairly different from previous hominids on our evolutionary line." *That's a relief!* "They're different from the last common ancestor we had with chimps, and they're different from other primates. We can track these differences back through time through this DNA record—genes that we don't use any more, but that some of our primate relatives still use. Capabilities that we have, but that others don't have. What we're trying to do," he said, "is reconstruct how we came to be, and how we came to be different from other things."

I just couldn't comprehend how we could compare the DNA of humans to the DNA of another species, so I came at it directly: "Okay, Sean, if you line up the DNA of a human next to the DNA of a chimpanzee, how do you know one gene on the human matches a gene on the next species over?"

He explained: "It would be sort of like if you were lining up different editions of the same novel. You might find that over the course of the years they had dropped out a few words or corrected a few typos or things like that, but generally the text of DNA—which is only four letters, A, C, G and T in all sorts of permutations—large blocks of it will align between chimpanzees and humans." Without skipping a beat, Sean added, "In fact, about 99 percent of it aligns.

What! What happened to "fairly different"? 1% doesn't sound like fairly different!

"There are vast tracks, where essentially all the letters of the chimpanzee's DNA and all the letters of the human's DNA are exactly the same, and about 1 out of 100 letters . . . change. So, it's very easy to align ourselves with chimps."

There was no stopping him. He continued. "It's also very easy to align our DNA even with a mouse. It's even easy to align stretches of our DNA with things like sharks. And parts of our DNA are even alignable with the DNA in plants and fungi and bacteria and all these other life forms, because some genes have been around really since the beginning of complex life."

Placing my alarm aside, it came to me that our current ability to suddenly see inside the DNA of all living things was like working a puzzle—only backwards. Looking back to our origins. And to our interrelatedness.

If no one had thought up the theory of evolution before, scientists would certainly start positing explanations now—simply because of the common overlap of all this DNA. Every scientist in his right mind would be gripped by the question: There has to be some explanation of why every living thing looks so much like every other living thing. You might call it a scientific parlor game. "Here are ten different sets of DNA. Are they related? And if so, who split from whom and at what point?" The first person to come up with the answer gets to say, "Elementary, my dear Watson." Only you don't get the honorific of being Sherlock Holmes. You get to be Francis Crick. It's been fifty years since Crick and Watson won the scientific foot race to discover the structure of DNA. We've been told ever since that the discovery of the double helix was sensational. Only now is it becoming clear to the layperson that it really was.

We had the science, but what we didn't have was the technology. And now suddenly, we do. We can comprehensively analyze the DNA of humans and any other living entity.

"For the first time ever," as Sean explained.

"Forty or fifty years ago, some of the big pioneers in evolutionary thought did not think this was the way it would be. They thought that the sequence of DNA turned over so much that [typical and constant] mutation was sufficient to simply erase this record. That all the letters would be gone and changed, and there would be nothing really to compare between say, a human, and a fish, let's say.

But they were wrong. Some of this code persists over hundreds and hundreds and hundreds of millions of years, and really, the number of genes that we have is very similar to the number of genes in a chimp, in a mouse, in a fish, etc.

We are really just another animal with a really similar-looking genome."

I pointed out to Sean, that for some people, those are fightin' words.

"Well, I guess you could say . . . sometimes the truth hurts," he said. "But, for biologists, it's a great starting point, because it says, in understanding how we became human, we have to figure out the meaning of the differences—not so much worrying about the rest of that 99 percent that is similar.

Now, to put this in mathematical terms, to do the arithmetic, there are about three billion letters of DNA code in our genome. The chimp, on average, let's just say differs a little more than one percent of those positions. Well that's still about 30 million differences between us and chimpanzees.

Now most of those differences we think don't amount to anything, because there's places in the DNA where if a change happens, there really is no consequence on how animals appear or behave or anything like that. But somewhere in there are the changes that mean all the difference [between] us holding this conversation and still living in trees."

That got me to wondering. Let's say we see an obvious mutation between one of our genes and one of the chimpanzees. How do we know when they're actually using the gene, while we no longer use it, yet still carry it?

Sean responded:

"The obvious signature is that the gene had mutations in it that disrupts its code. For the DNA information to be decoded, it's read three letters at a time. If you were to insert a letter into that code, that shifts what we call the reading frame, and now it can no longer be read. It's nonsense. Or [in the case of] a deletion, it doesn't mean anything. It still has the letters that will align, but there's some hole in it, or there's some insertion in it, or there's some change in the meaning of the code, so the gene can no longer function. So it's very easy for us to spot a gene that looks pretty good but actually has a fatal flaw in it.

And these 'fossil' genes—we have about 900 of them in the human DNA alone, out of about 20,000 or so genes . . . and about 70 of those have evolved since our last common ancestor, the chimpanzees. So this is a process that is still going on. And it goes on in every species . . . some genes are mutated at random. This is something that happens in every generation: every new individual carries new mutations that neither of its parents had, and sometimes those mutations *hit* in the meaningful part of genes. If there's no consequence to that, if there's no penalty, no performance disadvantage or anything like that, those mutations are carried in the population.

What's happened over the course of millions of years is that a variety of human genes are no longer really relied on by us for performance, whether that might be [developing] a sense of smell or forming a particular muscle, or triggering some sort of immune defense, or something like that. These genes have sort of gone out to pasture.

Maybe it's easier to describe [in terms of] other animals. Think about any change in lifestyle. Let's suppose the animal [species] shifts from living out in broad daylight to using color vision to being nocturnal. Well, it changes a lot of the pressures on the animal's senses. What happens is that the genes for detecting various wavelengths of light . . . go to pot. And this has happened again and again and again. I give a number of examples in the book. Animals that have shifted to living in caves, to being primarily nocturnal, living underground, or living in the deep ocean—a lot of them evolved from ancestors that lived in the daylight or lived in shallow water or lived above ground, but now what we see in the genes that otherwise would equip their sense of vision, those genes have accumulated mutations—they are 'molecular fossils.'

And that's what I mean by allowing us to trace these shifts in lifestyles in the evolutionary process. They have sort of the defective version of what their ancestors had."

○   ○   ○

ANOTHER GREAT example Sean talks about is the ice fish:

"I think this is one of the most amazing animals I know about on the planet. This fish—called the ice fish—lives in the southern ocean, around Antarctica actually. It has abandoned a way of life that all other vertebrates have, and that is we have red blood cells. All other mammals have red blood cells, all birds, all reptiles and all fish have red blood cells—except for the ice fish. What appears to have happened is that as this animal adapted to very cold water—it lives in water that is as cold as 30 degrees Fahrenheit, subfreezing. Having lots of red blood cells would make its blood too viscous. It has abandoned that way of life. It makes no red blood cells. It has very dilute blood, and it pumps this very dilute blood around with a big heart much more rapidly than other fish, and it just extracts oxygen passively from the water around it. It's completely changed the way it gets oxygen.

"And the signature of this big change is all over its DNA record. You look at the DNA of the ice fish [and you see that] the genes for hemoglobin—which are genes we have, because hemoglobin is the oxygen-carrying protein in our red blood cells—one of them is gone completely from the ice fish and the second is just a little remnant."

"And we know," I surmised, "because most of the sequence is the same?" At that, he said:

"You have it! Its ancestors had it! That's right, the ancestors had it, but the ice fish has lopped it off.

When biologists first discovered [that there were] no red blood cells in this fish, that was pretty stunning. That was about fifty years ago, and then to discover that the globin genes are either missing or completely broken, that sort of flies in the face of all of our intuition. That's such a fundamental way of life. It's how vertebrates have lived for 500 million years, and these fish in the Antarctic have abandoned that way of life, abandoned the genetic machinery for that way of life, and there's no going back.

And that also sort of shatters our notion of evolution as being progressive."

Again. Another stunning pronouncement. If we made it here we may not be the fittest? Only different? We aren't the best? We don't have the best genes? He explained as follows:

"Current species aren't better. They're just different . . . from former species. They're just keeping up with the changing earth. Really, the general idea is that the earth and life evolve together. And the signature of the changing earth is really sort of etched also in the DNA record. When you look at the pertinent places in the DNA record, you can say, 'Ah! Here's an animal that was shifting its physiology.'

One of the other things that's in the ice fish genome is a really peculiar set of genes for making antifreeze. This fish lives close to the sea ice, and if it didn't have any kind of protection, it would freeze like a fish stick right up against the ice. But its tissues are full of this very peculiar protein that prevents ice crystal formation. That way it can live in this very cold water and bump up against the ice without freezing solid. I guess the other thing to think about [is] like that movie scene where the kid puts his tongue on the pole, and . . . *yyyeeeewww!!! Let's not go there* . . . It's very pertinent to people from Wisconsin."

Sean lives in Wisconsin. And while there's certainly a lot of ice fishing going on in Wisconsin, I wouldn't think it had a genetic basis. He continued.

"But anyway, the ice fish has to have lots of adaptations to live in this environment. Some people might say, 'Well, what is the ice fish trying to do, adapting to 30-degree water?' Other fish couldn't adapt, so it's an open opportunity. The winners are those who could come up with the genetic inventions that enable them to live in places that are otherwise quite hostile."

To the victor belongs the spoils. I asked him, "What does the ice fish eat?"

According to Sean, "The ice fish eats krill, a shrimp-like creature that is [plentiful] throughout the oceans, and the krill feed on algae that grow on the sea ice. So the ecological chain is this sea ice down there sort of nurtures the bed of algae, and the krill feed on the algae, and the ice fish feed on the krill.

"We don't necessarily need to go in this direction, but if there's less sea ice, that's not such good news for the ice fish, is it?"

○   ○   ○

WITH ALL this new DNA data, I wondered how Sean had gotten access to it.

> "There's a few findings out of my laboratory—but [the things I'm reporting in the book] are largely the collective findings of hundreds, if not, thousands of scientists. In the last few years, so many genomes have been completely sequenced, and then what happens is they are made into public databases. Really anybody with an Internet browser could do this type of research. They don't need any kind of special permit, or anything else like that. There's been a nice marriage between information technology [and the pure science.] Without browsers and information science we wouldn't be able to comb through this vast quantity of data at the speed that we do—but we now have the genome sequence of about 800 organisms. That might include a dozen or so mammals, and all sorts of other animals, all sorts of plants, many fungi, lots and lots of bacteria, and this material, really, anyone can tap it. It's public, freely available, and this is what the scientific community is mining.
>
> "There's been an enormous growth in the amount of the DNA record we have at hand. I couldn't have written this book a few

years ago. Really, five years ago we had just a tiny fraction of the data we have today, and the pile is growing so fast, it's sort of like drinking out of a fire hose. Even as an individual biologist, it's really hard to keep up with the opportunity. I hear every day about new genomes going online. What this means is that enough sequencing has been done that now that data has been put somewhere, that biologists can access it, and there's more mysteries to uncover with virtually every genome that's added to the pile."

And Sean's not just talking about existing species, either. In his words:

"I think one of the most exciting projects on the horizon is the sequencing of a Neanderthal genome. We're talking about sequencing ancient DNA from an extinct species of human. The Neanderthal bones have turned up for about the last 150 years. There's lots of specimens now. Svante Paabo and his colleagues at the University of Leipzig in Germany have gone through a lot of bone samples to see which ones have the highest quality DNA for sequencing. Not only are [they] going to sequence one Neanderthal, but his ambition is to sequence ten individuals, so we get a good sense of Neanderthal variation. Now that will give us a peek at a human lineage that kind of split off from *Homo sapiens* probably in the ballpark of about 500,000 years ago, and we'll be asking questions about what makes *Homo sapiens* different from *Homo neanderthalensis*. That's our closest extinct relative.

"It's actually a mass achievement because ancient DNA undergoes a decay and a transformation. With the DNA of a living species, we get long, long intact pieces of DNA to use to do our analysis. But you get just shrapnel out of a Neanderthal.

"So imagine this: You could reconstruct a book by having entire pages, working sort of a page at a time versus working a few letters at a time. Imagine how long it would take to put together a good size novel from just a few letters at a time. And that's really what the Neanderthal situation is. He's got really short pieces. He's got to figure out all of the overlaps among all the letters, to piece the whole thing together. Computers are doing it, but when you only have four letters in your alphabet? A lot of little pieces look a lot alike. So, it is not an insignificant challenge. As I understand, so far they have about a million bases put together, which is enormous. We only had a few hundred bases up through the 90s of Neanderthal DNA. This will be another project that's gonna make a lot of headlines."

I asked Sean to sum up the surprises that had come with the influx of this new data:

"I think there have been a huge number of surprises, and I'll try to tick them off in various ways. I think it's stunned us how similar gene content is across all domains of life: the fact that you can find pieces of code that are shared among everything from the archaeobacteria that live in the boiling hot springs of Yellowstone . . . right to humans.

It's surprising how similar the organization of genes is from, say, mice and dogs to humans. It's amazing how similar the sets of body building genes are between fruit flies and earth worms and humans and mice. That's sort of one dimension.

There are the little gems that we find in the DNA record, things like these fossil genes that tip us off to ways that we're different from our ancestors. We have a bunch of fossil genes for odorant receptors. Our sense of smell is inferior to that of other animals like dogs and mice, and that's very clear how that's happened in the DNA record. So I think we're sometimes surprised at the quantity of information we get, and at the quality of the information we get. You're staring right at the smoking guns of evolution.

Every change and every trait involves changes in DNA. So, DNA is a document of history—that's an easy thing to say, but in reality what it means is that there's thousands and thousands of pages to look through for any organism, and it's full of information about who it's related to, what's happened in the course of time, how it's different from other things. Biologists are having a field day. It's really a new golden age in evolutionary science."

If there's one thing that differentiates humans from other animals, it's our complex language skills, and also arguably the size of our brains. I asked Sean if there was any insight on these attributes.

"These capabilities which we consider uniquely human—this is sort of an extra level of sleuthing that's going on in the DNA record.

If we accept . . . that we and, say, chimpanzees—have pretty much the same set of genes—there's been some coming and going of individual genes, but the genes that build chimpanzees and build their brains, and the genes that build our brains are pretty much the same—I'm talking about the identity, the fact that there is a gene doing that. But there must be some changes in how those genes are used—either when, or in what parts of the brain, that have wired us up differently.

Biologists are using all sorts of methods to try to figure out—in a needle-in-a-haystack sort of way—which genes are involved in speech [and] in language, and whether or not there's any signature of evolution in that gene.

The way they're being led to this is by studying humans and small families that have some deficit in that capability. There's a family that was studied a few years ago where there's a problem, not with, say, the motor aspects of speech, but in formulating speech. So this is a wiring problem in the brain. And the gene responsible was tracked down and the mutation responsible was identified. And then that gene was studied from a more comparative perspective [to determine if there was] anything going on interesting in that gene in the course of evolution. Again, Svante Paabo and his colleagues in Leipzig turned up a signature that perhaps that gene had been a target of natural selection in the human lineage pretty recently. So, that long story is just to say that [it takes] detective work, among the 20,000 or so genes we have, [to] identify those that are important for our capability—speech and language—and then study them one by one for whether or not they have any kind of signature that they've evolved in recent human history. The way those genes are being identified is really through medical genetics. There are other syndromes, for example, that affect brain size, called microcephaly. Those genes are being identified first for clinical reasons, and then they're studied in an evolutionary context.

The two payoffs there are we're learning something [about] human biology and things pertinent to human medicine, and then using this genetic knowledge to ask questions about our ancestry."

○   ○   ○

I DEFINITELY had a better picture of how a particular gene might get lost. Either an extra letter is inserted in here, or a letter is deleted there. When that happens, the gene becomes a different gene, if you will. It's no longer the gene that it was, so it can't function the same way. But it's still a gene! I asked Sean, "Do these changed genes become new genes, so to speak? With new functions?" He answered:

> "Genes are born and die. If you think about a word processing analogy, you have this whole text, this three billion letters of DNA text, and sometimes there are just copy-and-paste errors and parts of that text get duplicated. And when genes get duplicated—and this happens very regularly—that creates sort of spare parts. What happens is those genes are free to explore a little bit, because as long as that other copy is there that carries out the long-standing function, then this gene has a free pass. And that's certainly a big story in evolution. There's all sorts of traits we have that are the product of this process we call 'gene duplication.' That's how new genes arrive, and that's an important contribution to evolution, and it is part of mutation. Gene duplication is a mutation—it's just a creative mutation, as opposed to a destructive one.
>
> The other aspect that enables genes to expand their functions is that there are all sorts of controls—switches, I'll call them—that are nested in DNA around the functional parts of genes, and they choreograph how genes are used. Determining whether this gene is used in the liver and in the blood and the brain, and at what times of development is it used. [Is it used] while we're a young embryo, or is it used only in adulthood? Is it used when we're replenishing our white blood cells, whatever it might be? And this choreography evolves. This is perhaps the most important part of our physical evolution, or anatomical evolution. Our brain got bigger, and our body changed shape, and our musculature changed, because the decisions, that go on in the choreography in the usage of genes, change. A gene might be on or functioning for a little longer period here, or functioning in a new place. And it's that choreography that makes a big difference—*now we're back to a big difference, instead of a small difference*—between very closely related animals like ourselves and chimpanzees.

What I'm getting at is—let's imagine two species with exactly the same set of those 20,000 genes, but look different. How does that happen? What happens is it's the choreography of their use that's different—not what the genes do themselves."

So there's the punch line. Genes don't tell us everything. We have to look at what they do in process. We have to look at these . . . switches . . . surrounding the genes.

"Right," said Sean. "And for genes involved in body building and organ building, they often have many jobs. They'll work many, many times in the course of developments. Some of the same genes build your pinkie as build your ribs as build the bones in your ear and even contribute to the formation of teeth. But, of course, to get the right pattern, that we call human, they have to work at the right place and time.

"Genes require that they be governed, that they be choreographed, be told when and where on the stage they should be acting. Otherwise, we don't come out the way that we do."

Well, I don't look like Sean, and few of us—even biological siblings—look like each other. But we're all still human.

○   ○   ○

IN MY INTERVIEW with Sean, I was sufficiently embarrassed about one question, that I claimed someone else had come up with it. People come up to me all the time and ask questions, so that much is plausible. But I should tell you that we interviewers sometimes use this device when we don't want to look stupid—or the question itself is pretty controversial. Controversial questions bring blasts of e-mail, so unless you're prepared to deal with that, you tend to couch the question as if someone else thought of it. In my case, I plead guilty to both.

I'd been cogitating on the small differences between humans and other primates, as well as on our ability to splice-n-dice genes. After all, it was over thirty years ago that Dr. Chakrabarty had taken one bacterium and inserted gene fragments from a set of other bacteria to make a new super-bacteria. That's old technology now. Look at what we can do today. And if there's one thing that happens when we get a technology, over time we make it smaller-faster-cheaper.

So I posed my hypothetical question to Sean: "Let's say we have the human sperm invade a human egg, and we come out with a fertilized egg. If we tinkered in the genetic engineering lab and changed the exact one percent difference, would we get a baboon?"

I could see Sean thinking it through as he answered.

"If you . . . if you changed all those differences back to what the sequences looks like in a baboon, you'd get a baboon. Yeah, so if you could—*reverse engineer*—if you could make those 30 million changes—out of the 3 billion—yeah, you'd get a chimp back out."

I was stunned. Since someone else has ostensibly thought up the question, I posited that it might be a weird way of thinking, until Sean said:

> "No, I think it's an imaginative way of thinking. When we think about changing DNA—and I think right now of people with hairs going up on the back of their neck [because they're thinking] that this is *Brave New World*—it's not gonna happen in the foreseeable future for lots of reasons. One is that we don't have those techniques. We don't have those techniques that ensure that we can do [these kinds of techniques] accurately and without mistakes. And those mistakes would otherwise be profound.
>
> And there would be a huge moral and ethical debate about that, that I think scientists themselves would have a significant amount of discomfort. So genetic engineering of humans, and engineering in various traits, I think we're way, way off in time from trying that."

I stopped him and asked him directly, "But the fact is, that if you could do it, you'd get a baboon?"

He responded without hesitation. "Yeah. That is true."

He went on. "If you want to just do that as a thought experiment, and say I'm gonna tweak those 30 million changes back into [baboon] DNA, I guarantee you, you'd get a baboon or a chimpanzee, whichever code you engineered in."

If you are wondering why I was pressing him, it's this. And frankly, it has nothing to do with science, and everything to do with our sense of ourselves as humans . . . and what we humans believe.

Take stem cell research. Some people think it's perfectly acceptable to take frozen embryos and then redirect them for scientific use. Others find it tantamount to murder. For some, it crosses an ethical boundary. For others, a moral boundary. And for others still, it is against their religious beliefs. For some, it's all three.

I never argue with a person's faith. Or lack thereof. People believe what they believe. And they have a right to that belief. Without hassle or being asked to defend it.

But what I knew was this: The hypothetical proposition I proposed presented a potentially colossal religious conundrum.

For those people who believe that human life begins when the sperm enters the egg, they frequently then say that we must protect and respect the human life developing from that moment forward. This point of view presumes that from that point forward we have a human life.

Let's run this baboon proposition out.

A human sperm enters a human egg, and human life has begun. Before the resulting cell split—which takes hours, we have learned, so we've got some time—the folks at the genetic engineering technology lab kick into overdrive.

With technology just like we have today, but smaller, faster, and cheaper than the technology which Dr. Chakrabarty used some thirty years ago, we splice in gene fragments, or we take out a letter that had been inadvertently inserted, or we insert a letter that had been inadvertently dropped—for 30 million such combinations. Then we let the fertilized egg divide again and again and again, and we implant it in a mama baboon. (Hey, it's my hypothetical! If we can put tigers in lions, this can't be too big a stretch.) Some number of months later, out pops a baboon.

Okay, would this be a baboon with a human spirit?

Now let's go the other way. We have a baboon sperm invading a baboon egg. A baboon's life has begun. The gene lab people turn on the gene-switching machine, turn the setting to human, and press Start. The fertilized egg does its thing, and we implant it in a human female. Nine months later, out pops a beautiful little baby.

Is this a human baby with a baboon spirit? Or is this a human baby with a human spirit? . . . because it's human?

You would be hard pressed to find anyone comfortable doing this kind of gene manipulation, but the fact remains that all living things seem to be related—from humans down to the tiniest bacteria. Not just structurally similar—*related*.

○   ○   ○

THIS IS NOT the first time that science has sent religion around the bend. It's not the first time that science has uprooted deeply held beliefs and caused a massive schism in our individual and collective perspective on all of life itself. No less a schism was felt by Western civilization in the sixteenth century when Copernicus figured out that the earth revolved around the sun . . . and not the other way around.

In his recent book, *Uncentering the Earth,* William Vollmann writes about the moral struggle, the ethical challenge, the prospective tear in the religious fabric of life, in addition to the scientific revolution that the Copernican insight brought.

Many people know William Vollmann as the winner of the 2005 National Book Award in the fiction category for his work *Europe Central.* The judges' citation tells us how richly researched his writing is: "Like an all-hearing intelligence agent, Vollmann occupies the minds of Germans and Russians, artists and generals, victims and torturers in impossible ethical quandaries. Scrupulously researched, rigorously designed, scarifingly (sic) voiced, this omnibus is heroic art, the writer's courageous immersion in totalitarian ugliness to retrieve forgotten moral heroes."

Bill also applied these skills in his non-fiction work about Nicholaus Copernicus. He wrote of the historical landscape at the time he published *On the Revolutions of the Heavenly Spheres,* and the bumpy road to the ultimate acceptance that the earth revolves around the sun.

When I questioned him on this topic, he said, "Essentially, science and the Catholic Church seemed to support each other in Copernicus' time." In the Book of Genesis, God created the earth and even placed the stars in the firmament. "In Ecclesiastes, for instance, 'and the sun also rises and it goes down.' And then in Isaiah, God tells the sun to actually retrace its course by ten degrees on the sun dial. There is every literal indication that the sun goes around the earth."

It was accepted that the earth was round, but they believed the earth was the center of the universe. Vollmann said, "As Ptolemy pointed out [in the second century], if it were off-center, then the stars would obviously be bigger, say, to the East than they were to the West, because we would be closer to them. They had no conception of how far away the stars were. But given that all the stars rotate around us in unison, every twenty-four hours, the same pace of every single star, it seems to make sense that they are all equidistant from us. They are lying on some kind of sphere, which is slowly rotating. And, of course, that's an artifact of our rotation every twenty-four hours. But if you believe that the stars are on this fixed sphere, then of course they're the same distance away, and they're probably not that far. And so, if you are off-center you would be closer to that sphere, so it makes a certain amount of sense."

Besides, there was little technology to show anyone any different. Copernicus in the sixteenth century has essentially the same equipment as Ptolemy in the second century—crude wooden instruments, at best, and little real science to assist. "It was amazing what the guy was able to do with no telescope, with no theory of gravity, no modern understanding of inertia and motion. In his day, motion was considered to reside with the specific bodies or elements that moved," said Vollmann.

Nicholaus Copernicus was also a canon of the Catholic Church, a man of religion. "All the scientists that Copernicus cared about in his time, and of course, Copernicus himself, were Christians, who believed literally in the Bible. The Bible was a literal scientific fact as far as they were concerned. And this caused great difficulties," Bill added.

This may be exactly why Copernicus shared only small portions of his work, and the complete Copernican system was not published publicly until 1543, at the very end of his life. The story survives that he was finally able to hold the book in his hands on his death bed. The facts show that this was possible, and indeed, it was likely. But there was also betrayal and subterfuge afoot. The preface that Copernicus had written for *On the Revolutions of the Heavenly Spheres* was replaced at the last minute by another one prepared by Andreas Osiander, a Lutheran theologian. Osiander had been left in charge of publication by happenstance, and he intentionally chose—without authorization—to shade the book as simply a convenient way to calculate planetary positions, not a fact, not a reality. Therefore, no controversy.

But soon, the telescope was invented and far more definitive observations and calculations could be made. While various popes continued to reject the notion of a heliocentric universe, there eventually was a softening. In 1624, Galileo was allowed by Pope Urban VIII to consider the work of Copernicus as a theory, but this proved to be a single moment in time. Within a decade, the Inquisition turned its sites on Galileo. According to Vollmann, "When it came time to interrogate Galileo, people were really starting to menace him. 'You know, it would be a lot better if, instead of insisting that the earth literally goes around the sun, you just try to speak hypothetically, the way that Copernicus spoke.' But he wouldn't take the hint, so he had to be punished." Galileo spent the remainder of his life under house arrest.

You would have thought that the new technology would have stood by Galileo's side, where it could not for Copernicus. In Vollmann's words, "Galileo kept saying 'Use the telescope! Use the telescope!' and these grave sages would say, 'No. I refuse to look through your telescope, because it's only going to confuse me and unsettle my convictions. I know that the earth is the center of the universe.'"

Perhaps, the most important lesson here, according to Bill, is that "people held out—some of them to the very beginning of the nineteenth century, which is amazing. So it's not something that can really be hurried, when you are asking people to abandon some fundamental conception of where they are in the universe."

And that's where we are today. With a fundamental concept of the universe challenged by the new DNA data that we have generated with all this new technology. And if history repeats itself, the acceptance of this data—just like the idea that the earth is not the center of the universe—will take some time. Likely, a long time.

Even without my hypothetical baboon, there is plenty new here to reset how we think about all living things on planet earth. Which gets us back to the questions: What is life? And when does life begin?

Sean Carroll stepped up to the plate again.

"I certainly understand the point of view that life begins at conception," he said. "A fertilized egg is a live cell that has human potential. If we manipulated the DNA, yes, it would have a different sort of outcome. But I still think I understand where those people are coming from in terms of their concerns about intervening after that moment—whether that's to intervene to freeze that embryo, whether that's to intervene to change the genetic material, or, of course, to not go forward with a pregnancy. Clearly, if we had the technology, we'd be right back where we are now, which is asking fundamental questions about what we think is ethically and morally acceptable."

As you can see, there are no answers here. We are simply at that point where the scientific evidence that is being provided by technology is coming at us fast. What it all means . . . well, that is unclear. And if this is like every other breakthrough, most of how we are interpreting this newfound information is right.

Let's remember that Copernicus didn't get *everything* right. He thought that the planets circled the sun . . . literally. It took a while for Johannes Kepler to jump in and show us that these were elliptical orbits. And so some of what we think we are seeing today will be re-thought and re-explained tomorrow, as more and more information presents itself. But the operative word in the previous sentence is *some*. There is a great undeniability of the basic truth of what we are now seeing with this filling in of the infrastructure of the DNA of all living things.

In the Book of Genesis, God created so much in a single week. Who would have suspected that so much of life, as it is described there, is actually related to each other? From a project management standpoint—given what we know now—it was a great design. Start things out in a particular way, get it going, give it some time, and the creation of all living things will take care of itself. It's the first cogent argument I've heard that suggests God could actually get his part of the job done in a week.

But where does this leave us?

For the science-minded, it is good to remember that the first job of science is to observe. It is a separate job, a subsequent job, sometimes an impossible job, to explain what it is we are observing.

For those of religious faith who are challenged here, there are many choices. At one end is the Dalai Lama. He says that when science comes into conflict with Buddhism, then Buddhism must change. But his is an exceptional view. At the other, it is simply a matter of faith.

No matter what you think or believe or fear, take comfort in this: God works in mysterious ways.

CHAPTER SIXTEEN

Another World

"YOU CAN SAY I am the chief of Aman-*chthck*"

This was the fourth time he had pronounced the name of his village, and for my part, I didn't come close.

"Ahh-man . . . clee," I said, slaughtering it again. I gave up. "You'll have to forgive me. Maybe you can come back and teach me how to say it another time." We laughed. He was a lovely man—Chief Advocate Mdutshane, the chief of the village of Amanci in Eastern Cape Province, South Africa. Advocate was his first name, and fortunately, his last name was workable. Moo-doo-sha-nay.

We were at BIO 2006 in Chicago, and I had burst into the press room that very morning—the last day of the conference—and announced to the communications staff on hand, "I want Africans. I know Africans are here, and I'm determined to find Africans."

The staffer looked up from her computer monitor, strategically placed to watch both the journalists walking through the door to her left and the sea of computer monitors inhabited by sedentary journalists to her right. She was also working on press advisories and back-up material on the computer monitor before her. The old saying "If you need someone to do something, ask a busy person" became immediately true.

Without blinking, she held my gaze and said, "Yes, we have Africans. You want Africans?"

"Yes. I noticed that there was a press announcement about Africans on the bulletin board here four days ago, and it doesn't seem to be here anymore. We want to get them on the radio, and today is the last day. In fact, we're breaking down early. It has to be before 2:00PM," I explained.

With that, she was back to her screen. "I know that announcement. I'll print another one out." She continued to concentrate on the computer, while behind her a printer started up with those whirring sounds that tell you it's about to spit something out.

I moved the three steps over to her table, having held this conversation from the middle of the aisle. She continued to squint at her screen and pound away at the keys. It wasn't one of those times, where someone *appears* to be competent, as in: "Let me create a flurry of activity to produce for you a totally useless piece of paper that is four days old, and completely worthless, and then declare complete victory, and pretend to turn to some other, more important work." Nope. That's not what was going on here. She had actually *heard* me. And was *acting*. I was stupefied. She looked up and said, "Why don't you just go on in. I've got the name of the PR person who's handling this. I'll call her now."

I was shocked. "Great!" I said, "Thank you!" And I went in to find my producer, who was madly creating a PowerPoint slide for a panel he was going to be on later that afternoon. I barely had time to tell him what had just happened, when from behind me came a quiet, hushed-press-room-or-public-library voice: "Dr. Gunn? I have the Africans." *If you really need to hire someone to do something, don't waste any time. Go track this woman down right now.* I stood up, turning around to face her. She was already turning and beckoning me to follow. "They're right here. The Africans are right here."

We walked to the front row of monitors, and there they were. Three of them. And a nice young lady, armed with three cell phones. She was just handing one of those phones to one African gentleman, while she picked up another. The two other African gentlemen were sitting there, politely and as quiet as can be. *How could this be? How could anyone—much less my Africans (I had begun to have a feeling of combined possession and destiny about this)—how could they have penetrated the press room?* In all my years in journalism, I knew of no one who wasn't with the press—no one seeking media attention and certainly no public relations person—who had ever made it into the inner sanctum of the press room. Yet here they were. Bright as day. Pleasant expressions on their faces. And very orderly. I don't know why I say "orderly," but it seemed that way to me, and I'm anything but orderly. Their PR gal was American, and like any PR gal worth her fee, she was on top of the whole scene, lightning fast, missing nothing, keeping everyone organized, and making it all work.

The PR gal got off the phone and proceeded to officially introduce us. That's when I found out I had an African chief.

"You are a chief?"

"Yes," he said.

"A real chief?" I repeated.

He couldn't hide his smile on his face. "Yes, I am a chief," he said, his eyes twinkling. I imagine that he had had this conversation repeatedly over the last several days.

The other fellow was just as interesting. Dr. Makhosandile Rebe. He goes by the familiar name of "Khosi" (pronounced "Co-see") and he was the assistant director of the Department of Agricultural Technology Development and Transfer at the Provincial Department of Agriculture in Eastern Cape Province, South Africa. It was a technological triumph to see it all fit on a single business card.

I conveyed all the logistics to their PR person and told her about our time constraints. For their part, they had a press conference scheduled for later that day, but we could agree on 1:00PM. We did mini-high-fives all around.

But now we were in the studio and out came the "Aman-*chthck.*"

They arrived together, and we could all just fit into the booth—my engineer, myself, and my two guests—having nabbed an extra chair from the nearby television control room. We decided that the Chief would go first.

As luck would have it, just as the Chief took his place, a television crew documenting the BIO "show within the show" showed up and asked if they could take some footage of us *pretending* to do an interview. *Of course!* Against this backdrop, I asked my guests, who were mightily accommodating and spoke in the cadence of a far more slowly paced life. I explained that we would start with a fake radio interview to be recorded by a real television crew for a partially fake documentary because we weren't actually recording at the time because we all couldn't fit in the recording booth together. Besides me, there was my engineer, Chief Advocate Mdutshane, Dr. Rebe, the cameraman, and the dual soundman/lighting guy—and all of our combined equipment—in a space smaller than a '62 Chrysler New Yorker. We were already squeezed for space.

The Chief and Dr. Rebe were the picture of cooperation. The cameraman was standing on a box, while his sound guy held a boom microphone that kept hitting the wall of the studio. The camera guy barked orders like "Move this," and "Remove that," all in the interests of getting a better shot. They started rolling and here we have separate audio and video recordings of me interacting with Chief Advocate pronouncing "Aman-chthck" and me repeatedly butchering it on-cue.

Finally, I surrendered and asked the Chief to tell us about his village, which I understood to be nearly 9,000 people. "Yes, almost 9,000 people," he said. "It's divided up into I think about eighteen smaller villages that make up this bigger area of Aman-chthck."

Finally! We were getting somewhere. He was saying the name of the village. I didn't have to! We could fix it in postproduction. And we were getting color!

With that, the television crew jumped up to set up a cross-shot and started re-arranging everything. Cables re-laid. Lights re-arranged. And new directions came like lightning from the cameraman. "Excuse me, Chief, I'm going to get out of your hair. . . . Right now, Moira, I want you to just listen to him a little bit. . . . I'm gonna get over his shoulder . . . and . . . just tell her [speaking now to the Chief] . . ." I leaped in. "Tell us some more about the village."

He proceeded calmly.

"The village is in Eastern Cape, South Africa, near the town of Flagstaff. The town is about twenty-six kilometers away from the village."

"And there's nothing in between?"

"There are other villages in between. Yes."

"But that's the closest that there's a bigger town."

"Yah, closest there's a bigger town. Yah."

This went on for a bit, and then the TV crew was out of there as quickly as they appeared. We all had a bit of a laugh over it all, I got the Chief to give me a few more lessons on how to pronounce Aman-chthck, gave up, and then we proceeded to settle down for the actual *BioTech Nation* interview.

For the record, I spelled the Chief's name, and suddenly I remembered to ask: "Is there a website? Or an e-mail address?" The Chief tried to suppress his mirth. "A website?" he asked. After a quick discussion among us, it was decided that we would use Dr. Rebe's e-mail address for both interviews. *And the winner of this year's dumbest question directed to a person from a developing nation is . . . Dr. Moira Gunn! Congratulations! You have topped even yourself! Who knew you would exceed that platinum standard—the time you prefaced a question to your interview guest by saying "Now, putting on your CEO hat" only to look up and realize he was wearing a turban. Every year, you manage to be an inspiration to us all!*

Then I decided to confess the truth. There was no way around it. I had to ask Chief Mdutshane to say the name of the village on-air and for the record.

"Aman-*chthck* village. Aman-*chthck*." We both laugh. "Okay, this village is in South Africa, in the Eastern Cape, next to the town called Flagstaff. It's got a population of about 9,000 people. . . . Yah."

"But it's a set of small villages, no?" I confirmed, since we were finally recording.

"Yah. The way we divide ourselves, you know. We divide it into smaller communities. Even this one is divided into various smaller communities, which is composed of about eighteen areas."

"How far is it from Johannesburg, a place that many people travel to?"

"It is about 900 kilometers away from Johannesburg."

"So, it's a long way," I said. "And what is the terrain and landscape like? Is it dry? Is it wet? What is it like?"

"It is a wet area. It is not dry . . . Although it is dry in winter, but in summer it is okay," he told me.

"Where does your food supply come from?"

"Food supply?"

"How do the villagers eat? Is there a big supermarket in the middle of the village?" *I knew there wasn't, but absurd questions yield precise answers.*

"No." You could hear him wondering if I was really clueless. "We don't have supermarkets there," he said. "We've got smaller shops, or some things that we call *spasser* shops . . . Yes . . . So the bigger supermarkets, you get them in town . . . Not in the village."

"So how do you provide food?"

The Chief said, "There's transport in between the town and the villages. So, you're using buses. You're using also what you call taxis, but they are different from the ones that you have in America, yeah?. . . So, these are different taxis that we're using. They go up and down during the day."

"But you've always grown a portion of your own food, no?"

"Yes. . . I always do. . . before I came back to the village. . . for a period of about twenty years," he explained. "And then after that, I went over as a community leader there, and my family was always doing farming. When I came back, then I continued also. So it was me now who was in charge of that. . . within the family."

"Usually all the family members within the community—not necessarily my family—all the community members are farmers," he continued. "So I used to get the seeds, using conventional or what we call traditional seeds. . . you know? Those that had not been treated. Or have not been tested, anyway. You just take it from the cob and then you put it on the field. But during the years—you know—we were not getting the good yield. So we tried on these tested ones that we buy in towns from various seed companies. You try this one and find that it's not working, [then] you use that one. Then after that we got to know about this 'Bt maize' (pronounced "bee-tee maize"), that we got from Monsanto. Then we used it. We tested it in field trials that we did for only one season. Then, thereafter, we continued using it because we felt that it is okay."

I asked him, "What was the difference in your crops before using genetically modified seeds and after?"

The Chief was a plainspeaker. "Before we used these GM seeds, you know we used to get a very low yield because the problem you find that harvest is having 'stalk borers,' you know? So, we don't want that for eating because it is not conducive."

"Are those little bugs that get in?" I asked.

"Yes. That get inside the cobs, and that affect the kernels. So you find that your yield is not good, and then you lose the crop. Then," the Chief said, "after we have used this GM crops, all that changed. You find that your crop is clean, it has got no insects, and then that increases your yield . . . after you have harvested. People were so disappointed about the results [from] the traditional seeds, but in the first year, at least, we got I would say about 100 percent of that. And after that, the yield increases from that 100 percent. . . because we usually get very low harvest. . . but after that it went up to about four times, five times, depending how you prepared your soil," he said.

"You could actually get four or five times as much yield compared to the traditional?"

"Yes. And no waste. Very little waste."

A new line of questioning occurred to me. I commented, "That would say to me that perhaps you had more food than you really needed."

"Yah. As a result of that . . . there are some communities surrounding us who don't have the opportunity of having this GM seed. So they don't have the yield. So we are selling to the neighboring communities," he said.

"You've become a business in yourself."

"Sort of. Yes."

I wondered if there was any concern about the safety of the corn.

"Not really . . . not really . . . there was none," Chief Mdutshane said, because after we've been informed about this type of technology, we said, 'Let's test it, and see whether, health wise, it's going to be good for us.' After some time, we used it and then no one is complaining of anything."

"How did you find out about it?"

He answered, "At that time I was doing the project management for one of the municipalities. We met this guy . . . from Monsanto. He's a Monsanto rep. He introduced me to GM seeds. And then we said, 'We are going to do field trials together, and see what is going on.' And then we found that people were so excited about it."

At that point, I decided to change course again because I just had to know, "How did you become chief?"

Chief Advocate laughed quietly. "It's a tradition . . . that you are born into the position. After your father has died, you take over the position. Then when I die, my son, my eldest son, will take over the position. That's how we do it."

Then I said, "Your family has lived in this village for many generations. How far back can you trace your father to his father to his father before him? How many generations do you trace back that you know?"

"If I trace it, I'm the seventeenth person in that [lineage,] meaning that therefore for a number of years which [he laughs] I cannot remember."

I commented that most people in the Western world could not trace their families back more than a few generations.

"But unfortunately for us, it's a tradition that you must keep," he said, "especially if you are a leader, because the lineage, I mean the success goes with the eldest son of the first wife in the family . . . so, others are not that important, but you—as the leader—you must know, because that lineage is very important . . . to you."

I thanked Chief Advocate, and invited him to return to *BioTech Nation* at any time. Polite to the bone, he said, "By invitation, I'll come. Thank you."

○   ○   ○

AND NOW it was time for the Chief to switch seats with Dr. Rebe.

I started the interview by saying, "There are many small farmers throughout South Africa, and I know that in your capacity with the government, you are trying to introduce genetically modified seeds. How do you transfer the technology of GM to a traditional farmer who's been farming in the same way for many, many years?" Dr. Rebe answered:

"It is not enough to go out to the farmers and tell them there is a new technology, and then it ends there . . . because the farmers, before they adopt anything, they want to see that it is working.

We have demonstration trials, whereby we're going to demonstrate the methods of planting that Bt maize, and also demonstrating the results of the Bt maize. In that case, we compare the Bt maize as well as the conventional way, the one they've been growing for many, many years. And how do we do that? We sort of organize the farmers. We select a suitable site, where we are going to have that trial. A trial is an experiment, and then we plant the Bt maize and the conventional maize together at the same time.

We know for a fact that when we grow conventional maize, during the process of growing it is going to be attacked by the stalk borers. Those are the insects that cause damage to the maize. In America, they call them 'corn borers.'

So, what we do, we have the conventional maize, we have the Bt maize, which is a new technology. And then we allow them to grow together at the same time under field conditions. We involve the farmers in those activities, because they have to be part of process, so that they can be able to see whether this new technology is working, by comparing that new technology with what they have been doing for many, many years. And in the process of doing that, we know that at a certain stage, the maize is going to be attacked. That is what we call a 'natural infestation.' It is going to be attacked by that corn borer . . . Then at the end, we are going to go and examine the damage . . . Then we are going to look at the leaf damage, the percentage of plants that have been attacked by the corn borer—that is, the conventional maize. We look at the percentage of the plants that have been attacked by the corn borer—that is, in the case of Bt maize . . . . We also look at the stem damage. How many plants have attacked by the corn borer in the case of conventional versus Bt. And how many cobs have been attacked by the corn borer in the case of conventional versus Bt. . . . We involve the farmers in actually calculating and make sure that they see those differences . . . and once they have seen those differences, we organize a 'field day.' That is where now we are going to look at those differences that have occurred from the start of the trial up till the end.

So the farmers will have the benefit of seeing the differences in leaf damage, because the corn borer attacks the leaves. They will have the benefit of seeing the stem damage, because the corn borer also attacks the stem of the plant, as well as the cobs. Once they have seen the damage, they can actually decide, and say, 'Oh. What we have been growing for years is completely damaged by the corn borer compared to the Bt maize.' So this is how we're introducing the new technology to the farmers."

I asked, "How impressive is the difference, when you go and observe it?" According to Dr. Rebe, "Yes, the difference is so impressive. For an example, in the case of a damage caused to leaves and to the stems, you find out in the case of Bt maize [that] sometimes you don't find any damage at all. Whereas in the case of conventional maize, you may find the damage. The differences are always significant. . . . In the case of yield, also you do find some differences . . . because you will get a high yield in the case of Bt maize . . . and the yield will be much lower in the case of conventional maize."

The Chief's numbers from the the farmers' yields from GM seeds were four or five times what they were from traditional seeds. But Dr. Rebe was a scientist. And he was also with the government. I wondered if he had a broader sense of productivity across the entire province.

"It differs from one place to another, and that is also determined by the conditions in one area. That is the environment," he said. "Some areas are dry, but you got areas that have got a fair amount of rainfall. In those cases, where you are growing maize in a fair amount of rainfall, the yield of Bt maize could be as high as ten tons per hectare, while the yield of conventional maize could be as low as eight tons per hectare. That is in a very, very good season. But then we have other areas where people are growing maize under the most severe conditions. The yield could be as low as four tons per hectare, [but] Bt maize will always have a high yield compared to conventional."

So, I had heard it twice now. The bottom line was that you grow more corn in every patch with Bt maize, and most, if not all, of the corn you grow is usable. Now, it was time to ask the million dollar question, once again: "Have there been any concerns about the health impact of using the genetically modified seeds?" On that subject, Khosi replied:

"Let me share with you one experience that I had. Honestly speaking . . . once people have seen the difference, they always accept that there are no problems. But for us, I think it is very much important that you should not decide for the people, when you're bringing in a new technology. You give the people as much information as you can about the new technology so that they could be able to make decisions for themselves. You don't actually, sort of, impose things. You give them as much information as you can.

"Now, coming to the question that you have asked . . . about the concerns. One question that was asked by one farmer when we had a field day was: If the corn borer dies when feeding on the Bt maize, ['am I not going to die when I feed on the Bt maize?']. A farmer who has enough information will never ask that kind of a question, because [he knows] what happens before that Bt maize is introduced. [He knows] it is tested by scientists and the scientists have said it is safe for us to feed on Bt maize. Once they have said that it is safe, it could be introduced to the people. . . . And therefore, it is our duty now, when we have a farmer who is concerned about himself or his health, it is our duty to teach that farmer and convince them that this Bt maize is safe. It only kills the corn borer, because the maize itself is 'pest-specific.' It kills that group of insects, and it has no effect on the human being."

Interesting. Several ideas pinged all at once in my head. Certainly, the farmer had raised an interesting question: If the corn borer eats the corn and dies, why won't humans? A really good question. A thinking person's question. I liked it. But there were two other points that really struck a chord.

The first was Dr. Rebe's statement that "you don't actually sort of impose things." You don't? Well, that's refreshing. And certainly he understood the science and believed in the science. But the policy of the first Bush administration was that genetically modified foods were safe . . . there being no scientific evidence to the contrary. Was that the science that Dr. Rebe was talking about? Was there better science that he knew of? Specific to Bt maize.

The bells went off right away, but as any interviewer will tell you, the questions don't always formulate on the spot. It was a question that would get asked in time, but not by me on this occasion. It was not unlike the story that Jim Lehrer told me.

The day that the Monica Lewinsky story broke, Jim had a scheduled television interview with President Bill Clinton. It was actually a re-scheduled interview—re-scheduled from much earlier at the White House's request, and so it was to go forward. The importance and proportion of the Lewinsky scandal was yet to reveal itself, and Jim's interview for the *NewsHour* was focusing on foreign affairs. [That's funny!] Still, Jim had a chance to ask about breaking news before moving on. The president could give a simple answer, and the bulk of the interview would take shape as planned.

We talked about this delay between what you hear and the formulation time necessary for the next question. Sometimes you get lucky, but many times you don't. Jim Lehrer was focusing on a very long and important interview on a completely different subject, and he did ask a quick early question about the Monica Lewinsky situation, and President Clinton responded simply by saying "There is no relationship."

Jim moved on, finished out the interview, and thanked the President, who then immediately left. Instantly, Jim was surrounded by *NewsHour* staff. They were apoplectic. They had caught it. "He said *is!* There 'is' no relationship! Why didn't you ask him if there *was* a relationship?!?!!!"

It's very simple. You're looking in another direction. You're focusing on something else. It's like that training video where they show a number of people bouncing a basketball between them and they ask you to count how many times they bounced it. Whoever is leading the group asks for how many bounces you counted. Different numbers are shouted out. Then the group leader asks: "How many of you saw the gorilla?" Almost no one, if anyone, knows what he means. They replay the video, and sure enough, some guy in a gorilla suit meanders right through the middle of the scene and you wonder how you could have missed it.

That's how it was with Jim Lehrer and the word "is."

Most of the time you have to wait for the MTFQ—the Mean Time to Formulate the Question. Luckily, there was another question for which the MTFQ has passed. A bell had rung earlier in the day. *How did these Africans get into the press room? And where had they been when we all had been looking around for them? And how could they be found so quickly when I asked the BIO staffer? Could they be special guests of BIO? Special guests of the conference? With special events to attend?*

Wouldn't you know it? President Clinton figures in again. The day before Clinton had come to the BIO 2006 conference, and it had caused quite a stir with the press.

You will recall that the press room comes equipped with a big screen—I mean a huge screen—and frequently, numerous smaller monitors so that the press can actually cover what's happening at various sessions without having to leave the press room. It behooves everyone. The host organization knows it's getting coverage. The press can file their reports without delay, and without having to brave the crowds to get the story. This is especially convenient if it's unlikely you'll get an original quote.

Still, at the BIO conference, it pays to check the calendar on the luncheons. They're huge affairs, with several thousand people jammed twelve to a table at ten-person table rounds. Usually there's good food—all things considered—and frequently, the opportunity to lay eyes on someone famous in the flesh.

The celebrity gives a speech, the sponsoring organization—who's buying lunch—gets to make a big splash, and everyone goes away happy.

That's the role that Brooke Shields played at BIO 2004, as have others along the way. Arnold Palmer. Patti LaBelle. Even Magic Johnson made an unexpected drop-in appearance. But the big kahuna of them all was Bill Clinton at BIO 2006.

Early in the conference, the rumor mill went on high alert. It was said that we—the press—would not be allowed to attend the luncheon Bill would speak at, *and* it was not going to be broadcast in the press room. Sure enough, it was true! The conference organizers claimed that this was a requirement of the Clinton people and that there was nothing they could do about it. The press was in an uproar. *What was the meaning of this?!?!!*

I don't know what the official word was, but the rumor mill's favorite went like this: Hillary was flying in with Bill, and she was making a luncheon speech on the other side of Chicago. Bill's people didn't want to inadvertently pull any press coverage away from Hillary, while Bill was pocketing a check for some multiple of a gazillion dollars. If this was so, it probably sounded wildly rational at the time when Bill and Hillary's people thought it up. Except that the biotech press had traveled half-way across the United States—or half-way around the world, depending on the person—to cover biotech related news. We couldn't care less about what Hillary had to say. She had nothing to say about biotech. We wouldn't cover her, even if she managed to slip into the press room as a groupie in the entourage of Africans.

Serious negotiations ensued. With the press, that's dicey. It doesn't mean we stand together and present our grievances in a collective-bargaining way, gaining strength in numbers. No. It means we individually make the situation a story in itself and threaten to run it in our various venues, which would all be accurate versions of the truth, but not the spin that the collective Clinton folks—or the BIO folks—would have in mind. Think about it. One of the first orders of business in a collective-bargaining situation is to work up a list of items and issue a distinct warning: "We'll tell the press!" Get a grip. We *are* the press . . .

By the morning of the Clinton luncheon, a new decision had been handed down. We could go hear Clinton speak, but there were conditions. 1) We had to have identification tags on our wrists, 2) we had to sit in a designated area in the room, 3) we couldn't take any recording equipment inside with us, 4) we couldn't exit and re-enter, 5) we couldn't take any pictures, and 6) we must certify that we were specialist biotech reporters; general reporters would not be admitted to the lunch. Period. We dutifully lined up between the velvet ropes of the press entrance. Legions of conference attendees had already been let in, and scores of women had scooted up front to get a good seat. Finally, they opened the velvet ropes that blocked us from entering. Huge bouncers with bright yellow plastic strips in the fists were greeting us as we filed through. We had to show our press credentials. We had to repeat what we would and wouldn't do. We got those horrid yellow strips slapped on our wrists and were told not to take them off. We sat in the back, which arguably was in the next county, given the expanse of the room at the colossal McCormick Place. And we suddenly realized that everyone who wasn't a journalist had cell phones that could take pictures and videos. Record sound. They could dial out and have their spouse listen to the speech live. Had no one on the rule-making committee visited a Best Buy in the last five years?

We sat and ate together, which is always fun, and the savage press beasts were momentarily tamed. The Clinton folks had made it a press event by making it a "non-press" event. There was some suspicion that this may have been intentional, but who knew? Mostly we were hungry and marginally interested in what Big Bill had to say. And every biotech journalist wanted to see him in the flesh, just like everybody else in the room.

Let's not forget that during his presidency—and certainly during the interminable Lewinsky months—Clinton didn't give any interviews. He barely held cabinet meetings. He was nowhere to be found in person. Yes, Jim Lehrer's interview was indeed an opportunity. It would be the last time anyone had a one-on-one with him for months. But even if Jim had known, even if he had challenged the "is" versus "was" nonsense (which even Hillary couldn't quite see through at the time), Clinton would have found a way to slip out of it. He was ready, no doubt, to handle a second, third and fourth question, and then make some final definitive statement. For all we know, he had already formulated the famous "I did not have sexual relations with that woman" claim, and was just waiting for the opportunity to roll it out. All we really have is the first public sighting of the "is" business. Given how it ended, what difference would it have made in the world? Clinton had months ahead of him to see if he couldn't slip out of the whole mess.

But at this luncheon and for this crowd—all was forgiven. Clinton appeared. The crowd went wild. Cameras flashed. People stood. There was applause and whistles. They kept it up. From way back in the room, the press could only see a tiny man up on the stage, but with all the jumbo screens hung throughout, we could see a giant video of his head and shoulders. He continued absorbing the applause and cheers. He did that old partial bite of the lower lip: "Aw, shucks! It's just me! You've really touched my heart!" The crowd finally settled down, and he began to give his speech. And it was masterful. If you were to dissect it for public-speaking class and somehow be able to teach it, we would become a nation of public speakers.

Clinton actually delivered one exceptional note in the middle of it all. He expressed concern about obesity in America, and especially obesity among its youth. He blamed a huge part of it on high-fructose corn syrup, which was first introduced during a much earlier administration, when the food industry, with government support, was looking for additional products that we might produce and sell . . . because we were able to grow so darn much corn. Clinton was dead against it. Hidden in all our packaged foods, our fast foods, our sugary sodas, our breads, and such. Maybe he should talk to David Kessler and get him to tell the Pepsi folks.

At any rate, in the end, the press had a good meal and the luncheon completely underlined the wild popularity of this man. One usually reserved female British scientist captured it in a nutshell later when she told us she had gotten in line early, rushed to get a great seat, and was overwhelmed with his presence. In her words, "I want to have his children."

Well, if Bill can stick close to Hillary, continue to do all the good works he's been doing in the world—and be a good boy—some of this fairy dust will rub off on the Senator. Besides being competent in her own right, she'll have a free ride back to the White House, and this time she can call which side of the bed she wants to sleep on.

○   ○   ○

THE CLINTON luncheon happened the day before I had found and interviewed Dr. Rebe and Chief Mdutshane. And I was suddenly overcome by a realization. *Where were these guys yesterday? They had incredible access to everything BIO and their now-you-see-us-now-you-don't capabilities were worthy of an underfunded sci-fi movie. I bet I know where they were! They were with President Clinton!* Obviously, they were at the luncheon, but I'll bet dollars-to-doughnuts that they were at some sort of personal meet-and-greet, while journalists like me were eyeing those horrid yellow plastic strips and being questioned by the bouncers recruited direct from the south side of Chicago.

So I asked Dr. Rebe.

"You were here yesterday?"

"Yes."

"And you got to see President Clinton?"

"Yes."

"What was that like?"

And so Dr. Rebe—Khosi—began in his soft, precise, respectful voice: "Oh, it was a great feeling for me. It was a blessing. It is something I never really expected to happen in my life. I mean it's always a great feeling when somebody meets a person like him. It's just like people who visit South Africa and happen to meet Mr. [Nelson] Mandela, so it was that kind of a feeling . . .

"I managed to shake hands with him . . . we had a chat . . . for one minute or two," he continued. "It was such a great feeling. And I'm looking forward for those pictures that were taken . . . and I hope that I get a clear picture. I will enlarge it and make it a very big poster in my house, so that my children could see that this is how far I've gone. For me, I think, . . . it is an achievement. It is something. And it also shows that . . . when you have dreams of doing something, you'll always achieve those dreams. And I think I achieved something yesterday."

You did, Dr. Rebe. You certainly did.

And Khosi? One more thing.

Next time you come on *BioTech Nation*? Try not to make the interviewer cry.

CHAPTER SEVENTEEN

Lessons Learned

"**WELL, GEORGE,** what did you learn today?"

That's George's wife, Mary, talking, and she asks this question every Saturday, weather permitting. You see, George is a pick-up golfing buddy of my friend, Jake, who tells me that every guy in San Francisco knows that if you get up really early on a Saturday morning and wend your way through the fog-rich dawn to the parking lot of the Presidio Golf Course, you have an excellent chance of being placed in a companionable four-some of singles just by showing up. And that's how he met George. And George's wife, Mary.

Whenever George plays golf, Mary shows up at the clubhouse around 11:30, and they have lunch. Frequently they are joined by one or more of the pick-up foursome, and that's how Jake learned of her ritual question. You see, George is a self-made man, and while comfortably retired, he has never lost the habit of trying to improve himself in every way. This applies in spades to his golf game. Thus, after every round of golf, Mary's question comes out, right on cue. The ensuing conversation is lively and enriching for all.

I thought of George, when I realized I have dutifully recounted a good deal of my biotech odyssey in these pages, yet I am still wondering what it is I have learned. Oh, I'm not talking about scientific details here—I've already shared the particulars with you. No, what I'm talking about is some grand overarching theme, a general field theory of biotech, or at least some deeper analysis about what's really going on, what it all means.

It's tempting to keep rolling out the notable experiences. The press tour of Australia, where they organized 15-hour days, the first one ending with crowded trays filled with numerous shots of vodka, but they forgot to feed us dinner. We called it "Death March with Cocktails." Or Puerto Rico, where we arrived to the pounding waves and high velocity winds of Tropical Storm Jeanne. The entire island then proceeded to lose its power grid and the airport shut down, but all was not lost. We were fortuitously quartered in the hotel where some long-ago bartender invented the Pina Colada. And then there was the clamor in Sweden when the science journalists all volunteered at once to test the new cholesterol-lowering beer. And that reception at the De Young Fine Arts Museum when Prince Charles and Camilla came to San Francisco . . .

But the question remains: What did I learn? In perhaps a bigger way?

I was about a year and change into the production of *BioTech Nation* when Dr. Gurinder Shahi came to see me again. He had been one of my guests during our initial marathon at BIO 2004, and by then he had moved from Singapore to Los Angeles. Now he was the Director of the Global BioBusiness Initiative and teaching at USC's Marshall School of Business. It was during our second interview that he said something which brought me up short:

"By my reckoning, biotech is now one-third of the world's economy."

What?!?!

"Well, yes," he said, "if you count all of the genetically modified agriculture, the new biofuels, manufacturing—like enzymes and such, healthcare, pharmaceuticals, personalized medicine, all the DNA stuff, biodefense . . . I figure it adds up to about one-third of the world's economy."

Hmmphh, I thought. One-third of the world's economy? I was skeptical until I thought about it. Even if he's off, he can't be off that much. Not only that—it's a sector that's growing by leaps and bounds. I *knew* I had heard something important. I just didn't know what to make of it at the time.

Eventually, other facts came my way that started to relate. For instance, there was the longevity folks. They tell me that with biotech, we are going to live longer and longer. For example, the baby boomers are going to live ten-twenty-thirty years longer then they originally expected. And fifty percent of the girl babies born in the United States in the year 2006 have a life expectancy of over 100 years of age. Even Congress is hip to the beat. In 2005, it raised the age at which a person could receive 100 percent of their Social Security and keep *all* of their outside income from age 65 to age 66 and you can count on it inching up a year at a time. It will still make for a good deal for the front-end of the baby boomers, but it might better be described as a consolation prize for their having to work so much longer than they ever expected.

For sure, this turns traditional financial planning on its head. Even those of us who haven't gotten around to doing any financial planning can do the math. If we're going to live ten-twenty-thirty years longer— well, that wasn't in the plan. Boomers have led their entire lives thinking they were going to retire at age 65, and pass away some tasteful number of years after that. Well, they still might, but how many will still be hanging around into their nineties and possibly beyond? One Stanford business professor told me that if you are working today, you will probably be working until you're 76. 76!?!? Well, of course.

So where does that leave the baby boomers? And the rest of the generations, for that matter?

Now, I really had to think.

Once you resign yourself to the fact that you might need to keep working, you focus on the basic challenge. As in, you need to have a job. Yet many organizations have a mandatory retirement age. For an example we need look no further than Intel. The CEO gets his gold watch at 65, unless the board repeatedly votes to ask him to stay on for short periods. Just don't count on Intel co-founder Gordon Moore's vote. He was chucked off the board in 2001 at age 72. And why? Yet another mandatory retirement age, one that he had a part in creating. Decades ago, at Intel's inception, he could have allowed for a founder's exception, but in his own words, "It seemed so far away then."

The real sticking point for me was that at 72 the fellow hadn't lost an intellectual step. So, if it can happen to Gordon Moore, one of the legends of technology, the creator of the famous "Moore's Law," a member of the National Academy of Engineering and a recipient of the National Medal of Technology . . . it can happen to you. And me. Which is obviously closer to my heart.

For the record, Gordon Moore still has a future with Intel. He became Chairman Emeritus and reportedly retains his famous cubicle. He says, "It's more for me to get educated than to help." So, here was a man who at 72 was being put out to pasture as an active director, but whose thoughts for his own future was about continuing to be educated. And, you know, I think Gordon's onto something.

When I was in college, I was young for my class. (That age thing is really a women's thing; I will repeat as long as there is a breath in my body that I was younger then everybody in my class.) But the actual point of the story is that I was able to join the first class of computer science majors at my university. And so, I was awarded my bachelors degree in computer science in...1970. *1970?* What could I possibly have studied? Brontosaurus computer science? In truth, a lot of what I learned is still very much applicable, only smaller, faster, and cheaper. But try shopping *that* degree around Silicon Valley!

So, let's back up. Everyone from the baby boomers to the Gen-X and Gen-Y-ers has thought that a college education was basically something you did after you got out of high school, and then it was supposed to carry you through the rest of your career—your forty-year career. Only now we find out, we're not going to have forty-year careers. We're going to have fifty-year and sixty-year careers.

If we want a good-paying job (and we want one for at least the fabulous medical benefits that go along with it) one way to do that is to go out and get a shiny new credential of some sort. Yes, that's right—go back to school. It almost doesn't matter what you study. It only matters that it's new. The best choice is something you might like and something an employer would like, as well. This is not the time to finally submerse yourself in your life long passion of the pottery traditions of ancient Babylonia, unless you are independently wealthy or have a line on a very unique job.

The good news is that it's not as hard as you think to go back to school these days. By coincidence, my beloved undergraduate university has in recent years also become my employer. In my particular college at the university, we *only* take adults and give them new degrees. We presume prior work experience, as well as life experience. And we presume our students have *lives*. They have full-time jobs. And families. In further good news, USF is not alone is creating such programs. There are many, many institutions of higher learning with similar programs, and they are becoming more plentiful every day.

So, if you've never completed that bachelors degree, do it now. And if you have a bachelors degree. Or even a PhD or a law degree? Try your hand at a new masters. In a growing area of the economy. Like . . . like . . . biotech! *Wow! There's an idea!* Remember, a third of the world's economy? Do the math. And there's also any part of the economy that serves the baby boomers. And why? They will spend an unprecedented number of years which were formerly described as old age. It will be the longest Act III on record, and they need products and services galore.

Here's a great example of transitioning jobs. A friend of mine was a nurse, who like so many nurses, threw her back out and every other part of her body lugging patients around and being surprised by their sudden moves. Add to this her arthritis, and she was in a fix. Working as a nurse was simply out of the question. So she went out and got a masters in recreational therapy. You should see her. She brings her music into a room of geriatric patients in wheelchairs and before you can say "Boo!" the place is rockin'. Yet everybody's sitting down. Even her. If you have a toe you can move, she wants you to move it. You might be spared if you're catatonic, but you might not be. She's a nurse, and she knows what ails you. She even brings her dog for comic relief. She can't help it if you're faking catatonia and her dog licks your face. He's just a friendly guy.

So just like always, you gotta go where the jobs are. And they're likely to be somewhat different jobs than you originally envisioned and they may be in different organizations than you ever imagined. And they just might be in biotech.

You see, I was fooled about jobs in biotech. I'd been interviewing the research scientists and CEO's, venture capitalists and policymakers. If you cover the media, that's who you talk to. They are the face of biotech. But these jobs are less than 1% of the people working in biotech. Most positions are in far more familiar terrain. Finance. Computers. Healthcare. Sales. Manufacturing. Marketing. Business analysis. Technical support. Administration. Operations. Law. Training. Industry associations. Non-profit organizations. You name it. And the good news? We already know these jobs. These are the jobs we already have. They just aren't in the area of biotech.

So, how do we transition over to those jobs? Ain't that a good question.

Are you prepared to stretch yourself? After thinking you had it made in the shade? I'm thinking that's the hardest part of all. I remember when I worked my way through college as a data entry clerk and then a programmer. Fellow employees—who I now realize were my current advanced age—would say things like "I can't use computers. I can't type." Or "I'm close enough to retirement. I've figured out a way to avoid computers altogether." And they would ignore computers. They were asked to do less and less as every month went by. But try to get a job now that doesn't require you to be facile with a computer. These folks were whistling past the woodpile, hoping to reach retirement before they had to make a change.

I wouldn't be surprised if we see the same pattern of wishful thinking around biotech. "I can't be in biotech, because I don't know any science." Or "I'm close enough to retirement. I've figured out a way to avoid biotech altogether." It would be a real shame if just as you resigned yourself to working another ten or twenty years, you became obsolescent.

Which begs the question: Is it possible to extend your traditional career into the new field of biotech? Well, are you a programmer, systems analyst or statistician? You could study bioinformatics. Are you a salesperson? Take some training as a pharmaceutical rep. Lots of biotech lingo there. Are you in finance? Learn the economics of biotech. There are constant and repeated rounds of investment and a long time to come to fruition. Are you a nurse? Help run all those clinical studies we need to get all these biotech miracles approved by the FDA. Are you in the media? Pick a biotech field close to what you already are reporting on—business, state affairs, social policy, even sports and sports medicine.

Yes, it's challenging, and here's one of the reasons why. I once checked out the website of a CEO business acquaintance of mine, and I didn't know what his company did. I knew I was going to see him, so I thought I'd check out the company website. I looked at it for some time, and I realized that I simply couldn't figure out what the company did. Built DNA data bases? Manufactured some kind of equipment? Provided DNA diagnostic services? Was it a biotech software company? Could have been all of the above and none of the above. I was completely puzzled. Later on, in the course of hosting *BioTech Nation*, I eventually learned that it was a very key biotech company, and it had made a major contribution to the field, enabling the Human Genome Project to be successful. I remember thinking: "How could I have been so clueless?"

It's easy. Because it's oh-so-hard to understand biotech. And I was tripped up by the notion that if I could locate the company's website, the rest would be a matter of reading. Not so in biotech.

The point is this: If you've got great chops in sales, and this same company was hiring salespeople, and you, too, went out to their website, there's a chance you wouldn't figure it out either. Can you imagine if you actually scored a job interview? How do you finesse that? How do you impress them when you can't figure out what it is they're selling? How do you relate your past experience to what you can do for them now?

For those of us who want to directly transition into biotech, we've got to figure out a way to learn what I call "BioTechSpeak." I have some ideas how to do it, but it's early yet, and it will take some effort.

The biggest change is that I've altered my mindset. If life is for the living, we've got a lot of life ahead of us. Think Clint Eastwood. He keeps coming back for more Oscar nods, even though he's well into his seventies. This is a man for whom age is not defining. Who would dare to tell him to cut back?

To be sure, I don't want to downplay all the science I've learned in these past three years. It's been wonderful, if unexpected, since a grade school aptitude test I once took placed me in the fortieth percentile for science comprehension. But the greater lessons—about myself, about my future, about our collective future—those are certainly new.

And I also know this. The lessons from this time will continue to reveal themselves. Who hasn't looked back at an experience years later, and had further realizations? Inspiring quests, never let you down. And so it is for me. I never know what I'm going to learn, and that keeps me in the game.

I'm betting that George, the self-made man, would agree. On one particular Saturday morning, my friend Jake went out early to the Presidio, and sure enough, there was George unloading his golf clubs. Together they sauntered into the starter's check-in desk, and right away they could see that the starter didn't look very happy, so they asked him what was wrong. As with many golf courses, the starter's desk is also a mini-golf shop, where you can buy balls and tees and all manner of things. This being a pretty swank setup, there was a full array of upscale merchandise. The starter grimaced and made a hitchhiker's fist with thumb extended. He pumped it twice toward the racks of women's clothes. Jake and George turned to see two mid-thirty-ish blonds, who looked to have been cheerleader material in their younger years. Even at that early hour, the girls were intently rifling the racks. Jake and George turned back to the starter, and said, "What's the problem?" The starter whispered, "Their husbands are here at a convention, and they want to play a round of golf. I've got to find them a foursome." George and Jake looked at each other, and then looked back at the starter. In unison, they said, "We'll take 'em."

Things started out politely with the girls in one cart and the boys in another. Within a few holes, the fellas were driving the carts, and the girls were passengers, personally chauffeured to every ball. The guys were buying them diet sodas, while the girls oohed and aahed at the boy's long drives. George made running commentary on his golf game, in preparation for his lunchtime analysis, while Jake recalled every golf joke he could think of. This happy round of golf concluded with Jake and George driving the golf carts directly up to the girls' rental car, where they gallantly loaded the ladies' clubs into the trunk. Side-by-side, Jake and George waved goodbye like two trusted family retainers, as the girls' car disappeared from sight.

Stowing their clubs, Jake and George started for the clubhouse. They could see Mary lounging on the ledge out front. As they approached, Mary spoke first.

"Nice foursome, George. Did you learn anything?"

"Yeah," George said, his smile brightening. "I learned it's impossible to hold your stomach in for four and a half hours."

ACKNOWLEDGMENTS

There's a whole passel of people who contributed to the success of this book, and you've already met some of them: trusty producer, Mark Andrews, of course, and Clive Cookson and Nuala Moran. There's also David Ewing Duncan, the chief correspondent for *BioTech Nation* and the person with whom I chat constantly on *BioIssue of the Week*. Which reminds me that I need to thank all the science journalists I've hung out with through it all, as well as the *BioTech Nation* guests themselves—no guests, no book.

Some of the people I need to thank read drafts, discussed the pros and cons of including this or dispensing with that, or provided essential assistance at key points. (One person helpfully provided a blue pen at a critical juncture, and the last corrections made it into FedEx with minutes to spare.) And while some folks were just around at a single point in time, others had an active part through it all. You know who you are if you provided an anecdote which appears herein, while some of you were just great friends, without whom I wouldn't have made it through—book, or no book.

In alphabetical order by first name (I know. It's kind of goofy, but I've always been a big fan of this format), let me personally thank:

Allison Young, Anders O. Field, Jr., Andy Ambraziejus, Annette Kaminsky, Arvind Bhandari, Bev Ziegler, Bob Alls, Bob Wild, Bonnie Shaw, Ceil Muller, Charles Polvino, Chris Langton, Christie Dames, Danny Bringer, Deirdre Kennedy, Dottie Johnson, Gleb Nikitenko, Greg Ryken, Gwen Risch, Howard Gelman, Irene Majuk, Jake Steinman (and Maggie, God bless her), Jason Pontin, Jennifer Holder, John Kingston, Kevin O'Malley, Kingsley Smith, Larry Brewster, Linda Bernardi, Liz Crilly,

Marilyn Field Wilson, Mark Huffine, Marlene Caldes, Matt Gardner, Monty Carlos, Neeta Bhandari, Paul Toulmin, Paula March Romanovsky, Pauline Shen, Richard Beer, Rocky, Steve Privett, Tara Lemmey, Teddy, Wilma Kay, and all the AMACOM staff, who got behind this book wholeheartedly. Thank you all!

I must give special acknowledgment to my sons: Nate and Jon. Even when times were tough—which meant it was tough on them, as well—they have been unwavering in their support of my work. I cannot imagine two more loving sons, nor could I ever have imagined how much I love them.

Finally, no one would be reading this book at all were it not for the "mastermind" behind *Welcome to BioTech Nation*. That person is AMACOM's Executive Editor Jacqueline Flynn. I had sent an admittedly dry, biotech book proposal into AMACOM, and it had somehow landed on her desk. She emailed back to me: "While your idea is interesting, I fear that it is just too narrow of a focus to produce a book that would be commercially viable." I nearly didn't read the rest. She's saying "No," right? I then realized she had invited me to call her to talk about it.

We spoke on the phone, swapped stories for half an hour, and laughed uproariously. Jacquie suddenly got quiet and spoke very seriously. "You know, I've read your book proposal through twice, and no one would ever know you were funny." That got another laugh. She asked me to write a chapter on how I started *BioTech Nation*, just to see if it could work as a book. Chapter One appears here, pretty much as written then. And that was all it took. And a little bit more, obviously. From that point forward, we've continued to laugh about all kinds of things, and she has been a font of sage advice for this first-time author, who feels smart about so many things and clueless about others.

At this writing, I must tell you that I've never actually laid eyes on Jacquie Flynn, but by the time you read this, I no doubt will. I'm sure you can tell I'm looking forward to it enormously.

Moira Gunn
San Francisco
March, 2007

INDEX

ABOUT THE AUTHOR

Dr. Moira Gunn is best known as the host of both *Tech Nation* and *BioTech Nation,* heard weekly on the National Public Radio (NPR) channels on Sirius satellite radio, on public radio stations nationwide, in 133 countries via American Forces Radio International, and to anyone over the Internet.

Dr. Gunn's work stands squarely at the nexus of science, technology, and society. She has done some 3,000 interviews with people ranging from well-known innovators who drive our fast-changing world to the everyday people who must cope with this change.

Her many public roles range from moderating opening panels at the Sundance Film Festival, the *Forbes* CIO Forum, and the Deloitte&Touche CEO Summit, to emceeing the entire three-day Pop!Tech Conference, to keynoting major events. The topics range from "The Facts of Life in the High-Tech Age" to "What You Need to Know About Biotech, and What Biotech Knows About You."

A former NASA scientist and engineer, Dr. Gunn was the first woman to earn a Ph.D. in Mechanical Engineering from Purdue University, where she also earned a Masters in Computer Science. In addition, Dr. Gunn shares a software patent in Nutrition Science with two USDA nutrition researchers.

Program Director for the Information Systems Programs in the College of Professional Studies at the University of San Francisco, Dr. Gunn also serves on a number of advisory boards, including the Dean's Science Advisory Council at Purdue University, the Advisory Board of the Department of Mechanical Engineering at Stanford University, the Anita Borg Institute for Women and Technology, the

Trusted Computing Group, Compumentor, and the Tech Awards' Global Leadership Council.

Dr. Gunn was named a Science Laureate for her contributions to science journalism, and she is a member of Phi Beta Kappa. She lives in San Francisco, California.